ST ANTONY'S COLLEGE, OXFORD

PUBLICATIONS

NO. I

CONFLICTS IN
FRENCH SOCIETY

St Antony's College concentrates on research in modern history and social studies, with centres or groups specialising in Europe, Russia, Africa, the Middle East, the Far East and Latin America. This new series is an expansion of *St Antony's Papers*, twenty-two volumes of which have appeared since 1956. It is designed to present a selection of the work produced under the auspices of the College, and it will include full-length books and monographs as well as collections of shorter pieces.

CONFLICTS IN
FRENCH SOCIETY

ANTICLERICALISM, EDUCATION AND MORALS
IN THE NINETEENTH CENTURY

ESSAYS EDITED

BY

THEODORE ZELDIN

LONDON
GEORGE ALLEN AND UNWIN LTD
RUSKIN HOUSE MUSEUM STREET

Printed in Great Britain
in 12 on 13 pt. *Fournier*
by T. & A. Constable Ltd.
Hopetoun Street, Edinburgh

CONTENTS

INTRODUCTION

Were there Two Frances?

When the sociologist Emile Durkheim was asked at the turn of the century how France's frequent ministerial crises could be ended, he replied that there was no simple solution, because her political troubles were the result of genuine and fundamental disagreements. This is a common opinion. The history of France, perhaps more than that of any other country, is usually presented as a conflict of opposed traditions and of inescapable divisions. Repeated revolutions have lent force to this picture of radical antagonisms. Frenchmen have been either for or against the revolution, for or against Dreyfus. 'Christian or republican,' said Proudhon, 'that is the dilemma.'

However, recent research is making it increasingly difficult to accept the old simple divisions, or the labels men have given themselves, as satisfactory guidelines. It is revealing the contradictions within parties, the complexities of individuals, the survival of traditional beliefs under the cloak of modern formulae and of traditional practices in nominally new institutions. The revolutions, viewed from a longer perspective, emerge less drastic, less violent breaks with the past, less revolutionary than participants in them thought they were. The original writers, whose works appear to be landmarks in social or political theory, and who give such richness and variety to modern France, were very often appreciated in their own day, not for the novelties which now fascinate students of politics but for those very aspects which were least original and which could fit most easily into the traditional framework of ideas. The poems of Lamartine, for example, which were most popular in his lifetime, are those now considered least new. The cult of novelty did indeed flourish in nineteenth-century France but so too did resistance to originality, and often in the same people. Who could be more revolutionary and more conservative than Proudhon? Men did not break away from their

9

past so easily. Underneath the dramatic conflicts which characterized the century, and which have drawn most of the attention of historians in the past, there were assumptions which people did not question and which are perhaps more difficult to write about. But these ideas that people had in common are as important as those on which they disagreed.

Detailed and numerous investigations will be needed before useful generalizations can be made about these common ideas. However, there has been an increasing interest in the study of popular and bourgeois mentalities and already many important monographs on different aspects of French society have been rapidly transforming and deepening our knowledge of it. The four essays collected here are intended as a contribution to this reassessment. They each deal with a particular and limited topic, but they have as their common theme what was possibly the major conflict of the nineteenth century—and one with many social ramifications—the struggle against the Church. They try to discover just how far this conflict went. It may appear that after 1789 and after Napoleon, the Church had become a department of state, that it had lost its old dominance, that faith in its teachings diminished and that it should not be considered of primary importance. But Madame d'Agoult was right when she wrote: 'The Catholic church still rules, not, to be sure, over the mind or the heart of French society, but over its habits. In a country in which principles are so weak and passions so changeable, is not command over habits really command over life itself?'

It is with habits and everyday life that the first essay is concerned: it investigates the extent to which the Church and its enemies wanted different forms of personal conduct, and had different values and moralities—not on the philosophical plane, but in terms of the life they offered to the ordinary man. The next chapter examines the educational system of the Church, against which the republicans fought with such vehemence, and which they accused of dividing France into two hostile camps. It asks how the pupil of the Catholic schools differed from the pupil of the state's schools and whether there is truth in the legend of 'the two Frances'. The third essay studies how the struggle for power between Church and state could take on an extreme form, how the Church could participate in politics with violent polemic and vigorous organization, but it also shows the ambivalent part in this of social antagonism and class ambitions. The last essay looks at the conflict in even greater detail, at the local level, and considers to what extent the squabbling of villages against priests had any element of principle in it. It tries to see just how small quarrels started, how they became irreconcilably poisoned and how they were fused with national issues.

These essays are intended also as a contribution to the study of anticlericalism. This is a somewhat neglected branch of the sociology of religion, which is now one of the most stimulating frontier areas in French scholarship and which is giving new insights into social history and the more obscure of human attitudes. Sociologists have written surprisingly little about anticlericalism, which has, until very recently, tended to be the preserve of protagonists in the conflict.[1] An attempt is made here to suggest and illustrate some possible new lines of approach: the investigation of the institution of confession—whose varieties may help to explain, in some measure, hostility to the Church—and the comparison of the attitudes of Church and laity when confronted by the same problems, which is possible when one obtains access to the bishop's archives as well as those of the prefect and police.[2] However, anticlericalism is a subject which has many facets to it; and the conclusion to this book can only point to some of the problems which still await further research.

T. Z.

[1] For bibliography, see the *Archives de sociologie religieuse*.
[2] I should like to thank H.E. the Apostolic Delegate in London and Fr Michael Hollings for their kind help in obtaining permission for Roger Magraw to consult the episcopal archives of Grenoble.

CHAPTER I

THE CONFLICT OF MORALITIES

CONFESSION, SIN AND PLEASURE
IN THE NINETEENTH CENTURY

THEODORE ZELDIN

The *Petition to the Chamber of Deputies in favour of the villagers who are being stopped from dancing* (1820) by P. L. Courier, the anticlerical polemicist, tells the story of a traditional community which suddenly stopped going to church. A zealous new curé refused absolution to girls who would not promise to give up dancing. By the end of the year the number of communicants was reduced by three-quarters.

The young man was in all innocence putting into practice the recommendations of nearly every textbook on moral theology used at the time and taught in the seminaries. In these, dancing was strongly discouraged because it might excite the passions. Most dances as 'ordinarily practised' were definitely dangerous and the 'German dance, vulgarly called the waltz, should never be allowed'. 'Honest dancing', where there was no danger of exciting passions, was permitted, but this seemed to be rare; it should preferably be in broad daylight and the open air. Priests should never partake in any form of dance, unless they danced privately amongst themselves—in which case they sinned, but not mortally.[1]

A certain Abbé Hulot, between the years 1821 and 1830, produced a series of little books, some of which went into several

---

[1] Even the chaplain to Napoleon III disapproved of dancing: *Pensées d'Humbert sur la religion appuyées de faits et d'exemples par l'abbé Mullois, premier chapelain de l'empereur* (1855), 154-7.

editions, devoted to analysing the sins that could be committed in each form of popular entertainment, from singing and dancing to novel-reading and theatre-going.[1] Courier protests that the clergy are forcing people to opt between their religious duties and 'their dearest affections of this present life'. The old curé in this village had indulgently tolerated dancing, saying it was best that courtship should take place publicly; but his successor was laying himself open to counter-attack. Was it worse, asked Courier, for girls to dance openly with men who will become their husbands, than for them to have 'secret talks with young men dressed in black', under the pretence of auricular confession?

The confession was one of the most common objects of anti-clerical attack in the nineteenth century. The probing into the private lives of individuals, the restriction of daily pleasures, the interference in sexual relations, married life and personal conduct roused violent resentment. The great public issues—the Church's struggle for political power, its electoral activities, its efforts to control education, were often less important to many people than the pressures exerted by the Church on their everyday behaviour. There is a considerable literature on this subject which has never been studied by historians or sociologists. Through it, one can investigate the growth of one form of hostility to the Church. One can also discover what the clash of Church and state meant in terms of private morality—whether the anticlericals were demanding a more or less liberal code of moral conduct. At the same time one can obtain a wealth of information about those personal aspects of life for which historians can normally use only police records and the testimony of novels.

The best-known attack on the confession as an instrument of clerical domination was made by Michelet in 1845.[2] He objected

---

[1] Abbé Hulot, *Instructions sur la danse* (Charleville, 1821, five reprints 1823-42), *Instructions sur les mauvaises chansons* (Paris, 1824, three reprints, 1825-36), *Instructions sur les spectacles* (1823, reprinted 1826), *Instructions sur les romans,* (1825), *Instructions sur l'abstinence et le jeûne, sur la sanctification des dimanches et des fêtes* (Sedan, 1830).

[2] J. Michelet, *Le Prêtre, la femme et la famille* (1845), reprinted at least eight times by 1875.

above all to its use on women, who, he assumed, were the part of the population which principally submitted to it. Through it, he said, the Church obtained control of women, and this was the vital basis of its power. It was the priest, not the husband, who controlled a man's wife. As her confessor, the priest received her in church, alone, at fixed hours. In addition, as her spiritual director, he visited her at her home whenever he pleased. He asked her questions on matters about which she would never dare talk to her husband. As spiritual director he demanded to know not just her sins, but everything about her, and in this role, he was not obliged to keep her secrets. He might postpone absolution to wring information out of her, facts about her husband, the name of her lover. Husbands no longer used fear as an instrument for keeping the love of their wives, but priests did: the priest 'always has the stick of authority in his dealings with the wife, he beats her, submissive and docile, with spiritual rods. There is no seduction comparable to this.' The wife is isolated; her will and personality are destroyed. Families are divided. 'The home [becomes] uninhabitable.' A man cannot express an opinion without the certainty that his wife (and daughters) will contradict him, and report him to the curé.

Michelet protested on two grounds, in the name of the family and in the name of morality. The family needed to be transformed and the Church stood in the way of this. The husband must be master in his own house, but he must not repress his wife to such an abject role that she sought protection and consolation from the priest. Women should be the associates of their husbands, a condition so far seen only among small shopkeepers. This was Michelet's ideal. Men must learn to explain their work to their wives, instead of priding themselves on their specialized know-ledge and taking refuge in technical language. Women should rear their families with the advice of their husbands and family unity—destroyed by disagreement on religion—would be restored. 'May the religion of the home replace religion.' Seen from this point of view the emancipation of women, as a liberal ideal, involved strengthening the rights of men as well as those of women. Likewise, it was not a relaxation of stringent moral laws that Michelet demanded in his protests against priestly rule but, on the contrary, greater puritanism. He wished to protect women from new temptations. Priests had confessors' manuals filled with lists of sins which no honest woman would think up on her own, and in their questioning they 'put terrible ideas into innocent minds'. There was a strange contrast between the education the laity received, which carefully omitted all reference to sex, and that of the priesthood, which involved a full diagnosis and classification of every known sexual practice and perversion. These might have been a problem in previous centuries, 'horribly corrupt and barbarous', but from which 'thanks to God, we are now far'. Worst of all, the casuistry of the Jesuits—for whom Michelet had a special antipathy—had modified the teaching of the Church on the subject of sin, to find increasing excuses for immoral conduct. By their laxity they had increased their influence and popularity. But this was part of a great conspiracy to 'weaken the will'. The Church indeed needed to be protected against itself—it was polluting the minds of the innocent young men it trained. Michelet was thus on the side of puritanism. He laments the victory of the Jesuits over the rigorist Jansenists, who, whatever their theological views, were 'the party of virtue'.

There were many attacks on the confession in the name of morality. Comte C. P. de Lasteyrie, in a social history of the sacrament, accused it of inspiring either terror or alternatively a relaxation of morals, because of the assurance of pardon. Its questions enabled priests to excite and seduce oversexed women. It was an obstacle to true religion, to intellectual liberty and the progress of civilization; it had been invented to give power and riches to the Church.[1] Confession, wrote Edgar Monteil, later to be one of Gambetta's prefects, involves the delation of the most intimate secrets of families and the loss of all chastity and all honour. His novel, *Sous le Confessional*, attacked priests on puritan grounds, 'for their worldly existence, their love of luxury, good living, idleness and all evil passions'.[2] 'Many women and

[1] C. P. de Lasteyrie, *Histoire de la Confession sous ses rapports religieux, moraux et politiques chez les peuples anciens et modernes* (1846).

[2] Edgar Monteil, *Sous le Confessional* (1873), 62, 67.

most girls are in love with their confessors', wrote two other authors, who declared themseves to be in favour of Christianity but against the clergy who have spoilt it. The confession 'by the habit of avowal falsifies the moral sense of women, spoils their innate sentiments of modesty and places them, through fear, under the dependence of the priests'.[1] The anticlericals seized on the dubious but vivid polemic of a temperance-preaching Canadian priest defrocked for immorality, Père Chiniquy, who denounced confession as 'the cornerstone of [priests'] stupendous power: it is the secret of their almost irresistible influence. . . .' A woman's most happy hours, he admitted,' are when she is at the feet of that spiritual physician showing him all the newly made wounds of her soul, explaining all her constant temptations, her bad thoughts, her most intimate secret desires and sins'. But the Church was thus making her speak 'on questions which even pagan savages would blush to mention among themselves. . . . Whole hours are thus passed by the fair penitent in speaking to her Father Confessor with the utmost freedom on matters which would rank her among the most profligate and lost women, if it were only suspected by her friends and relatives'.[2]

What confessors said to their penitents could be guessed from the manuals published by the Church for the guidance of curés and for the education of seminarists. These were avidly studied by the anticlericals and denounced as immoral. Ecclesiastical treatises on sins against the sixth commandment were particularly condemned as obscene, polluting not only the minds of the clergy and those of penitents but of a large number of salacious readers: it was claimed that the best known of these, by the Bishop of Mans, sold 200,000 copies, even though it was in Latin. Dog-Latin was what all the manuals slipped into when they discussed sex, but it is significant that all but one of the anticlerical critics

---

[1] Emile Faure and Thomas Puech, *Le Confessional* (1869), 41. See also, for example, Francisque Bouvet, *De la Confession et du célibat des prêtres* (1845), 275-82.

[2] Père Chiniquy, *The Priest, the Woman and the Confessional* (London, 1874), 7, 103-4, 122. (French translation 1880.)

prudishly kept to this language for at least the more intimate details of intercourse and perversions.

It is instructive to see exactly what the critics objected to. Paul Bert, Professor of Physiology at the Sorbonne, and another of Gambetta's lieutenants, minister in 1881-2, published a study of a leading manual of moral theology by the Jesuit Gury. He complained that the book lacked general principles, inclined towards the most lenient solutions, found excuses for many crimes and always took the side of the sinner. It showed a profound contempt for women; it did not know what love was, only fornication. 'It is not only the mysteries of the bed of young couples that he scrutinizes with an insatiable lubricity, at the bottom of which jealousy quivers; it is the chaste conversations of fiancés that he surveys obliquely, the kisses of sister and brother, of father and daughter, of mother and child, that he condemns with his impure suspicions. . . .' It was a treatise on morals, but it said nothing about virtue—Gury 'does not know what love is, nor even decency; he does not know what delicacy, generosity, devotion, friendship, personal dignity, civic duty or patriotism are. He is so ignorant of these noble things that he does not even know their name. You will not find a single one of these words in the *Morale* of Gury. All that makes the heart of humanity beat leaves him cold. Do not speak to him of progress, fraternity, science, liberty, hope; he does not understand; in his obscure corner he chops away minutely at erroneous consciences, secret compensations, mental reservations, shameful sins and out of this he tries to compose I know not what kind of concoction to brutify and enslave mankind. For he lowers everything he touches— abolishing conscience, delivering free will into the hands of a director, making delation into a means of governing souls. . . . Beware husbands . . . beware fathers. . . .'

Paul Bert also published an analysis, partly in Latin and partly in translation, of Soettler's commentary on the sixth commandment, revised by Rousselot, Professor of Theology at the seminary of Grenoble (1844). He insisted that he was not just concerning himself with the education of priests: the enumeration and explanation of different forms of sexual activity were rapidly communicated by them to children. He claimed to have before him an exercise by a schoolgirl aged fifteen called 'The Empire of Vice'. This was divided into seven provinces, the largest of which was Lust. It had a river running through it, The Filth, its capital was Lewdness, it had nine major towns: Debauchery, Voluptuousness, Immorality, Adultery, Incest, Prostitution, Cynicism, Violation, Impurity; and eleven communes: Seduction, Evil Desires, Laxity, Turpitude, Fornication, Depravation, False Pleasures, Orgy, Sensuality, Immodesty and Rape.[1]

An anonymous criticism of Moullet's *Compendium Theologiae Moralis* (1834), used in the seminary of Strasbourg, likewise complained of its relaxed moral standards. If a girl, for example, was pursued by a man having evil intentions, she commits a sin unless she tries to flee or cry for help. But, says Moullet, if by her flight or by her cries she is exposed to having her life endangered, or to losing her reputation, she is not required either to flee or to cry out. If an innkeeper sells wine to men who are half drunk, with the probability that they will be made completely drunk, he commits a grave sin, 'except however if by refusing to give wine, he exposes himself to injury or to notable unpleasantness'. If a man commits improper acts with a married woman, not because she is married but because she is beautiful and putting completely aside the fact that she is married, these relations 'according to certain authors do not constitute the sin of adultery, but simple impurity'. If a man swears an oath, but without the intention of swearing, and only using the formula of an oath, he is not fully bound by his word. If a man kills a thief in order to preserve property necessary to his life, he is in effect saving his life as well as his property, and the killing is not sinful. But what if the goods threatened are not necessary to life? The probable answer is that it would be lawful to kill the thief in such a case, 'because charity does not require that one should undergo a notable loss of temporal goods to save the life of another'. Moullet's book is denounced as a justification of vice.[2]

---

[1] Paul Bert, *La Morale des Jésuites* (1880), preface xxxiv, and 523n.

[2] [F. Busch?], *Découvertes d'un bibliophile ou lettres sur différents points de morale enseignés dans quelques séminaires de France* (Strasbourg, 2nd ed., 1843).

19

Though these anticlericals are prudes, they are not opposed to sex in marriage; indeed, they object to the Church's hostility to it. Another anonymous author, 'Le Curé X', attacking Bishop Bouvier's treatise on the sixth commandment, complains of the interference in the rights of husbands. The message of the bishop's book, he claims, is that 'to be agreeable to God the conjugal duty must be performed weeping and praying; a truly chaste husband must neither put his hand into his wife's blouse in the daytime, nor lift her nightgown in bed.' They must resign themselves to living like brother and sister if one or the other is impotent. A woman must, even at the price of her life, refuse the conjugal act if her husband does not carry it out according to the rules. But she is herself threatened, because Bouvier's book concludes with a treatise on Caesarian operations, to enable priests to cut her open, so as to baptize her child.[1]

The accusation that these divines were hypocritically peddling pornography is immediately shown to be false if one examines their works. Bouvier, Bishop of Mans, has not the slightest trace of salaciousness. His book, given its premises against carnal pleasure, is a very logical, straightforward work, which reads like a legal or medical textbook, with precise and careful definitions. He makes sex sound very grim. Moreover, he warns confessors to be extremely careful in the questions they pose, lest they put bad ideas into innocent heads. If a child has not reached puberty, he warns the confessor, he is unlikely to masturbate: so do not ask about this. When you do ask, enquire in a roundabout way, to avoid making suggestions, for example, 'Have you felt movements in the body, agreeable delights in the private parts, followed by calm?' It is true there were cases of priests who were prosecuted for pointing out to children those parts of the body which they must not touch, and for posing questions, as one court ruled, of 'an undoubtedly licentious character . . . likely to overexcite the imagination of very young children and of developing unhealthy ideas in their minds'.[2] But they were defying the warnings

[1] Le Curé X, *Les Mystères du confessional par Mgr. Bouvier* (n.d., Brussels).
[2] Cases of 1879, quoted by Bert, 523n.

frequently given to priests by their teachers. Abbé Gaume's popular manual for confessors urged them to take special precautions with women: not to call them 'My dear daughter'; to be modest with married women, asking them only whether they have obeyed their husbands, and remaining silent about the details, unless questioned. They should take care not to teach them sins they did not know; they should be brief about 'impure matters', to show the horror they felt for these and also to protect themselves against temptation.[1] But that there was some justification in the complaints about the use to which confession, and these guides to it, could be put, is seen in Bishop Pusey's preface to his translation of Gaume's *Manual*. His translation was purposely incomplete, leaving out Gaume's sample questions to be posed to penitents, which he considered improper. 'The English clergy', wrote Pusey, 'are gentlemen and I do not believe that they could ask such questions.' He urged even greater care than his French colleagues, especially in dealing with women who confessed details of domestic life 'which have not a right or a wrong'; the clergyman's aim, he said, should be to strengthen the sense of personal responsibility in those who consult him.[2]

It is clear that different methods were employed by confessors. It is possible that in England, and in Italy, for example, questioning was far less severe than it was in certain regions of France. In Spain there is a tradition in some areas for people to confess not to their own parish priest but to go to the neighbouring town —which must reduce tensions and clerical power considerably. In Colombia, many priests in this century have been trained in France and have brought back a severity in their methods which contrasts notably with that country's laxer Spanish traditions, and this has inevitably had repercussions in the form of increased anticlericalism. A comparative study of the intimate relations of priest and penitent has never been undertaken. These generalizations are very tentatively offered as possible hypotheses. If there

[1] J. J. Gaume, *Manuel des Confesseurs* (1st edition 1837, 9th edition 1865) 157, 191.

[2] E. B. Pusey, *Advice for Those who Exercise the Ministry of Reconciliation through Confession and Absolution* (London, 1878), preface.

is truth in them, some explanation of the different amount of anticlericalism found in various countries might be sought in this personal, rather than the traditional, political context.

In France there were two attitudes to confession which at their extremes were pretty different. One school of theologians urged laxity and gentleness towards sinners. They drew their inspiration from Italy, and particularly from St Alphonse of Liguori. Gaume's *Manual*, which based itself on him,[1] urged confessors to avoid imposing excessive penances, particularly on new converts, and penances should not be public. Excessive penances, he insists, are not carried out and the penitent simply reverts to sin. The best one is therefore the frequentation of the sacraments. If in doubt, incline towards leniency. Do not forbid a drunkard to drink altogether, but only limit the amount he must not exceed. Do not show anger or astonishment at sin. Do not refuse absolution except in very exceptional circumstances: if you defer it because you doubt the penitent's contrition, defer it say for fifteen or thirty minutes, at most for a week.[2]

The extent to which laxity could go is seen in a guide written by an appropriately named Abbé Léger, director of the seminary of Nimes (1864). It carried the approval of his bishop and it shows what some provincial priests were being taught. Léger was opposed to severity. 'It is better to allow the penance for a sin to be completed in purgatory than to expose the sinner to damnation by setting a penance he will not carry out.' He firmly says that serious sins deserve heavy penances, but the worst he can think of are the recitation of a few prayers, psalms or the rosary, the reading of one or two chapters of the *Imitation*, or a long period of kneeling.[3] Fasting should not be required of

---

[1] As well as on various other authors, for example St Francis of Sales, St Francis Xavier, and St Charles (Archbishop of Milan): with the last named, Gaume says his reputation for severity is due to faulty translation, which he remedies.

[2] Gaume, 348-50, 421-33.

[3] See J. B. Bouvier, *Traité dogmatique et pratiques des indulgences des confreries et du jubilé, à l'usage des ecclesiastiques* (1826, 10th edition 1855), 10, on the stern penances imposed in the Middle Ages: 'but, so as not to discourage sinners, the church allows them to be treated nowadays with greater leniency'.

those who are delicate or working. No long penances, for six months or a year, should be set; they were rarely fulfilled. Abbé Léger believed in the most discreet questioning at confession. Ask only, he says, if peace reigns in the home, if there are children and if they are being raised in the Christian way. 'Has the penitent anything to reproach himself for on the subject of conjugal duty or the sanctity of marriage? It is better in this matter to ask less than too much. . . . It is best to leave them in good faith than to instruct them, with the danger that they might sin formally, be scandalized and that their idea of the priest's holiness should be weakened. In fact, many people do not reveal certain acts, because they fear they would scandalize the priest. The confessor must therefore demand only what is strictly necessary and forbid every explanation which would be improper.'

The abbé took a very practical view of sin. Do not refuse absolution to all who dance, he says. Discover first what kind of dance was involved, the reason for participating in it, and if the dance actually caused a sin. 'If you do otherwise, you will force people to abandon the sacraments which were their only chance of salvation and they will fall into all sorts of trouble.' Dishonourable dances, like the waltz, must not be tolerated, because even if the penitent commits no sin, he may have caused another to sin. But people who have to dance because of their social position, or to please a husband, may be absolved, provided no sin was committed and that the woman was not too indecently clothed. The theatre, as all authorities acknowledged, was morally dangerous, and 'you should as far as possible turn everybody away from it, but not under pain of total refusal of absolution'. Bullfighting, again, was a popular sport in Nimes. Pius V had forbidden it on pain of excommunication. Clement VIII had suspended this prohibition in Spain only. What were the people of Nimes to do? 'In France, this excommunication is generally unknown, and as people often do not think they are doing wrong by watching bullfights, the confessor must not bother those who say nothing to him about it; but if they express doubts to him, he must tell them to keep away from this sport, when there is danger of death or scandal, and this on pain of refusal of absolution.' If the toreadors were good, and there is no danger of their being killed, people may watch; 'if someone was killed or wounded, it would be an accident and one is not required to foresee an accident. But fights held in the country, where everybody goes into the arena and where it is rare for someone not to be wounded or killed, one may not attend, because one may not contribute without reason to the death or injury of anyone, even if this contribution is distant.'

Another serious local problem was the avoidance of tax. Léger found the authority of an archbishop to encourage him to leniency. Generally in France, says this Mgr Gousset, people do not think themselves obliged to pay excise duties, state and local taxes, except in so far as they are unable to avoid the vigilance of those who are charged to collect them. They reassure themselves that, despite these frauds, the state always gets its money, either because it is careful to increase taxes in proportion to the frauds it foresees, or because it compensates itself by fines on those whom it catches red-handed. On this reasoning, those who act in this way in good faith in tax matters, either because they do not consider taxes to be obligatory, or because they think they have contributed enough to the expenses of the state, in keeping with their means, through other taxes, must not be disturbed in their good faith nor bothered. If they ask the confessor's advice, they should be urged to pay, but not on pain of refusal of absolution 'because it is not certain that *all* tax laws are rigorously obligatory on the conscience'. Now if a smuggler, for example, listens to the exhortations of his confessor to make restitution for his crimes, he should be urged to make this to charity rather than to the government, 'because the government does not suffer from his fraud, it is society which suffers through the taxes which are increased because of the fraud'. Smugglers who, despite their breaking of the law, have difficulty in earning a living, should be urged to change their profession, but they need make no restitution, because natural law comes before human law, that is, 'that one must get a living from one's work and even a certain comfort'. As for those who cheat the state by declaring a sale or an inheritance to be less than it really is, they should be left alone, because one is only required to execute a law in the manner in which it is customarily executed, and the general usage is that one does not declare the exact price of a sale or the real value of an inheritance. For this reason, confessors should not bother either notaries, buyers or sellers, or heirs.[1]

This was a religion which almost allowed people to do more or less what they pleased. It was one way of modernizing religion. The archbishop whom Léger quotes freely, Gousset of Reims, played an important part in giving widespread currency to this lax attitude. He published a treatise on moral theology in French —one of the few not in Latin—and this was much appreciated by priests whose Latin was weak.[2] But the seminaries could not adopt it as a textbook, because it was not in Latin. It was to meet this need for a modern lax text that the Jesuit Gury—whom Paul Bert dissected—produced his manual, to revive that 'consoling doctrine which our ancestors had and which had too long been banished from our schools by the influence of the Jansenists'. His book, published in 1850, sold about five or six thousand copies a year and in 1866 on his death reached its seventeenth edition. He based himself on St Alphonse of Liguori and used all the skill of casuistry for which his order was famous, but he tried to bring his sources up to date. However, it was leniency rather than an understanding of modern thought that inspired him, for his biographer states that 'a stranger to the politics of this world, he did not read newspapers, or if sometimes after recreation, sitting by the hearth, it happened that he opened one, he did not delay to fall asleep'.[3]

The relaxation of the Church's moral requirements had begun a couple of centuries before, under the leadership of the Jesuits, whom Michelet attacked for this very reason.[4] The effects of

---

[1] Abbé D. Léger, *Le Guide du jeune prêtre au tribunal de la pénitence, ou devoirs du confesseur* (1864).

[2] Mgr T. M. J. Gousset, *Théologie morale à l'usage des curés et des confesseurs* (3rd edition 1845), 2, 333.

[3] *Vie du R. P. J.-P. Gury de la compagnie de Jésus*, par un père de la même compagnie (Paris and Lyon, 1867), 63n, 83, 119-21.

[4] Jules Michelet, *Les Jésuites* (1843).

original sin were minimized, a more optimistic view of man was adopted, that he was not radically corrupt and that conformity to the commandments was enough to save him. The Jesuit ideal was the *honnête homme* and no longer the saint. There was hope for man, and individual merit counted for something.[1] Against this the Jansenists revived the doctrine of the basic corruption of man, who was capable of salvation only through grace, and only if he has this (which means God's choosing him in preference to others) can he, by the practice of severe asceticism, accomplish the will of God. Conversion therefore implied the total transformation of an individual. Only the most holy were worthy of approaching the altar; frequent communion was discouraged; severe penances expected for sins; and repeated deferment of absolution was urged, to make sure that the penitent was in every way fit to receive communion. Arnauld's *De la Fréquente Communion* (1643) argued that if a man sinned, he should not simply be forgiven and allowed to take communion, but should be kept away until the habit of sin was destroyed—against the orthodox view that communion was a principal method of destroying sin. The penance must be accomplished before the priest gives absolution, and the penitent must appear at least twice before his confessor. These 'melancholy sectaries', as Joseph de Maistre called them, got the reputation of making religion rebarbative and difficult. Moral rigorism was by no means the most essential part of the Jansenist doctrine. Jansenism had many interesting varieties, which make it an ancestor for example of decentralization and individualism in France. It formed alliances with other creeds, such as Richerism—advocating equality between priests and bishops—which increased the appeal of the heresy to the lower clergy. Jansenism survived longer than is usually realized. There were still periodicals defending it under Louis Philippe and Napoleon III,[2] and the

---

[1] Cf. the defence of the Jesuits by the Père de Ravignan, S.J., *De l'existence et de l'Institut des Jésuites* (1844, seventh edition 1855).

[2] *La Revue Ecclésiastique* (1838-48) and *L'Observateur Catholique* (1855-64).

Jansenist order of the Brothers of St Antoine at St Mandé did not collapse till 1888.[1]

The really important instrument of the survival of Jansenist rigorism, however, was Louis Bailly's treatise on dogmatic and moral theology, first published in 1789 and reprinted, in various editions, twenty times between 1804 and 1852. This book was used as a standard text in nearly all the seminaries of France during the first half of the century; it was considered the main obstacle to the resurrection of the doctrines of Liguori; it was to replace it that Gousset and Gury wrote their works. The strength of the objection to it can be seen in the fact that in 1852 it was placed on the Index. This is a date that ought to be added to the histories of the Jansenist controversy, which is normally assumed to have lost its importance by the end of the eighteenth century.[2] In contrast to the lax manuals urging moderation and leniency, he has long lists of cases in which absolution should be deferred, and he insists on sufficient proof of reform before it is granted. In contrast to their feeble penances, he would impose three years of penance for fornication, between five and ten years for adultery and penance for life for fornication with a nun. Dancing in front of the church should get three years too, and talking in church ten days of bread and water. The cursing of parents received forty days of bread and water. 'If any woman bedaubs herself with white lead or any other pigment so as to please other men', she should undergo three years of penance.[3]

This book had considerable influence in continuing Jansenist or rigorist practices among many parish priests, particularly in areas in which the heresy had been most firmly implanted. In the diocese of Nevers for example, the curé of Alluy was in the

---

[1] Augustin Gazier, *Histoire générale du mouvement janseniste depuis ses origines jusqu'a nos jours* (1922). Cf. also M. D'Hulst, *Conférences de Notre Dame: Carême de 1892* (1912, 3rd edition), 458-9.

[2] Chanoine Gousset, *Le Cardinal Gousset* (Besançon, 1903), 464-73; Abbé Le Noir and Bergier, *Dictionnaire de Théologie* (1873), 2, 33. For Jansenist opinion of Gousset see *L'Observateur Catholique*, vol. 6, 142.

[3] *Theologia dogmatica et moralis ad usum seminarium auctore Ludovico Bailly* (new edition, Lyon, 1804), 4. 283-4.

1860s still refusing communion and absenting himself from his parish for a fortnight before Easter, so as to avoid hearing confessions, saying his flock was sacrilegious. The way these rigorists heard confession is told in the case of the curé of Saint Médard en Forez, who died in 1835. He demanded a complete change of behaviour before he granted absolution. He listened silently without interrupting the confession, but then took up each point and discussed it 'with the most pathetic gestures'. The confession would take at least one hour and the penitent emerged 'very moved by the eloquent unction of his exhortations'. He demanded as penance reading of the Bible, prayer morning and evening, and a period of contrition lasting six to eight weeks, after which he would tell the sinner how much further he had to go in his progress towards humility and self-knowledge. Only if the penitent showed he had followed his instructions and had not relapsed would he be granted absolution.[1]

The reasoning behind this attitude can be seen in a work published in 1865 and reprinted in 1872, by the abbé Laurichesse, professor at the *petit seminaire* of Pléaux (Cantal). There are those who claim, he says, that people are stopping to go to church because its doctrines are too opposed to human passions and that they are therefore no longer in harmony with the needs of modern civilization. The priest, the representatives of laxness have argued, must keep quiet on subjects on which he formerly preached. But what good has this done? Laxness has not strengthened the Church. The right method therefore is to preach the word of God fearlessly. 'The world does not wish to believe; let us tell the world that there is no salvation except in the most abhorred dogmas, in the free submission to beliefs which are most formidable and best made to dominate and to check human thought. Then the world will believe, and the world will be saved, the day it admits that the majority of things it pursues with ardour are satanic, and that divine, on the contrary, are the majority of things it overwhelms with its contempt.' The modern man, besotted by sensualism, does not confess, but society needs rules and restraints against impure passions. Discipline must be restored.

[1] Léon Séché, *Les Derniers Jansenistes* 1710-1870 (1891), 72.

'Now Christiantiy is law, rule, restraint. Confession is in Christianity the severest form of repressive force. Through it, Christianity captures man and dominates him. . . .' Pleasure and beauty, the joys of friendship all pass. 'Pain alone does not pass; it lives in everything mortal. Pain is the sole reality of this world.' As a result, the priest must inevitably have control over 'the magnificent empire of souls. . . . Without pain, there would be no church.' The source of all pain is sensualism, the greatest illness man suffers from. Confession is the only way chastity can be preserved. Marriage is holy and must be protected from gross sensualism. 'The secret of love is in the act of self restraint.' Marriages fail and produce such sad and bitter homes, with hate and servitude, because they are too often based on the egoistic satisfaction of sexual desire. Only the priest can cure this evil. He can set limits to it. 'The priest is the law, prohibition, for-biddance.' Far from destroying the family, the confessor saves it. 'Do you know how much effort your wife needs not to hate you, and to recover from the wounds you inflict?' 'But for the con-fession, you might lose your wife', for the priest stresses duty. In confessing, the woman cures herself of unhappiness, escapes from the servitude of the flesh and regains her personality. The inner life she acquires in this way allows her to bear the daily chores. Women are not enslaved by confession, but given entire possession of themselves as independent souls. Christianity gives women an internal asylum against all the oppression they receive from outside. Confession, he concludes, is thus essential for the individual, for the family and for society. Society can only punish crimes—priests can prevent them. 'The best of all governments would be a theocracy in which confession is established as the tribunal.'[1]

The effect of such doctrines, and of the denial or deferment of absolution, was frequently to cause people to give up going to confession and to church. The curé Millet of St Amand en Puisaye (Nièvre) wrote in his parish register in 1855 that the hostility of his parishioners was a result of Jansenism, and this must indeed

[1] Abbé A. M. Laurichesse, *Etudes philosophiques et morales sur la con-fession* (1865, overprinted 1864).

be considered an important cause of anticlericalism.[1] It is no accident that the diocese of Auxerre, where the Jansenist Caylus was bishop from 1705 to 1754, became an area of strong anticlericalism.[2] If a map could be drawn of the spread of Jansenist influence in the eighteenth century and another of anticlericalism in the nineteenth, there might well be some concordances between them. It is no accident, again, that Voltaire, one of the leading intellectual founders of anticlericalism, should have been the son of a Jansenist family, so that his hate of the Church was initiated not so much as an attack on Christianity, but as a rebellion against the fanaticism of his Jansenist father and elder brother.[3] It is no accident that the eighteenth-century writer on libertinage, Restif de la Bretonne, should have come from one of the most Jansenist areas of France of a very rigorist family, that his half-brother should have been a model Jansenist curé, and that he should have had a grandfather nicknamed 'The Severe' and a father called 'Honnête Homme'.[4]

In the Second Empire there was still a party among the clergy— its size can only be guessed—in favour of using confession as a severe instrument of repression.[5] Mgr de Ségur—a best selling popularizer, some of whose works ran into seventy-five editions— used a telling phrase in defending it: 'Let yourself be taken by the good God's police; they will take you not to prison but to paradise'. To those who complained that they did not like priests to meddle in their affairs, he stated that 'the priest has not only the right but the rigorous duty to teach you in general and in detail what you ought to do and what you ought to avoid'.[6] A work recommended by Bishop Pie of Poitiers insisted on the importance of confession as 'the most powerful dyke opposed to

---

[1] Abbé J. Charrier, *Histoire du Jansenisme dans le diocèse de Nevers* (1920), 140.

[2] Pierre Ordioni, *La Survivance des idées gallicanes et jansenistes en Auxerrois de 1760 à nos jours* (Auxerre, 1933).

[3] Réné Pomeau, *La Religion de Voltaire* (1956), 30-6.

[4] Ordioni, 129.

[5] Cf. Anon.; *Quelle est la bonne confession et quelle est la véritable absolution* (Valence, 2nd edition 1848), 2.

[6] Mgr de Ségur, *La Confession* (1862), 21.

the overflow of human passions' and pointed to the 'terrible moral degradation' of England and Germany, where it had been largely abandoned.[1]

The questions which confessors implementing this policy asked might relate to business activities. Merchants would be questioned about excessive profits, innkeepers about whether they had adulterated their wine, tailors whether they had returned the extra cloth and ribbons left over from each garment, barbers whether they did ladies' hair 'following the cursed custom recently introduced in our time by the devil'.[2] 'A Christian should never seek pleasure for its own sake, but always relate it to some useful and legitimate end.' He should take pleasure only by necessity, like sleep, to enable him to work better. So it was the duty of the confessor to discourage many normal recreations. Travel simply for pleasure, said a guide on *Relaxations Permitted to Pious Persons*, was undesirable; and if it had to be undertaken for business or other reasons, conversation with fellow-travellers should be avoided and limited to the needs of politeness: the best course was to read or pretend to be asleep. But great care should be taken in what was read. Novels 'exalt the imagination, trouble the heart, spoil the judgement . . . and produce boredom and distaste for the real world. . . . The number of young people who have been ruined by the reading of novels is incalculable.'[3] The aim of the confessor should be to keep his penitents in ignorance of sin as long as possible.

A treatise on the confession of children and young people, by the director of a church working-class youth organization in Marseille, published in 1865 with recommendations from five bishops (and still being used in 1924, when it was reprinted for the fourteenth time) warns sternly against sex education. A child often asks, it says, why there are two sexes. 'If you cannot elude the question, which is always the best thing to do, if he is

[1] Abbé Jarlit, *De l'institution divine de la confession* (Poitiers, 1858), 371, 383.

[2] J. J. Gaume, *Manuel des Confesseurs* (9th edition 1865), 205-6.

[3] R. P. Huguet, *Des Délaissements permis aux personnes pieuses appelées à vivre dans le monde* (Lyon, new edition, 1857), 21, 60-3, 108.

31

certainly likely to ask the same question of others, reply that God has arranged it so because it seemed right to His wisdom. Let him think you have told him everything. . . . So many children naïvely ask questions on which any answer satisfies them: therefore it is unnecessary to say more. . . . A prudent mother used invariably to reply to the embarrassing questions of an extremely inquisitive child: You will know when you get to the upper sixth form (the philosophy class); and this child, satisfied, patiently awaited this happy hour.' The author somewhat contradicts himself when he goes on to describe, on the basis of his experiences in the slums of Marseille, the sexual licence of children he knows, the mistresses they have at fourteen, their experimental visits even earlier to brothels, full of secondary schoolboys on the *jours de sortie* (holidays), the widespread homosexuality, which he regards as a major problem and to which he devotes over twenty pages.[1] Not just obscene books should be avoided, but also 'indecent pictures and sculptures' and 'evil newspapers, that is to say, newspapers hostile to the Church, to the Pope, to priests, to monks and those which do not hesitate to publish serial stories contrary to good morals'. Greed, the desire for riches, for the goods of this world, for honour and esteem were all of the same kind.[2] Women's clothes were a constant source of danger. Married ones who dressed to please their husbands, or girls who dressed in order to win husbands should be given some concessions, but not if they sought to please others apart from their husband, or if their aim was not to get married. Those who leave their arms or shoulders naked or only lightly covered were, if they were following the fashion, not guilty, but those who invented these fashions were guilty of mortal sin.

There were formulae in the manuals for the investigation of the most intimate details of sexual relations. There were questions about the exact postures adopted in intercourse, because only one

[1] Abbé Timon-David, *Traité de la confession des enfants et des jeunes gens* (1865, 14th edition 1924) 2. 180-262.
[2] See Mgr de Ségur, *Aux Enfants: Conseils pratiques sur les tentations et le péché* (1865), 25.

32

was approved, as being the most likely to produce conception. The procreation of children should be the aim: married people who had intercourse for pleasure committed a sin, though a venial one. The authorities were divided on whether intercourse to avoid incontinence was permissible. 'A woman was not required to fulfil her conjugal duty to a husband who demanded it too often, for example several times in the same night, because this is contrary to reason and because it could become very dangerous. The wife must however, as far as it is in her power, lend herself to the libidinous needs of her husband when he suffers violent desires of the flesh: for charity obliges her to save him as far as possible from the danger of incontinence.'[1] She may not refuse her duty for fear of too many children: she ought to confide herself to God. But some authors thought that if they could not afford more children, she could refuse, provided there was no danger to the husband of incontinence—but there always was. This problem of birth control worried the Church. 'Nothing is more frequent among young couples today,' wrote Bishop Bouvier, 'than the detestable practice of onanism.' He accordingly sent a petition to the Pope. 'One can hardly find any young couples who wish to have too numerous a family,' he wrote, 'and yet they cannot reasonably abstain from the conjugal act. They normally feel very offended when their confessors interrogate them on the manner in which they use their matrimonial rights; they cannot be got by warnings to moderate their exercise of the conjugal act, and they cannot decide to increase the number of their children too much. To the murmurs of their confessors, they reply by abandoning the sacraments of penitence and Eucharist, thus giving bad examples to their children, their servants and other Christians: religion suffers considerable prejudice from this. The number of people who come to confession diminishes from year to year in many places and it is above all for this reason, according to a large number of curés who are distinguished by their piety, their learning and their experience. How did confessors conduct themselves in former times, many

[1] J. B. Bouvier, *Dissertatio in sextum decalogi praeceptum et supplementum ad tractatum de matrimonio* (10th edition 1843), 149 ff.

people ask? Marriages did not generally produce more children than today. Spouses were not more chaste and yet they did not miss the obligation of Easter confession.'

The Sacred Congregation replied in 1842 that the confessor was not normally required to speak about sins that spouses commit regarding their conjugal duty and it was improper for him to pose questions in this regard, unless to the wife, who should be asked as moderately as possible whether she had fulfilled her duty. He should keep silence on everything else, unless he is questioned. This was the reply of the moderate party, but it is clear from Bouvier's letter that many curés did seek to control the sexual behaviour of their flocks and that many people broke with the Church for this reason. The cures they offered for the reduction of sexual urges—sobriety, abstinence from hot foods and spirits, little sleep, hard beds, cold baths, meditation on the dangers of sexual licence, on the prospect of death, divine judgement and hell, frequent prayer and the reading of works on *The Dangers of Onanism*—do not seem to have provided satisfactory alternatives.[1]

Michelet's fury against confession was unleashed not by theoretical considerations but by personal experience. He wrote his book on it soon after the death of his mistress, Mme Dumesnil, of cancer. During her illness she had resorted to a confessor, the Abbé Cœur, later bishop of Troyes. He won a great ascendancy over her and stimulated bitter jealousy in Michelet, who was often refused admission to her sick bed.[2] The autobiography of George Sand shows how much rested on the tact of the confessor in seeing how far he could go. She had an idyllic relationship with a sympathetic Jesuit confessor at her convent school, to whom she was quite devoted; but when she went home the local curé, whom she barely knew, 'thought I was

---

[1] Bouvier, *op cit.*, 172-3. The recommended works on onanism are by Tissot and Doussin-Dubreuil. For a non-religious study of this subject see Dr A. Mayer, *Des Devoirs Conjugaux* (1874).

[2] Jean Pommier, Les Idées de Michelet et de Renan sur la confession en 1845, in *Journal de Psychologie normale et pathologique* (15 July to 15 October 1936), 520-2.

falling in love with someone and he asked me (in confession) whether this was true. It was not, I replied, I have not even thought about it.—Nevertheless, he insisted, people assert . . . I rose in the confessional without listening any more and was seized by an irresistible indignation. All the purity in my being revolted against a question which was indiscreet, impudent and in my view irrelevant to religion. . . . If I had some chaste confidence to make, I saw no reason why I should address myself to him, who was not my director and spiritual father. I considered he had confused his curiosity as a man with his function as a priest.' He was so unlike her Jesuit, who 'scrupulous guardian of the holy ignorance of girls, once said to me: One should not ask questions; I never do'.[1]

All this evidence suggests that conflicts about morality were a significant element in the growth of anticlericalism. However, these conflicts were not simple, and neither side had a monopoly of any one set of principles. On the one hand, anticlericalism was stimulated by the excessive severity of some priests in enforcing unpopular moral standards through the confession. But the use of the confession as a means of interfering in private conduct was itself possibly an equal source of resentment. For, on the other hand, the anticlericals also protested against the laxness of the moral standards of other priests. There is the paradox that the Jesuits were singled out as the object of the most vigorous criticism by the enemies of the Church; but the Jesuits were leaders of the movement for the modernization and humanization of Catholic moral doctrines. It is too subtle to suggest that the anticlericals feared them most because they were most likely to save the Church. It is more probable that they did not see the issues clearly.

In the middle of the nineteenth century, a wide variety of practice and teaching coexisted in the Church in France. Anticlericals in different regions and with different personal experience were attacking different things. The Church was itself far from static, and not untouched by the intellectual and scientific developments of the eighteenth and nineteenth centuries, but not all the

[1] G. Sand, *Histoire de ma vie* (1904), 3. 192 ff., 327.

clergy were equally affected. The Church had its progressives, who appeared excessively radical to many republicans. It should not be forgotten that some clergymen in the eighteenth century had anticipated Rousseau's idea of the natural goodness of man. There were Jesuits who argued that human nature should be cultivated rather than denied, that man was not irretrievably fallen, that rational, as opposed to saintly, living was a commendable ideal. Such men should not be simply classified with those who tried to prove the literal truth of every fact in the Bible (as for example a certain Abbé Calmet did, in twenty-two volumes), but they clearly often were.[1] In the nineteenth century some ecclesiastical teachers were giving a considerably larger part to reason in religious education, without discarding revealed truths, but rather adding rational proof of these. They reacted to the romantic movement by adding appeals to the heart and the emotions, though this was largely dropped after 1830, when the emphasis on reason was revived. The popularity of science led to the greater use of arguments based on the marvels of nature; in reply to the enlightenment's hostility to dogma, a considerably larger place was given to the teaching of Christian morals.[2] This does not mean that the clash of reason and revelation, liberty and authority, progress and original sin, was unreal, but it was not as clear-cut as the polemicists lead one to believe.

To a certain extent the battle between Church and anticlericals was blown out of all proportion simply by anger. The need to be in either one party or the other concealed the fact that many people in both parties had a lot in common, particularly if abstract principles were put aside and their actual practical conduct was compared. This can be seen by examining the question of just how different the morality of the anticlericals was from that of the Church. Did the republicans, who were so firmly determined to found an independent state lay system of

[1] R. R. Palmer, *Catholics and Unbelievers in Eighteenth Century France* (Princeton, 1939).

[2] C. E. Elwell, *The Influence of the Enlightenment on the Catholic Theory of Religious Education in France 1750-1850* (Harvard, 1944).

moral education, in fact wish to give the individual greater freedom in his personal conduct? How puritan or how liberal were the republicans?

Edgar Quinet, one of the first advocates of lay education, lamented that 'there is no popular book in which the people can, without danger, receive their first moral education'.[1] This always remained true, and no single moral code was ever evolved by the republicans, who were even more disunited than the Catholics. The vast majority were not interested in producing new rules of conduct. Jules Ferry said that his lay schools had the duty 'to teach only one morality, that is to say the good old morality of our fathers'. Buisson, his director of primary education, likewise insisted on the traditional character of the ethics schoolmasters should instil. 'The only elements of morality that a society should transmit to the young generations are those which it has itself received from a long past, which constitutes the heritage of the centuries and the patrimony of humanity.' He defined lay morals in fact as that body of 'rules of normal conduct . . . on which all men of the same age and the same country cannot differ, any more than they can dispute the four laws [of arithmetic] or argue about geographical facts'.[2] The aim of this great consensus was to produce unity and harmony in France. Quinet had written in 1852 that there were several religions fighting each other, but beneath them lay a single morality and it was the function of the state to reveal this.[3] In 1914 Gustave Belot, who rose to be Inspector-General of Public Instruction, was still saying the same thing. All religions merely consecrate rules of conduct established by tradition: the only difference between lay and religious morality is therefore in motivation. Belot conceded that 'lay morality, as it is too often presented, is nothing but religious morality without the religion', and he was honest enough to admit that nothing had come of all the proposals to change this situation. The desirable changes 'not only still needed to be carried out, they had

[1] Edgar Quinet, *L' Enseignement du peuple* (1860 edition, vol. 14 of his Œuvres Complètes), 136.

[2] F. Buisson, in G. Belot *et al.*, *Questions de morale* (1900), 313.

[3] E. Quinet, *L'Enseignement du peuple* (1860 edition), 127.

yet to be discovered'.[1] This shows the bankruptcy of lay morality and explains why it was inevitably conservative.

The majority of republicans were far from advocating pleasure as the main purpose of life. The people who got nearest this were the St Simonians and the Fourierists. They were of course small sects but some of their adherents were influential, and some of their ideas gained popular currency. The philosopher Renouvier was probably as much responsible for their diffusion among the republican masses as any man, for he was patronized by Carnot in 1848 and by many leaders of the Third Republic. He wrote popular moral manuals, which can be compared to those of the Catholic confessors, though it is clear that his ideas were not as uniformly reproduced by the *instituteurs* as the hierarchy's doctrines were by the curés. His main interest is that he illustrates what intelligent and advanced anticlericals were thinking. 'Religion,' he wrote in 1848, 'teaches you how to conduct yourself in this world in order to render yourself worthy of eternal felicity. I speak in the name of the republic, in which we are going to live, and of that morality which every man feels at the bottom of his heart. I wish to instruct you on the way to be happy on earth, and the first thing I would say is this: Improve yourself. You will only become truly happy by becoming better.' This is the doctrine of the republic of professors. Realize your full capacities, help others to realize theirs, be just, fraternal, tolerant, and in this way the world will gradually become better. Love God is the first commandment, love your neighbour is the second. 'The Republic of 1792 established the morality of Jesus Christ in society.' The disagreements with the Church which had arisen since then should be ended; and France will then become the Promised Land.[2]

Twenty years later in his *Science of Morality* (1869) he was still repeating that reason approves of religion, and that religious indifference was undesirable; religion's only fault is intolerance,

[1] G. Belot, L'Efficacité pratique de la morale laïque, in R. Allier *et al.*, *Morale réligieuse et morale laïque* (1914), 51, 95.

[2] C. Renouvier, *Manuel républican de l'homme et du citoyen*, publié sous les auspices du ministère provisoire de l'instruction publique (1848).

its claim to absolute knowledge. In this work he gives more details of his view of pleasure. Pure pleasure is not to be condemned, he says, provided it is limited and ruled by reason, so that it does not lead to the forgetting of duty or to laziness. Sexual pleasures are aesthetic and there is nothing immoral about them, nor is there any need to restrict intercourse to the needs of procreation. Marriage is desirable but it is difficult to work because equality between the sexes has not been established. Adultery should not necessarily involve the dissolution of marriage. The education of children of both sexes should be reorganized to avoid the inculcation of shame and secrecy. Obedience is incompatible with the moral law. Parents must not abuse their authority, they must respect their children, bring them up as rational people, free to reject or accept their teachings.[1]

Now this latter part of Renouvier's doctrine was very advanced for any party in France at this date, and it was pushed into the background by most of his readers. He owed these ideas partly to Fourier but partly also to his own experience, for this respected pundit of morality, in his obscure retreat from which he wrote thirty-two volumes and articles enough to fill another eighteen, lived unmarried with two women in a somewhat phalansterian way and produced an illegitimate son by his cook. This explains, to a certain extent, his attack on Catholic doctrines on matrimony. Otherwise he was a Christian, and after breaking with Catholicism he became a Protestant, as did quite a few intellectuals who wanted to reconcile religion and freedom of thought. He approved of Combes, but he always kept a Bible on his table. In his later years when his son came to live with him he was converted to the idea of the creation, and rediscovered God as the 'paternal creator'. In 1894 he wrote 'Everybody seems to believe in progress, despite everything. I no longer do. At our age, one should try to believe in a better world than this.' Renouvier, the son of a Rousseauist father and a Jansenist mother, a romantic and St Simonian in his youth, ended up a Christian heretic. His tormented life shows the difficulties anticlericals had in breaking

---

[1] C. Renouvier, *Science de la morale* (1869), 1. 436, 547, 578, 584, 607.

away from their past. Renouvier wrote of a Utopia, but at bottom he was a pessimist.[1]

Pessimism indeed continued to permeate much republican thinking, so that in this respect there was no sharp break with Catholic teaching. This was due partly to the long-surviving influence of eclecticism and Kantism among the philosophers and so in the schools in which they taught, and partly to the conscious desire to produce a new morality which was all-embracing and therefore containing elements of Christianity in it. The philosophy master at the Lycée Condorcet, who produced an anthology of moralists in 1897, on the one hand praised Comte as one of the greatest philosophers of the century, Rousseau as having had an influence almost equal to that of a religious reformer, and Voltaire as the apostle of all liberties, but he also recommended Bossuet, as the representative of the Christian tradition ('so full of truths and reason, that even outside Catholicism, he has great moral and philosophic interest'), Bourdaloue ('having none of the laxity with which the Jesuits are often reproached'), Charles Rollin, the Jesuit educator whose *Traité des études* he calls a masterpiece of pure reason, St Francis de Sales 'author of gently and elegantly mystic works', and Malebranche 'who makes conformity to the universal order the essential rule of conduct'. He even includes Chateaubriand, Veuillot ('a great writer') and de Maistre ('theoretician of absolutism who pushes to . . . brilliant and revolting paradox all the arguments he supports'). He condemns not the Christians but Helvetius, 'advocate of the grossest sensualism'. He finds room for a large number of middle of the road eclectics like Cousin, Caro, Jouffroy, Jules Simon and Bersot, whose influence in the nineteenth century he rightly stresses. The republicans did not break with the past.[2] The Catholics who attacked Paul Bert's manual of civic education found fault with his politics and the accuracy of his historical facts, but they did not accuse him of immorality. It shows how the Catholics for their part belonged to the same classical tradition, that the first two chapters of one

[1] Marcel Mery, *La Critique du christianisme chez Renouvier* (1952).

[2] R. Thamin, *Extraits des moralistes* (1897).

attack on Bert criticizes first of all his French style, his colloquial-isms and his mistakes of syntax and spelling.[1]

The consequences of this attitude for daily life may be seen in the manuals of practical morals published by some leading republican philosophers. Ferraz, professor of philosophy at Lyon, may be taken as a middle of the road example. He begins by refuting St Simon and Fourier's view that pleasure or passion should be the guide to life.[2] There was no harm in seeking pleasure, provided it was realized that some pleasures were better than others and that intellectual pleasures were best of all. There was nothing wrong with 'our primitive tendencies . . . provided they were kept in their place and did not exceed the limits fixed by nature'. In other words the inferior ones—those which represented our animal side—'should be repressed' and the best way of doing this was by cultivating our higher sentiments. This was not totally different from the Church's recipe for enforcing chastity. Ferraz, like the Catholics, insists that reason should triumph not only by being assiduously cultivated but also by avoiding occasions which might damage its sway, for example, 'bad company, bad books, excessively free dances and licentious spectacles'. Christianity urges men to keep away from the world: he recommends only 'careful choice of company'. After a long discussion on the theatre, he concludes that occasional attendance is desirable. The total prohibition of dancing is excessive. Meditation was a good thing, but it should be lightened by physical exercise—mountaineering, shooting, hunting, riding, swimming and military manœuvres. This book shows how gradual was the move away from Catholic morals. Ferraz calls himself a rationalist, but his masters are Plato, Malebranche, Kant and Jouffroy.[3]

---

[1] Ch. Bellet, *Le Manuel de M. Paul Bert, ses erreurs et ses falsifications historiques, suivi d'un examen de la morale laïque de M. Jules Ferry* (Tours, 1882), approved by the vicar-general of Valence.

[2] Compare his criticism with that in Abbé Migne, *Dictionnaire des heresies* (vol. 1 of the first series of the Encyclopédie théologique) (1847), 2. 43.

[3] M. Ferraz, *Nos devoirs et nos droits. Morale pratique* (1881), xix, 100, 139-143, 216.

Paul Janet, professor at the Sorbonne from 1864 to 1899, has a similar inspiration though he quotes from an even wider assortment of Christian thinkers. He also believed in the rule of conscience: men should seek neither pleasure nor the useful but what was 'honest', preferring what is best in us, the noble affections over egoism, human dignity over animal passion. This could be called justice when applied to our attitude to others, and piety when applied to God—giving God his due. The superior sanction of religion was needed, because not all merit was equally rewarded in this world, and above all because hope in a supreme being was necessary to console man for his sins and suffering. 'We seem to be masters of the universe,' he wrote, 'but experience proves on the contrary how weak we are. . . . Life, despite the great side of it and despite some exquisite and sublime joys, is bad; all ends badly. . . . Deliver us from evil, that is the cry of every religion. God is the liberator and consoler.' Resignation to the will of Providence was the ultimate rule, but this did not mean fatalism. To love God is to love men. It is important to remember that God, as opposed to Catholicism, was not expelled from the lay schools. On a more mundane level, Janet counsels moderation in all things. Work is a pleasure and the cultivation of the faculties necessary to human dignity. Thrift is a virtue. Workers should not 'systematically feel hate, envy, covetousness or revolt against their employers. The division of labour requires that some direct while others are directed.' Workers have a right to equal respect, but they must make themselves worthy of respect by 'educating themselves and their children, occupying their leisure with family life, reading, innocent and elevating recreations (music, theatre, gardening if it is possible)'. They must not hope for equal salaries, however, because 'nothing is more contrary to the modern spirit which wants every man to be treated according to his achievements . . . otherwise there would be a premium on carelessness and idleness'.[1] Bersot, one of the most fashionable moralists of the Second Empire, perhaps summarized this

---

[1] Paul Janet, *Eléments de morale protique* (1889).

philosophy best when he said, 'Man is not born to be happy, but he is born to be a man at his own risk and peril'.[1]

There were lay moralists who were more 'advanced' than these men, but their radicalism concerned only their attitude to God, whom they sometimes left out altogether from their books: their aim was only to make morals entirely independent of religion. None of them advocated pleasure, or even utility, as the criterion of conduct.[2] They wished to make men act rationally, but they did not expect this use of reason to produce wildly different results in different individuals. Marion, Professor of Education at the Sorbonne, warned against allowing reason to get out of hand. In a lecture to schoolteachers on the moral education syllabus, he insisted that the new lay system involved the training of the intelligence, to enable it to make moral decisions, as opposed to the Catholic catechism, which relied on the memorizing of rules. However, children must not be turned into 'little reasoners who will grow up into sophists. . .'. 'Great circumspection should be used in the choice of occasions which will be given to the child to use his judgement.' He must not get into the habit of judging his schoolmates, nor must he be allowed to lose his feelings of shame or honour. 'What would one do when the child avows his mistakes without blushing?' It would be improper to ask him to judge directly his parents, neighbours and people to whom he owes respect. 'It is better to transport him at once to another sphere and give him very elevated thoughts, so that he does not, as it were, see the faults and ugliness in the middle of which he lives; but so that, when he does come to see them, he will judge them implicitly and from above, without discussing them. Inspire in him by example such a great respect for the law, that when in his turn he is tempted to become a poacher or to defraud the tax collector, as is so often done in the countryside, the majesty of the law will rise before him, so to speak, and restrain him.' Science was no way to inculcate such ideas into him. It teaches the struggle for existence and the brutal

---

[1] Felix Hémon, *Bersot et ses amis* (1911), 334.

[2] Emile Boutroux, *Les Récents manuels de morale et d'instruction civique*, *Revue pédagogique* (15 April 1883), 322.

triumph of force. Much better therefore to rely on the old syllabus of literary *culture générale* to instil morality.[1]

Madame Gréville, whose republican textbook on morals for girls (1882) was immediately condemned by the Church, did indeed leave God out, but otherwise she advised behaviour of a pretty traditional kind. She talked of the development of equality between the sexes and lamented that much still needed to be done to improve the lot of women, but meanwhile women's function was to please men. 'Men demand of women, first of all, that they should have the virtues and appearance of women.' So women should not be too masculine. They should guard their virtue, for faults considered insignificant in men are catastrophic for women. 'Their delicate sentiments will disappear in proportion as they show a little more of their necks and their arms': it is undesirable that they should cease to be ashamed and to blush when people look at them. To keep themselves virtuous, Madame Gréville recommends that they should examine their consciences every time they wash their hands. Their place was in the home; if they got bored and wandered in the streets, they would encounter temptations which would lead them to far worse evils. Those who were not interested by housework 'could not long remain honourable women'. It was their fault if they did not make their homes attractive enough to keep their husbands there. Even though they did not have the vote, they should have an opinion on politics, but if this differed from that of their husbands, they should keep it to themselves, to avoid discord. Women unfortunately had the not undeserved reputation of being chatter-boxes; so they should get into the habit of speaking only when they had something worth saying.[2]

Maria Deraismes, editor of *Le Républicain de Seine-et-Oise*

[1] H. Marion, L'Enseignement moral, *Revue pédagogique* (July-December 1882), 5-21. That the books on morals discussed here were widely available may be seen, for example, from Ministère de l'instruction publique, Exposition universelle de 1889 à Paris, *Trois types de bibliothèques populaires* (1889), which gives three interesting catalogues.

[2] Madame Henry Gréville, *Instruction morale et civique des jeunes filles* (1882), 139-77.

(1881-5) and organizer of anticlerical congresses in 1881 and 1882, inveighed against novel-reading with almost as much wrath as the clergy, though with more discrimination. In a lecture to the Freemasons' Grand Orient, she deplored the immoral influence of novels, with their contemptible heroes, their exploitation of scandal and their destruction of 'principles and sentiments'. Almost like a rigorist preacher, she attacked the age for devoting itself to the unthinking pursuit of pleasure, neglecting the superior pleasures of 'the intelligence and the heart' for the inferior satisfaction of the senses, idle amusements and temporary distractions. 'The phalanx of bastards and foundlings are the innocent victims of this pleasure.' Pleasure, she insisted, must be enjoyed within the limits of duty, or the family would be destroyed. The feminists were nearly all republicans, but for them the winning of women's rights went hand in hand with the suppression of vice.[1]

The Church told people what to do when they were married. The republican state, even when it took over the teaching of morality, was too prudish to do so. The hints it gave suggested that it was legitimate to enjoy sex in moderation but that it was best not to talk about it. Janet wrote: 'The honourable man enjoys his pleasures with simplicity and without thinking about them'.[2] A best-selling guide to the *Hygiene and Physiology of Marriage*, by a retired army medical officer, which between 1848 and 1883 went through 172 editions, is as near as one can get to enlightened lay opinion on this matter. The author dispels the myth that women do not enjoy intercourse, and his book is designed to show how both sexes can derive pleasure from it and maintain their enjoyment into old age. He urges women to satisfy their husbands, if they want to keep them; but he advises husbands to win their wives by affection and caresses, rather than by force or command. But he too counsels moderation. (Copulation more frequent than two to four times a week for those under 30, twice a week between 30 and 40, once a week till 50, will destroy the freshness of women's charm and possibly give them cancer of the

[1] Maria Deraismes, *Nos Principes et nos mœurs* (1868), 208-250.
[2] Janet, 250n.

ovaries; it will make men impotent.) He is not willing to discuss the details of 'permitted postures', as the Catholic casuists do: 'Where the devil were they sticking their noses?' he asks angrily. And he says not a word about contraception.[1]

Another doctor, a member of the inspectorate of public health, said it 'would dirty his pen' to describe contraceptive methods. However, his book on *Marriage Relations*, which went through six editions, was an attack on conjugal onanism, which he declares, was 'an almost universal usage' in every social class. He condemns it as the scourge of the times, in language which is just as vigorous as Bishop Bouvier's. He reaches the same conclusions as the Church, though by a different route. He quotes the latest scientific publications to argue that conjugal onanism produced appalling nervous disorders (though he does not say these were universal: he cites only a few cautionary examples). He recommends the rhythm method as a substitute—'chastity within certain limits', moderation once again. It is interesting that in theory this doctor was liberal, indeed advanced. He sings the praises of Fourier, who had believed in free love and trial marriages; he thinks that sexual instincts should be satisfied from the outset of puberty and he condemns the law against marriage before eighteen. However, like the radical party in politics, which had the most advanced ideals in theory but practised the most prudent moderation, he is in no hurry to put Fourier's ideas into effect. Contradicting himself he insists, like the Church, that the purpose of sexual relations should be reproduction.[2]

The ordinary man was thus not presented with alternatives which were wholly clear cut. Proudhon might say that the masses looked on the Church as an institution that stopped them from being happy, but his own moral code was asceticism itself. Comte likewise did not attack Catholicism in order to foster moral licence: he invented frightening totalitarian schemes to

[1] A. Debay, *Hygiene et physiologie du marriage* (n.d., 54th edition), 94, 103, 135-9.

[2] Dr Alex. Mayer, *Des Rapports conjugaux considérés sous le triple point de vue de la population, de la santé et de la morale publique* (1874, 6th edition), viii, 76, 221, 254.

instil altruism into everybody. The republican attitude was well put by Louis Havet, professor at the Collège de France and later a leading Dreyfusard, who thus defined how France should be saved 'by the republic and by free thought, by morals and by *discipline*. ... We must free ourselves from all authority and all tradition that is not based on reason; we must at the same time govern ourselves severely, repress every weakness and every petty interest, practise respect and obedience to every proper command.' The function of philosophy was to establish the rule of truth and duty. 'The best religion is that which keeps moral character in its greatest purity and which prescribes to people the most *severe* rule of morals.'[1]

Did the masses know what they were doing when they gave their support to the anticlerical leaders? Did they believe that liberation from the Church would give them freer lives? Were the bourgeois morals which the intellectual anticlericals dispensed to them a disappointment, so that they were cheated by the Third Republic, as they had been cheated in 1789? Or were the masses so indoctrinated by traditional values that they did not want a moral revolution? Louis Veuillot, one of the most influential Catholic journalists of the century, said that he was opposed to anticlericalism not least because he was 'a son of the *petit peuple*' and anticlericalism was a bourgeois doctrine.[2] Many socialists said the same thing. It is certainly impossible to isolate anticlericalism from the social and moral conflicts of the nineteenth century.

This essay has put forward a number of hypotheses which, it is hoped, further research may test and amplify. The first is that the confession is an institution the study of which could reveal a great deal to historians and social scientists; and that it is an institution which has taken on a variety of forms at different periods and in different regions of France and of the world. It requires—and indeed seems an ideal subject for—both comparative and interdisciplinary research. The methods of sociology and social

---

[1] L. Havet, *Le Christianisme et ses origines* (3rd edition 1880), i. xi. (My italics.)

[2] Louis Veuillot, *Les Libres penseurs* (1850, 2nd edition), i.

anthropology are needed to discover how the confession has been practised over the last fifty years, to see not only what questions were asked, how careful and prolonged the scrutiny and how severe the penances, but also what the attitudes of the faithful to confession have been, how they have altered, how they compare with their attitudes to, for example, psychoanalysis, how they relate to other attitudes, for example, to authority and pleasure, and what connexion they have with the rest of the penitent's behaviour. It would be useful to contrast the French situation with the Greek Orthodox one, where there is far less anticlericalism and where confession is made not to the village priests but to specially authorized monks with a reputation for holiness, outside the village community.[1] It would be worth investigating further the view put forward by an anthropologist studying an Italian village, that the confession is a key factor in explaining the power of the priest in social relations: the priest is able to act as arbitrator because he knows his parishioners' difficulties more intimately than anyone else; in disputes, since he knows the hidden motives and private histories of those involved, he can often offer fairer justice than the police or the law courts.[2] At another level, the historian of art and architecture would find fascinating material in the variations of the confessional box, which has known surprisingly many shapes. At one extreme is the *confessional à surprise*: one such had a painting of Christ on a panel which, at the touch of a button, changed into a picture of the devil with flaming eyes and gnashing teeth the size of tusks, to the accompaniment of frightening noises produced by whistles and organ pipes.[3] Some confessionals offer privacy; others, such as those in some shrines to which peasants still come crawling on their knees, have the priest illuminated as though on a throne, while the penitent weeps publicly in full view of the crowds. It may be that these variations could be related to changes in the emphases of Catholic moral theology. Again, there are an

[1] I am grateful to Dr J. K. Campbell for this point, and for other helpful comments.

[2] A. L. Maraspini, *Calimera* (Oxford D.Phil. thesis, 1962), 354.

[3] *L'Observateur Catholique* (1856-67), 12. 165.

enormous number of caricatures about the confession—descrip-
tive, suggestive or bawdy—which would repay study: the history
of humour, one may add, is still in a very primitive state.

The second hypothesis is that the rigour of inquisition in the
confession and the severity of sanctions may have some relation
to the spread of anticlericalism and the decline in church attendance. Much has been written about the interference of the clergy
in political disputes, but very little so far about the effects of its
probing into people's private lives. However, in France it seems
that the tenacious survival of Jansenist rigorism in certain areas,
and its propagation well into the nineteenth century through
Bailly's widely used seminary textbook and other works, did
produce a clergy who were particularly repressive in dealing with
sin and with pleasure. Sexual behaviour may have been an
important subject of dispute between the priest and his
parishioners, in a way which has not hitherto been realized. Bishop
Bouvier's letter to the Pope, quoted above, is an extremely
valuable piece of evidence. It asserts without hesitation that the
prying by confessors into sexual habits and their prohibition of
birth control was producing protests and driving people away
from church. Naturally, it is impossible to generalize from this
about the whole of France. More information will first be needed
about how confessors behaved in different regions, and local
factors may make it difficult to isolate the effects of their
behaviour. In Brittany, for example, the existence of *pardons*
(pilgrimages and feasts involving communal confession) com-
plicates the issue; there also, though the priests fulminated
against dancing, their pious flocks nevertheless made dancing
one of their major recreations—a contradiction explained by the
fact that the dances they indulged in were communal and totally
without erotic content. In Lorraine the formerly Jansenist
regions have not abandoned religious practice: repression does
not necessarily produce protest. The confession needs to be
studied within the context of local traditions. But it is interesting
to find a bishop pointing to sexual conflicts as a principal cause
of alienation from the Church and this deserves investigation.
As a preliminary, the chronology of the Church's teaching needs

to be established: there is still no adequate history of Catholic moral theology, let alone of its application in practice. A recent doctoral thesis on the origins of sexual taboos in France and Germany—unfortunately unpublished and written in Dutch— has discovered a battle against masturbation in the eighteenth century. The author likens the ferocity of this campaign to the witch hunts of the Middle Ages and to modern anti-Semitism.[1] This enquiry would be worth pursuing into the nineteenth century. It leads one to wonder whether the opposition to birth control may similarly have been especially powerful in some particular periods. It would be interesting to know which clergy initiated this opposition, or whether they simply joined in an outcry started by others. An understanding of the nineteenth-century position would be greatly helped also by a comparison with reactions to puritanism in the seventeenth century.

The third suggestion is that these problems of anticlericalism can be used to shed light on the development of the family. Michelet's hostility to the confession is linked with his concern for the emancipation of women. But he makes it clear that he is anxious not just to liberate women from clerical oppression; he also wants to strengthen the family and in particular the power of the husband in it. The confessor appeared to him as the great enemy or rival of the husband. Now in the nineteenth century the idea was frequently put forward that paternal authority was on the decline; and it may be that hostility to the confessor and anticlericalism was some form of rearguard action to safeguard or preserve this authority. The French family, however, is yet another subject on which practically no research has been done. It is extraordinary what large areas of French life still await investigation.

[1] Josef Maria Willem Van Ussel, *Sociogenese en evolutie van het probleem der seksuele propaedeuse tussen de 16de en de 18de eeuw, vooral in Frankrijk en Duitsland. Bijdrage tot de studie van de burgerlijke seksuele moraal.* Amsterdam University thesis for the Doctorate of Letters, defended 28 February 1967.

CHAPTER II

THE CONFLICT IN EDUCATION

CATHOLIC SECONDARY SCHOOLS (1850-70):
A REAPPRAISAL

ROBERT ANDERSON

Catholic secondary schools in France have had a troubled history. The loi Falloux of 1850 inaugurated one of the few periods in the nineteenth century when they were able to expand with relative freedom from official interference and hostile criticism. The aim of this essay is to trace the effects of the loi Falloux in the first twenty years of its operation on boys' secondary education. How did the new Catholic schools grow, and what different types of school were there? Why did parents choose Catholic rather than state schools, and how far was the division between the two sectors a social one? What education, moral and intellectual, did the Catholic schools give, and how did it differ from that of the state's lycées? Finally, why did the development of these schools come to be seen, even by the conservative government of the Second Empire, as a threat to the social unity of France, so that the granting of 'liberty of education' led in time to a new cycle of repression?

It may be as well to say something at the outset about the provisions of the loi Falloux itself and the intentions of the men who made it. Their first aim, of course, was to remove the restrictions on private education which had existed since the creation of the University by Napoleon. The University had been intended to take over the Church's functions as dispenser of education, and Napoleon's legislation did not provide for any large-scale revival of private education; such private schools as were permitted to exist were regarded as ancillary to the University, which authorized their opening and supervised their conduct. One provision in particular hindered the formation of a rival system of schools: candidates for the baccalaureate had to attend the two higher forms of a state school, and to produce a 'certificate of studies' attesting this. Only a small number of private schools were allowed *plein exercice*, the right to give the full range of education.

Even before the loi Falloux, the appointment of ministers of education sympathetic to the Catholic cause had led to the relaxation of these restrictions: the number of schools with *plein exercice* rose from twenty-seven on 1 January 1848, to forty-one in June 1849,[1] and the certificate of studies was abolished in 1849. The loi Falloux confirmed the freedom of private schools to teach what they liked.

The law also destroyed the 'monopoly' of the University: to open a school became a right, subject to certain legal safeguards, instead of a privilege. Certain restrictions imposed in 1828, which had cut short the first revival of Catholic education after the Restoration, were now implicitly repealed. First, the Jesuits, excluded from teaching since that date, had full rights under the new law.[2] Secondly, the bishops were given freedom to develop their *petits séminaires* as ordinary secondary schools: the 1828 ordinances had sought to confine these to their original role as schools for potential seminarists.

The emancipation of private education was, however, not complete, for the University retained some control: directly, because its officials still supervised the private schools and retained powers of inspection and discipline; indirectly, because the University ran the baccalaureate, whose requirements inevitably dictated the syllabus of all secondary schools. The loi Falloux provided safeguards for the Catholic schools by putting representatives of the Church (and other outside bodies) on the various councils of the University—the local *conseils académiques* through

---

[1] Archives Nationales (AN) F[17] 6839, list for 1848; F[17] 6833, note for President of Republic, 3 June 1849.

[2] Under the Restoration they had not had their own colleges, but had run eight of the *petits séminaires*.

which the University's supervision of private schools was exercised, and the *Conseil supérieur* at Paris which the minister of education was obliged to consult on syllabuses and examinations. But these provisions lost much of their value after changes in 1852 and 1854, which remodelled the councils and destroyed their independence of the government.

Nevertheless, the way was now open for the growth of a strong system of Catholic schools which could compete with the University on equal terms. The supporters of the loi Falloux claimed that this competition was desirable in itself, and would lead to a general improvement of standards. This argument was calculated to gain support for the law in intellectual and parliamentary circles, where the liberal ideology of the political economists was increasingly popular. Indeed, the whole concept of a state system of education and of a state-financed teaching corporation was now questioned, and the failure of the University to adapt its education to the needs of a scientific age was presented as an example of the evil effects of monopoly.

The destruction of the monopoly, it was claimed, would bring a new dynamism into the development of education. The loi Falloux introduced fair competition between state and private education, and allowed the consumer—the *père de famille*—to choose between them. The pressures of the market would be enough to bring about the reforms which were needed. When introducing the bill, Falloux defended in this way its failure to provide for the changes which were admittedly necessary in the lycées: 'these questions . . . will be more promptly and more decisively solved by the rivalry of the new establishments than by legislative means'.[1]

Something of the kind was to happen. In 1852, Hippolyte Fortoul (minister of education 1851-6) introduced a reform of the syllabus of the lycées ('bifurcation') which strengthened their scientific teaching. One motive for this was alarm at the loss of pupils to Catholic schools, which was to be countered by emphasizing one of the fields where the lycées were clearly superior. There were other reforms of the lycées introduced by

[1] H. Michel, *La loi Falloux* (1906), 483.

Fortoul and his successors (Gustave Rouland, 1856-63; Victor Duruy, 1863-9) which were stimulated by Catholic rivalry, although at times competition inhibited rather than encouraged change. In 1868-9, for example, Duruy's plans to reform the teaching of the classics were opposed by teachers and administrators on the grounds that innovation would alarm parents and drive them into the Catholic fold.[1]

The loi Falloux might have done more to stimulate the modernization of the French educational ideal if it had given the University rivals who were more forward-looking than itself. But in fact Catholic teachers were even more conservative than *universitaires*, and such progress as there was was chiefly on the part of the University. The fact that the Catholic schools were successful while offering a traditional education shows also that the parents were unlikely to play the positive role foreseen by the liberals: most of them were content with the classics, and their choice of school was rarely made on purely educational grounds. In any case, it will be seen that in practice competition was imperfect.

The creation of two rival systems of education had implications of a graver kind. The fear of such rivalry as a threat to the moral unity of the nation lies behind the whole history of conflict over education in France. Education was not thought of as a matter to which society could be indifferent, or which could be abandoned to haphazard development as in England. It was seen as one of the means of preserving national identity and creating a common set of beliefs and ideals which would unite the educated class; this concept of unity, of an education which would be 'comprehensive' ideologically if not socially, has haunted the minds of French thinkers (especially on the left) since the Revolution. In a nation where political and religious divisions were deep, the danger of educational rivalry was that schools teaching different systems of values would form *deux jeunesses* (the phrase is famous from a speech of Waldeck-Rousseau, but the idea is much older) who would grow into two hostile nations within the nation.

The debates on the loi Falloux showed that there were already

[1] AN F^{17} 6872^2, reports from academies on proposed reforms, 1868-9.

two parties with separate and irreconcilable 'ideas of France'. The republican view, as expressed in Hugo's speeches on the bill or Quinet's *L'Enseignement du peuple* (1850), was that the function of a national system of education was to keep France true to her revolutionary heritage and preserve the principles of liberty and reason. Catholics believed with equal passion that France's special mission was a Christian one, and that a return to the faith was the means of regaining national unity and greatness. Catholic schools were a first and necessary instrument of this regeneration.

Most Catholic teachers belonged to the second of these parties, but it would be wrong in this period to identify the University with the first. Many individual teachers were republicans and freethinkers; but the University as a whole—following the lead of Victor Cousin—saw its task as the promotion of national reconciliation and unity. It based its opposition to separate Catholic schools on the claim that its own teaching (even Cousin's philosophy) rested on principles which could be accepted by all Frenchmen whatever their beliefs, and contained nothing to offend Catholics. The *laicité* of the University in 1850 was a doctrine of tolerance and comprehension based on the concept of natural religion, not the anti-religious ideology which it later became.[1] Despite this, it was clear by 1850 that a large part of Catholic opinion found the University's education unacceptable, and it was therefore difficult to deny Catholics the right to have their own schools.[2] But it is they, with their rejection of a common education and their insistence on exclusivism, who must bear the first responsibility for the disruptive effects of the loi Falloux.

The defenders of the law, indeed, claimed that it would not

[1] See for example A. Garnier, *Morale sociale* (1850), 143-53; Jules Simon in *La liberté de penser*, v. 206-7 (February 1850). Cf. J. Barthélemy-Saint-Hilaire, *M. Victor Cousin, sa vie et sa correspondance* (1895), i. 464-6; A.-J. Tudesq, *Les grands notables en France (1840-1849). Etude historique d'une psychologie sociale* (1964), ii. 711-12.

[2] Large numbers of Catholic parents, of course, continued to use the state schools. The word 'Catholic' is used throughout to refer to *separate* Catholic schools and those who favoured them.

have such effects. Politically, it had been made possible by a coming together of old enemies in the face of a common danger. It was hoped that this compromise symbolized the healing of old wounds, and that the removal of Catholic grievances against the University would create a new atmosphere of harmony in which the two sectors of education would be friendly rivals, not bitter enemies. The liberal Catholics who were the strongest supporters of the law looked forward to an era in which Catholicism would become more liberal and open to modern ideas, while the bourgeoisie, and the University itself, returned fully to Catholic beliefs. This prospect had a strong appeal to the many Catholics within the University.[1]

But in fact the law inevitably favoured divergence of ideals rather than reconciliation: for example, when the Catholics had their own schools, the University had less obligation to respect the susceptibilities of ultra-Catholic parents, and was freer to develop its liberal tendencies. Moreover, the fate of the law was bound up with the fate of liberal Catholicism, and this current was now weakening. Those who ran the new Catholic schools were mainly men of the ultramontane and intransigent wing of the Church. We shall see that, as opponents of the law feared, Catholic and state schools did develop a different ethos, although the difference between them was perhaps not so great as to justify alarm about the political consequences in any country but France.

After this introduction, we may turn to discuss the growth of the Catholic schools. Statistics collected by the government allow us to measure this, although they are incomplete and unreliable. Table 1 shows the position before the loi Falloux came into force; in these figures Catholic schools were not distinguished from other private schools. They show first of all that private education was not a creation of the loi Falloux: by 1848, the University, despite its 'monopoly', had fewer than half of all secondary school pupils—considerably fewer if we add to the private total some 18,000 pupils in the *petits séminaires*, which were excluded from the educational statistics. But the fact that few private schools

[1] For example, A. de Margerie, *De la réforme universitaire* (Poitiers, 1850), 6-8, 15-27, 39-42.

gave a complete secondary education meant that the state schools were far superior in point of quality: in 1840-2, the private schools

Table 1. *Pupils in different types of secondary school*[1]

	State	Private
1842	45,281 (51%)	43,195 (49%)
1847-8	51,592 (48%)	56,494 (52%)
1850	*c.* 50,000[2]	52,906

provided only 295 of 5,038 candidates for the baccalaureate.[3] We may also note from these figures that by 1850 all schools had suffered from the political and economic crisis.

After 1850, there are no figures until 1854;[4] but the intervening period was clearly that when Catholic schools expanded most rapidly. The most significant single result of the loi Falloux was the reappearance of the Jesuits, and their new schools were founded rapidly: the demand for schools by local groups of Catholic parents was more than the resources of the Order could cope with.[5] Ten schools were founded in 1850, four more in 1851-2; between then and 1870, only two more were to appear.

The second feature of the period immediately following 1850

---

[1] Sources: for 1842, *Rapport au roi sur l'instruction secondaire* (1843), Tables 7, 14, 19, 21; for 1847-8, for private schools figures for December 1847 and January 1848, in AN F¹⁷ 6838 and 6839, and for state schools *Statistique de l'enseignement secondaire en 1865* (1868), Tables 13, 23; for 1850, AN F¹⁷ 6839, unpublished statistical report for 1850, Tables 5, 10, 14, 15.

[2] Official sources give at least five figures for this, ranging from 47,941 to 52,755—an example of the unreliability of this evidence.

[3] *Rapport au roi sur l'instruction secondaire* (1843), Table 27 (average annual figures for 1840-2). There are unfortunately no similar figures for later years.

[4] In 1853, Fortoul estimated the numbers in Catholic schools at 17,000 (almost certainly too low a figure), against 50,000 in state schools and 43,000 in lay private schools. At that time there were 158 Catholic schools, of which 62 had been opened since the loi Falloux. Report to Emperor, 19 September 1853. (Official documents of this kind are to be found in the *Bulletin administratif de l'instruction publique* and other collections.)

[5] J. Burnichon, *La Compagnie de Jésus en France. Histoire d'un siècle 1814-1914* (1914 ff.), iii. 374-5. This book includes brief histories of each school.

is that Catholics were then in a strong position in local politics, and were able to exploit provisions of the loi Falloux which allowed local councils to subsidize private schools[1] and to withdraw their municipal colleges[2] from the University and transfer them to the Church or to private teachers. By 1853, out of 307 colleges in 1850, thirty-seven had become Catholic schools and nine lay private schools.[3]

Detailed statistics of the effects of the loi Falloux were collected for the first time in 1854, and the results seem so to have alarmed the government that it manipulated the published figures in order to conceal the state's losses. On Fortoul's reckoning, the Catholic schools had 21,195 pupils (19 per cent), the lay private schools 42,462 (38 per cent), and the state schools 48,981 (43 per cent).[4] Another set of figures would give the Catholic schools 26,205 pupils (23 per cent) against the state's 46,440 (40 per cent).[5]

In either case, the Catholics had clearly made substantial gains, and their success was probably as great as was expected by reasonable Catholic opinion—Falloux himself had feared that the difficulty would be to find enough pupils;[6] but those who had hoped that the loi Falloux would lead to a rapid withering away of the University were disappointed. The Catholic schools grew quickly after the law because there was an unsatisfied demand for them; but once the demand had been met, and the schools had

[1] Up to 10 per cent of their expenses. A similar power was given to the central government, but was never used. In 1865, 120 private schools received subsidies from local councils; *Statistique de l'enseignement secondaire en 1865* (1868), Table 27.

[2] The state schools were either lycées, run directly by the Ministry of Education, or municipal colleges, where the Ministry was responsible for the teaching but the money came from the local councils.

[3] Report to Emperor, 19 September 1853. Cf. J. Maurain, *La politique ecclésiastique du Second Empire de 1852 à 1869* (1930), 140-1.

[4] Report of 4 April 1854.

[5] Figures for state schools from *Statistique de l'enseignement secondaire en 1865* (1868), Tables 13, 23. The higher figure for Catholic schools is obtained by adding up the totals for each department of France in Fortoul's table: the printed totals and sub-totals showing the lower figures are incorrect. Fabrication is the most likely explanation of the discrepancy.

[6] H. Michel, *La loi Falloux* (1906), 208-9.

reached the limits of their natural clientele, the situation stabilized itself. By 1854-5, the lycées were recovering, and after that the relation between lycées and Catholic schools remained the same for many years, both sharing in a general expansion of secondary education. This is shown by Table 2.

Table 2. *Pupils in different types of secondary school*[1]

	Lycées and colleges	Lay private	Ecclesiastical private[2]
1855	47,981 (42%)	40,506 (36%)	25,613 (22%)
1857	52,853 (44%)	41,889 (34%)	26,819 (22%)
1861	58,288 (44%)	43,351 (33%)	30,824 (23%)
1865	65,668 (46%)	43,009 (30%)	34,897 (24%)
1867	68,565 (47%)	41,989 (28%)	36,424 (25%)
1876	75,259 (49%)	31,249 (20%)	46,816 (31%)
1887	89,902 (56%)	20,174 (13%)	50,085 (31%)
1898	86,084 (53%)	9,725 (6%)	67,643 (41%)
1899	82,489 (51%)	10,182 (6%)	68,825 (43%)

The figures given for the Third Republic show that only at the end of the century did the Catholics gain at the direct expense of the state schools: under the Second Empire, both grew together. Moreover, the Catholics founded relatively few new schools, and most of the expansion was within the existing ones: there were 256 Catholic schools in 1854, only 250 in 1857, 278 in 1865.

For its part, the University had practically regained by 1865 the proportion of pupils which it had in 1848 (although the competition was now of a different order) and was soon to exceed it. It is therefore wrong to suppose, as anticlerical writers did at the time, that the loi Falloux struck state education a mortal blow.

[1] Sources: for 1855, 1857, 1861, 1867, AN F¹⁷ 8847; for 1865, *Statistique de l'enseignement secondaire en 1865* (1868), Tables 11, 19, 26, 27; for 1876, *Statistique de l'enseignement secondaire en 1876* (1878), Table 35; for 1887-1899, printed diagram in AN F¹⁷ 6859. Cf. A Prost, *Histoire de l'enseignement en France 1800-1967* (1968), p. 45. All these figures exclude *petits séminaires*, where the estimated total remained static at around 23,000 from 1865 to 1899.

[2] The official definition was a school run by a minister of religion. It included Protestant schools, but the numbers involved were insignificant (in 1865, 13 schools with 935 pupils).

Edmond About, for example, asserted in 1860 that 'the influence of the clergy, preponderant for the last ten years, has killed the state's education, and our lycées are in a very bad way'.[1]

Certainly, the expansion of Catholic education was alarming many observers: in his *Carnets de voyage*, based on his journeys around France in 1863-5 as an examiner for St Cyr, Taine gives a vivid picture of the success of Catholic schools in the provinces. But his pessimism about the future of the University was not shared by the University's own officials, consulted by Duruy in 1864. Duruy sent out a long questionnaire on many aspects of secondary education; on the private schools, it asked what the current position was and what factors caused their growth or decline. The general tone of the replies was one of reasonable confidence. The Catholic schools were generally prosperous, and the Jesuits were the chief danger; but they were gaining new ground only in certain areas. The University's place in public esteem and its competitive position were felt to be secure, and there was no real alarm.[2] The rector of Lyons even declared that private education had been stationary since 1850, and the academy of Paris reported that the loi Falloux had not affected numbers in the University's schools. Other rectors, however, were concerned, as we shall see, about the long-term political dangers of educational rivalry.

The Catholic schools were of different types and unequal quality. The important ones fall into four categories: schools run by teaching orders; a number of independent schools established before 1850; the *petits séminaires*; and 'diocesan colleges' run by the bishops. The first two types tended to be more exclusive and expensive than the last two. The orders had an advantage because they could supply trained and experienced teachers, and after 1850 some new orders were founded and many of the old independent schools were taken over by teaching orders.

[1] M. H. de la Garde, *Considérations sur la liberté d'enseignement* (1860), 46 (letter from About to the author).

[2] Replies in AN F¹⁷ 6843-9, arranged by academies. This will be referred to as '1864 enquiry'. The officials concerned were the rectors of academies and the *inspecteurs d'académie* (IA) in each department.

In 1865, the orders ran forty-three schools with 9,475 pupils. The Jesuits led the field (fourteen schools, 5,074 pupils),[1] followed by the Société de Marie, an order founded in France in 1817 (fifteen schools, 2,255 pupils).[2] Of the new orders, the most significant were the Assumptionists, founded in 1850 by the legitimist and ultramontane priest Emmanuel d'Alzon to run a school which he had opened at Nîmes. D'Alzon had ambitions to unite and lead the Catholic educational movement and to make Nîmes its centre: in 1851, he founded a periodical, the *Revue de l'enseignement chrétien*, as an intellectual forum for Catholic teachers, and he hoped to turn his school into a sort of Catholic *Ecole normale*. But these initiatives failed—the review never had more than 200 subscribers, and ceased publication in 1855.[3] In fact, the Catholic schools never achieved any organizational unity, and did not present a common front;[4] they followed different teaching traditions and represented different tendencies within the Church.

The influence of the orders meant that Catholic education tended to be ultramontane. On the liberal side, Lacordaire encouraged the formation of a Third Order of the revived Dominicans to work in secondary education, and in 1853 himself became head of the celebrated Catholic school at Sorèze (Tarn). This attracted much attention because of Lacordaire's personal fame (Matthew Arnold visited and described the school), but Sorèze passed out of the Order's hands after Lacordaire's death in

---

[1] The Jesuit schools in the period 1850-70 were at Amiens, Avignon, Bordeaux, Dôle, Metz, Mongré (Rhône), Paris (Sainte-Geneviève), Poitiers, Saint-Affrique, Saint-Etienne, Sarlat, Toulouse and Vannes. The Jesuits also took over an existing school in Paris (Vaugirard), a municipal college (Mende, until 1864), and two *petits séminaires* (Moulins, Montauban). A school at Le Mans was planned in 1868 but vetoed by the government.

[2] *Statistique de l'enseignement secondaire en 1865* (1868), Tables 26, 27.

[3] S. Vailhé, *Vie du P. Emmanuel d'Alzon . . . fondateur des Augustins de l'Assomption (1810-1880)* (n.d.), ii. 92-102, 105-12. The Assumptionists also opened a school at Paris (Clichy), but this closed in 1860.

[4] A *Comité de l'enseignement libre* formed after the loi Falloux is last heard of in 1853. No similar pressure-group existed until the creation of the *Société générale d'éducation et d'enseignement* in 1867.

1861.[1] The liberal tendencies in the Church were also represented by two famous independent schools: the Collège Stanislas at Paris, where the teachers were laymen and there was a special connexion with the University;[2] and Juilly (Seine-et-Marne), which was taken over in 1867 by the revived Oratory.[3]

The *petits séminaires* and the diocesan colleges were the 'standard' Catholic schools to be found all over France. The diocesan colleges (seventy schools and 9,107 pupils in 1865) included most of the transferred municipal colleges. Both sorts of school were under the immediate control of the bishops, and were usually staffed by the ordinary clergy of the diocese, though they might be entrusted to an order or to a society of secular priests, such as the Société de Saint-Bertin, which ran a number of schools in the Nord and Pas-de-Calais.[4]

Between 1850 and 1865, the number of *petits séminaires* grew from 121 to 137, and of their pupils from 18,549 to 23,000.[5] As significant as this increase was the change in their character: in 1853, it was reported that 'nearly all the *petits séminaires* have transformed themselves, taking advantage of the new law, and have become the Catholic colleges par excellence'.[6] This development was not really new. In the forties, the *petit séminaire* of Saint-Nicolas at Paris had enjoyed success as a general secondary school under the direction of the Abbé Dupanloup—to whose qualities as a headmaster his pupil Renan paid a celebrated tribute.[7]

---

[1] M. Arnold, *Democratic Education* (Ann Arbor, 1962), 271-8. B. Chocarne, *Le R.P. H.-D. Lacordaire, de l'Ordre des Frères Prêcheurs, sa vie intime et religieuse* (2nd edition 1866), ii. 267, 270-1, 276 ff. The Dominicans also took over a school at Oullins (Lyons) and founded one at Paris (Arcueil).

[2] L. de Lagarde, *Histoire du Collège Stanislas* (1881), 239 ff., 261 ff.

[3] C. Hamel, *Histoire de l'abbaye et du collège de Juilly depuis leurs origines jusqu'à nos jours* (1868), 554 ff., 665-72.

[4] C. Guillemant, *Pierre-Louis Parisis* (1916-25), iii. 230 ff.

[5] For 1850, AN F^{17} 6839, unpublished statistical report for 1850, Table 15.

[6] *Rapport au comité de l'enseignement libre sur l'exécution et les effets de la loi organique de l'instruction publique du 15 mars 1850* (1853), 68.

[7] *Œuvres complètes de Ernest Renan* (ed. H. Psichari, n.d.), ii. 805-19.

Dupanloup's policy was to mix the sons of the rich with the future seminarists, so that the former acquired a tincture of piety, the latter of good breeding. He applied the same principle in his *petits séminaires* when he became bishop of Orleans in 1849, and succeeded in attracting the aristocracy and upper bourgeoisie of the district to them.[1] Some bishops opposed such 'mixed' schools on the grounds that contact with rich pupils endangered the vocation of the seminarists,[2] but the majority seem to have followed Dupanloup's example, though rarely with his fashionable success.

As an additional category of Catholic schools, one should mention the boarding-schools run by the Brothers of the Christian Schools. These *pensionnats* were theoretically primary schools, but in fact gave a form of modern secondary education without Latin, which appealed to the lower middle class in the towns.[3] These schools expanded after 1850, despite official disapproval, and their education was good enough to be a challenge to the University. Their rivalry was one reason for the introduction of a similar type of education in the lycées (*enseignement secondaire spécial*) by Victor Duruy.

It will be recalled from the statistical tables that a large number of pupils were in lay private schools. But few of these schools were of real importance. The early organization of state secondary education in France prevented the development of private secondary schools run by individuals. It was difficult to compete with the lycées' subsidized fees, the more so because parents were reluctant

---

[1] F. Lagrange, *Vie de Mgr Dupanloup* (1883-4), ii. 106 ff.; C. Marcilhacy, *Le diocèse d'Orléans sous l'episcopat de Mgr Dupanloup, 1849-1878. Sociologie religieuse et mentalités collectives* (1962), 83-90, 394, 403.

[2] C. Guillemant, *Pierre-Louis Parisis* (1916-25), iii. 671-2; E. C. M. Husson, *Le Petit-séminaire de Tours depuis son origine, 1690, jusqu'à ce jour, 27 juillet 1875* (Tours, 1875), 18-19; J. Burnichon, *La Compagnie de Jésus en France. Histoire d'un siècle 1814-1914* (1914 ff.), iii, 416-17 (on Montauban).

[3] A. Prévot, *L'Enseignement technique chez les Frères des Ecoles Chrétiennes au XVIIIe et au XIXe siècles* (n.d.), 139 ff. History of the individual schools (some twenty by the 1860s) in G. Rigault, *Histoire générale de l'Institut des Frères des Ecoles Chrétiennes*, v (1945), 387 ff.

to patronize schools which did not have the sort of intellectual and moral authority provided by the University. Only the Church could compete in this respect, and between the two great teaching corporations the private schoolmaster was squeezed out. Independent lay schools at the level of a lycée or a Jesuit school did not exist, and the successful lay schools were those with a specialized function: cramming establishments, a few schools specializing in scientific or technical education, and the private boarding institutions connected with the lycées in Paris and other large towns. Apart from these, there were many small schools giving an inferior education and having a precarious, sometimes ephemeral, existence.[1] Lay private schools of all types declined from the 1860s because of Catholic competition and the improvement of the lycées, so that they suffered rather than gained from the loi Falloux.

The histories of Catholic colleges and biographies of priests and teachers which are the principal secondary sources for the history of Catholic education tend to be more edifying than informative; they are particularly silent about such matters as the social origin of pupils or the place of the schools in the local community. For this we must turn again to the government's statistics and the reports of its officials.

The figures given previously have been for France as a whole. But the political and religious geography of France was complex, and it is not surprising that the popularity of Catholic education, and the type of parents who used it, varied widely between departments—and within departments, as in the Ariège, where 'families from the plain areas turn by preference to the public establishments, while the clientele of the *petit séminaire* is drawn particularly from the mountains'.[2]

The adjoining map shows what proportion of the total number of secondary pupils in each department was in Catholic schools in

---

[1] For an example of a complete survey of lay and Catholic schools in a single department, see M. Chabot and S. Charléty, *Histoire de l'enseignement secondaire dans le Rhône de 1789 à 1900* (1901), 129 ff.

[2] 1864 enquiry, IA Ariège.

PROPORTION OF ALL SECONDARY SCHOOL PUPILS
IN CATHOLIC SCHOOLS, 1865

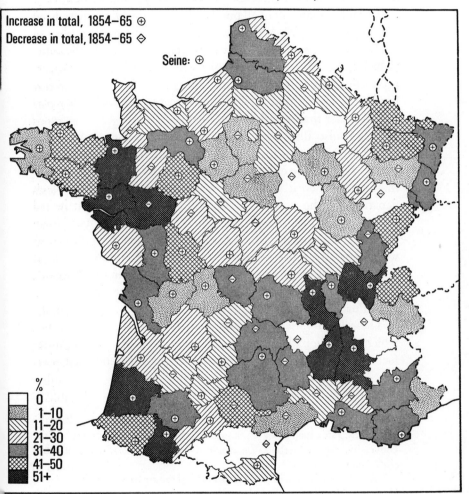

Increase in total, 1854–65 ⊕
Decrease in total, 1854–65 ◇

Seine: ⊕

%
0
1–10
11–20
21–30
31–40
41–50
51+

1865.[1] The areas where they had most pupils were, on the whole, the usual centres of Catholic strength in this period: Brittany and the west, Provence, an area around Lyons, Lorraine, the Massif Central, and the south-west. In sixteen departments, the Catholic pupils outnumbered those of the University,[2] and in nine they formed more than half of all pupils. On the other hand, there were nine departments where there were no Catholic schools at all, and twelve more where their share was 10 per cent or less. In the Seine (which lacked the smaller Catholic schools found elsewhere) the proportion was only 11 per cent. Duruy's officials were therefore justified in feeling that the Catholic threat to the University was a local rather than a national problem.

This is also illustrated by a comparison of the departmental totals[3] for 1865 with those of 1854, as shown on the map. If the vitality of Catholic education can be measured by the growth of these totals, then it was by no means uniform. In twenty-seven departments, the number of Catholic pupils had fallen; it had grown in fifty-five, though often only by small amounts.[4] Moreover, the departments where Catholic education expanded most were generally those where it was strongest in 1865, while it declined in the areas where it was weak in 1865: in other words, Catholic and 'dechristianized' regions of France drew further apart during this period.

These local variations meant that, for the parent, the choice which the Falloux had intended to make available was an imperfect one. Only those who were rich enough to send their sons

---

[1] The *petits séminaires* are excluded. Being organized on a diocesan basis they were fairly evenly distributed. Their inclusion would accentuate the tendencies shown by the map, as they had most pupils in areas like Brittany and Lyons. For a map based on the same figures showing the strength of the University, see P. Gerbod, *La condition universitaire en France au XIXe siècle* (1965), 430.

[2] Apart from those with over 50 per cent, these are Basses-Pyrénées, Gers, Morbihan, Moselle, Pas-de-Calais, Rhône and Somme. The department with the highest figure was Ardèche (66 per cent).

[3] Not proportions, which cannot be established for 1854.

[4] This leaves out departments where the Catholics had no pupils in either year, and the departments acquired in 1860.

away from home had real freedom of choice: but large numbers of pupils were day-boys (about half in the state schools, a third in the Catholic schools), and even boarders were usually from local families. Only a few towns had competitive schools of equal status. In some departments, the lycée provided the only form of first-class education, and lacked real rivals; in others, there were no municipal colleges, so that those who could not afford the lycée had no choice but to turn to the Catholic schools.[1] We may note, incidentally, that the transfer of a municipal college to the Catholic sector was a question of local politics—the parents had no choice in the matter.

The 1864 reports suggest that only a minority of parents chose Catholic schools on grounds of principle, and that most chose state or private education indifferently according to cheapness or convenience. In this period, when religious orthodoxy was maintained in the state schools, there was often little difference between them, especially in the smaller schools. The free-thinking professors of philosophy who alarmed Catholic parents were to be found only in the important lycées, while some of the municipal colleges had priests as principals, and were run on the same lines as Catholic schools. Such a college was Tourcoing, the largest municipal college in France: the Abbé Leblanc found thirteen priests teaching there when he became principal in 1858, and conducted the school on clerical principles for twenty-five years.[2] There were similar colleges at nearby Hazebrouck, and at Lesneven and St Pol in Finistère (which helps to explain why that department needed few private Catholic schools).[3]

A sharp division between a Catholic and a 'lay' system of schools was therefore not yet general. In 1864, however, the classic pattern was already apparent in Brittany, where it was reported that:

---

[1] This was the case in several departments where Catholic education was strong: Rhône, Loire, Ardèche.

[2] H. J. Leblanc, *Le collège communal de Tourcoing pendant les vingt-cinq dernières années du régime universitaire (1858-1883)* (Lille, 1885), 97.

[3] See description of Lesneven in 1853 in F. Sarcey, *Journal de jeunesse de Francisque Sarcey (1839-57)* (n.d.), 222 ff. For others, 1864 enquiry.

'Apart from the state scholars, the establishments of the state get only the children of the liberal families, who are loyal to the government and to modern institutions, friends of progress and of the principles of 1789. All those who dream of a return to the past, all those who desire the restoration of what is called legitimacy, entrust their sons to the priests.'[1]

The same was true in the Vendée, and it was pointed out that this situation limited the scope for competition between the two sectors: 'In a region where opinions are clear cut, the lay and the ecclesiastical establishments each have their fixed clientele, and there is little movement between them'.[2]

In the west, the division was political as much as religious: the Catholic schools were legitimist, the state schools 'blue'. One may also notice the role of scholarships and 'loyalty to the government' in keeping certain families loyal to the University. Officials, magistrates and officers tended to patronize the lycées—there were, perhaps, bonds of fellow-feeling between the University and the other corporations whose members formed a distinct society in provincial life. More important, pressure was put on them to use the state schools, though with limited success, for the ministry of education lacked the political weight to enforce this.[3] Securing the sympathies of high officials was one of the permanent tasks of the University's administrators, and the sons of the prefect, the *premier président* or the *procureur général* were major prizes in their battle with the Catholic schools. For many officials, the pressures of local opinion and their links with *bien-pensant* society prevailed over their loyalty to the state, and in 1864 the 'desertion' of the University by officials was reported in several academies.

Some state schools, then, were 'official' islands in a Catholic sea—like the lycée of Brest, where nearly all the pupils came from naval families. Others were islands of a different kind: in areas

[1] 1864 enquiry, rector of Rennes.
[2] *Ibid.*, IA Vendée.
[3] For example, Duruy in 1864: J. Maurain, *La politique ecclésiastique du Second Empire de 1852 à 1869* (1930), 683-4.

with a large Protestant population, the University's schools tended to become the Protestant schools[1]—to the chagrin of the University, for this frightened Catholic parents away.[2]

These cases indicate that the division between state and Catholic schools was not drawn on simple class lines. The classes which used secondary education were divided vertically as well as horizontally: religious allegiance, occupation, or local loyalties might be as important as class feeling in determining the ethos of a particular social group. This diversity was perhaps greatest where ethical and cultural values were concerned, and these are the substance of education. Schools not only represented national systems, but were part of the fabric of the local community, and reflected the divisions within it—Catholic against Protestant, liberal against legitimist, town against country. In this period, town and country were distinct worlds, and it would be possible to argue that the Catholic schools, with a clientele drawn from the landed nobility and the peasantry, stood for the values of the rural world, while the state schools were urban.[3]

To some extent the division was certainly a class one. As is well known, the Catholic schools especially attracted the old nobility and the richer bourgeoisie, impelled, in the words of one rector, 'either by political principles, or by religious inclinations, or by fashion'.[4] The Assumptionists and Jesuits aimed deliberately at this clientele. The Jesuit college at Vannes was the favourite choice of the Breton nobility, and in towns like Poitiers or Toulouse the Jesuits were closely connected with the local versions of the faubourg Saint-Germain.[5] This movement away from the

[1] J. Maurain, op. cit., 299 (Tournon), 304 (Castres), 315 (Valence). These towns were all in departments where Catholic schools were strong. In Alsace, however, the Protestants often had their own private schools.

[2] AN F^{17} 2481, monthly reports of rectors, Gard, August 1852 (Nîmes), F^{17} 2482, monthly reports of rectors, Lozère, December 1852 (Marvejols), Meurthe, January 1854 (Phalsbourg).

[3] But this was only partly true, for the smaller state colleges were also rural and had a peasant clientele.

[4] 1864 enquiry, rector of Besançon.

[5] AN F^{17} 2649, quarterly reports of rectors, especially Poitiers, 10 May 1858 and 11 July 1859; Toulouse, first quarter of 1859.

University had begun well before 1850.[1] The ministers of the Second Empire tried to reverse it, making a deliberate attempt to attract the rich back to the lycées. But their success was limited, and in 1864 some rectors felt that the University was losing further ground, as in Alsace, where 'an increasingly powerful current is carrying a notable portion of society towards the Jesuits'.[2]

For the legitimist nobility, the Catholic schools were a means of conserving their values from one generation to another even when the world was changing, and of insulating their children from anti-religious influences and the principles of 1789. In Taine's words, such parents found in the Catholic schools 'well-arranged hothouses, with the chinks carefully stopped up to keep out modern draughts'.[3] For middle-class parents, the attraction of the Catholic schools lay in the presence there of the sons of the aristocracy. Their own sons would learn good manners and form useful friendships, and would be protected from 'the mingling, the *promiscuity* of the state institutions'.[4]

A parallel may suggest itself with the English public schools, which assimilated the newly rich into an older élite in a similar way. There were indeed several respects in which the French Catholic schools resembled the public schools more closely than did the lycées. But there were differences in the situation: the values of the French landed aristocracy, unlike those of their English counterparts, were inward-looking, committed to a sterile political creed, and increasingly out of touch with and hostile to the evolution of French society.

Moreover, the Catholic schools did not form a privileged sector of education in the same way as the English public schools. The hope of doing so had lain behind the agitation for 'liberty of teaching', and was one reason why the liberals of the July Monarchy had opposed the Catholic claims so strongly. The

[1] A.-J. Tudesq, *Les grands notables en France (1840-1849). Etude historique d'une psychologie sociale* (1964), i. 202-5.

[2] 1864 enquiry, rector of Strasbourg.

[3] H. Taine, *Les Origines de la France contemporaine. Le régime moderne* (1894), ii. 249.

[4] 1864 enquiry, IA Haute-Garonne.

leaders of the campaign were members of that upper class which had been attempting since 1815 to reassert and consolidate its social influence. The middle-class liberals, on the other hand, saw the lycée as a symbol of the conquest of privilege in 1789 and as a guarantee of the new social order. The state school was open to all who could pay, free of social snobbery, and closely connected with the system of public examinations for entry to various careers. The reconstitution of a Catholic system of education seemed to threaten the return of a social order in which birth, patronage and religious affiliation would have more influence than talent or money.

This was not in fact to happen. A Catholic education might give social and professional advantages in certain circles, and the schools helped to maintain feelings of class solidarity among the nobility.[1] But the lycées retained many of the advantages which in England belonged to the public schools: they gave a better intellectual education, enjoyed greater prestige as national institutions, and had closer connexions with higher education and with the careers which mattered.

Some Catholic schools, then, gave an exclusive education to the rich and served as refuges from the more democratic lycées. But this was by no means the whole picture: these schools were a minority, and taken together the Catholic schools, like the lycées and colleges, served a fairly wide social range.

Many officials in 1864 attributed the popularity of Catholic schools to their cheapness, and their fees were in fact lower than those of the lycées. In 1865, it was estimated that the average fees for boarders and day-boys were 739 francs and 110 francs a year respectively in the lycées, 649 and 72 in the municipal colleges, and 630 and 97 in the Catholic schools.[2] These averages concealed local differences (in Paris, the Catholic schools cost more than the lycées), and variations between schools. But even the Jesuit schools were not very expensive: in 1858 they charged an average

---

[1] See the example of Pontlevoy in G. Dupeux, *Aspects de l'histoire sociale et politique du Loir-et-Cher 1848-1914* (1962), 145-6.

[2] In the lay private schools, 680 and 110. *Statistique de l'enseignement secondaire en 1865* (1868), Table 29.

of 764 francs for boarders, seventy for day-boys—comparable to a medium-rank provincial lycée. They also provided 212 free places, 125 of them at Vannes[1]—though the older Jesuit tradition of charging no fees could not be generally revived.[2]

The saving on salaries gained by employing priests was the chief reason for these low fees. There were no secret clerical funds subsidizing the Catholic schools. Indeed, most schools, even the successful ones, suffered from periodic financial crises, usually solved by the intervention of rich local sympathizers, old boys or parents, who subscribed to a society which owned and supported the school.[3] Most of the Jesuit schools were run in this way, and it was to prove useful later as a way of keeping schools open in the face of legal persecution.

The cheapest schools were the *petits séminaires*, where potential seminarists received scholarships from the Church's funds. Most of these pupils were drawn from the peasantry, and in areas where the Church retained its hold it was easy for priests and teachers to pick out promising pupils and arrange financial help for them; there were parts of France where to have a son become a priest was the great object of family ambition, and justified any financial sacrifice.[4] The paying pupils of the *petits séminaires* also came from the peasantry as well as the bourgeoisie, and it seems to have been common in all Catholic schools to adapt the fees charged to the means of the parents, and to make large reductions for the poor. In Savoy, 'the *petits séminaires* attract the young people from the countryside by their cheapness; they collect their fees in kind (a few loads of corn or of wine) in order to put themselves within reach of all'.[5] This was a backward area, but payment in kind was reported elsewhere.[6]

---

[1] AN F¹⁷ 6833. note on private schools, 3 April 1858.

[2] J. Burnichon, *La Compagnie de Jésus en France. Histoire d'un siècle 1814-1914* (1914 ff.), iii. 382-3, 462-3.

[3] See the example of the Assumptionist college at Nîmes in S. Vailhé, *Vie du P. Emmanuel d'Alzon . . . fondateur des Augustins de l'Assomption (1810-80)* (n.d.), ii. 236 ff.

[4] 1864 enquiry, IAs Cantal, Lozère.

[5] *Ibid.*, rector of Chambéry.

[6] *Ibid.*, IAs Aisne, Hautes-Pyrénées.

The Catholic schools fell, then, into two broad categories from the social point of view: the schools run by the orders catering for the rich, and the *petits séminaires* for the poor. The University might come between: in Provence, it was reported that the rich favoured the Jesuits at Avignon or the Dominicans at Oullins, the *classes aisées* used the University's colleges, and the *petits séminaires* served those who could afford nothing else. The pattern was similar in Savoy, except that the rich divided their favours between the Jesuits and the lycées. In the Somme, Catholic education served the rich in the large towns, the peasants and 'industriels' elsewhere.[1] These examples are enough to show that the choice made between state and Catholic schools was not purely a matter either of class or of ideology, but a combination of the two which depended on a multiplicity of local factors. In only a minority of cases can it have been a dispassionate choice made on educational grounds after comparing the merits of the rival schools.

An attempt to assess the merits of the Catholic schools is somewhat hampered by a lack of first-hand evidence about their internal life and teaching. What follows is based on a synthesis of two main sources: the histories of individual schools,[2] generally presenting a picture idealized by pious nostalgia, and the writings and speeches of Catholic teachers.

Among the latter, the works on education published by Dupanloup hold pride of place. These widely read books, published

[1] 1864 enquiry, rector of Aix, IAs Savoie, Haute-Savoie, Somme.

[2] Among the more useful ones are: J. P. G. Blanchet, *Notice sur les écoles secondaires ecclésiastiques du diocèse d'Angoulême au XIXe siècle* (Angoulême, 1891), F. Butel, *L'Éducation des Jésuites autrefois et aujourd'hui. Un collège breton* (1890), F. Choiset, *Le petit séminaire Saint-Bernard de Plombières-lez-Dijon. Histoire et souvenirs* (Dijon, 1896) A. Du Bois de la Villerabel, *L'École Saint-Charles à Saint-Brieuc. Souvenirs et récits* (Saint-Brieuc, 1891), *L'École St-Thomas d'Aquin à Oullins de 1833-36 à 1886* (Lyons, 1886), C. Hamel, *Histoire de l'abbaye et du collège de Juilly depuis leurs origines jusqu'à nos jours* (1868), L. Jénouvrier, *Un collège français et chrétien. Saint-Vincent-de-Paul de Rennes (1842-1923)* (Rennes, 1924), J. Lataste, *Histoire du Petit Séminaire d'Aire-sur-l'Adour* (Aire, 1935), A. Leistenschneider, *Un petit séminaire du diocèse de Lyon. L'Argentière* (Lyons, 1905), A. Rosette, *La Compagnie de Jésus a Dôle après son rétablissement. Un siècle de labeur 1823-1920* (1945), L. Viansson-Ponté, *Les Jésuites à Metz* (Strasbourg, 1897).

between 1850 and 1866,[1] were based on Dupanloup's experience as a headmaster, and were planned as a practical guide for those setting up new schools under the loi Falloux as well as a general educational treatise. In them the Catholic teacher could find advice on almost any conceivable problem, from the planning of a syllabus to the arrangement of dormitories to guard against the dangers of *amitiés particulières*. Dupanloup was perhaps strongest on the problems of moral education: his views on intellectual education were rather old-fashioned, and his conception of the role of Catholic education—to minister to the upper classes and restore their social leadership—was limited. But all teachers—including *universitaires*—echoed Dupanloup's words on the practical problems of education time and again in their writings and speeches.

The headmaster, or *Supérieur*, is the central figure in Dupanloup's books, and this in itself draws attention to one of the differences between Catholic and state schools. The *proviseur* of a lycée was simply an administrator, an individual school only one stage in his career: he did not teach, or have any moral influence over his pupils, or even meet them very often. The University ran by routine and by central direction, and the *proviseur* was not expected to innovate. The head of a Catholic school, on the other hand, could put his personal stamp on his school and his pupils, and only among such men do we find equivalents of the great English headmasters (in the lycées it was the professor of philosophy who might have a comparable personal influence). The Catholic head could teach, he could be a friend to his pupils (and their confessor), he could preach (as did Lacordaire at Sorèze—no wonder Matthew Arnold felt at home there),[2] he could work out his own disciplinary system and syllabus.

[1] F. Dupanloup, *De l'éducation* (1850-61), and *De la haute éducation intellectuelle* (1855-66). Some other representative works by Catholic teachers: E. Dauphin, *De l'éducation, discours prononcés aux distributions des prix du collège d'Oullins* (1860), H. Gras, *Famille et collège, leur rôle dans l'éducation* (1861).

[2] For Lacordaire's personal influence on his pupils, see B. Chocarne, *Le R. P. H.-D. Lacordaire, de l'Ordre des Frères Prêcheurs, sa vie intime et religieuse* (2nd edition 1866), ii. 295 ff.

The Catholic system also laid emphasis on the personal influence of the assistant teachers, the majority of whom were priests (2,420 out of 3,258 in 1865).[1] Catholic teachers were expected to devote themselves wholly to their work. In the lycée, the professor taught set hours, his relations with his pupils were formal, and discipline was in the hands of an inferior grade of personnel, the *maîtres d'études*. In the Catholic schools, the teachers shared the communal life of the school, were responsible for their pupils' moral as well as intellectual development, and even helped to organize their games and outings. The discipline of the Catholic schools was strict, but it was paternal where that of the lycées was formal and mechanical.

In their campaigns against the University, Catholic propagandists had long condemned it for putting too much stress on intellectual training (*instruction*) and neglecting the moral side (*éducation*). After 1850, the latter became the strong point of the Catholic schools, the centre of their appeal to parents, and, as it were, their speciality. While the books and speeches of *universitaires* dealt with questions of scholarship or literature, those of Catholic teachers tended to be devoted to moral and disciplinary problems.

It goes without saying that religion was all-important in the Catholic schools. Catholic teachers thought that children should be brought up in an entirely Catholic atmosphere and protected from any hostile influence. Doubt and scepticism were to be rigorously excluded from the schools, as were all potential sources of moral corruption. The idea of an education based on isolation from external influences was originally worked out by the Catholic teaching orders of the ancien régime,[2] and it survived into the nineteenth century with little change: indeed, it acquired new force in an age when both teachers and upper-class parents were hostile to the values of the world around them. The traditional pedagogy was enshrined in Dupanloup's works: for him,

[1] *Statistique de l'enseignement secondaire en 1865* (1868), Table 26. Cf. in 1854, 1,796 of 2,478 teachers.

[2] G. Snyders, *La Pédagogie en France aux XVIIe et XVIIIe siècles* (1965), 35-48.

even parents, with their tendency to indulgence and laxity, were a danger to a good education, and the child was safer in the vigilant atmosphere of a boarding school than in his own home.

In the lycées, religious instruction was somewhat desultory and confined to formal periods; the chaplains felt themselves isolated in a hostile or indifferent milieu, and lacked the support of their colleagues.[1] In the Catholic schools, religion permeated the ordinary subject teaching, and, in addition to services and the usual devotional practices, the emotional and demonstrative piety of the age was cultivated by such means as pilgrimages to local shrines and religious fraternities confined to an élite of pupils.

The Catholic schools tended to put the formation of character before intellectual education, and this was one of the ways in which they resembled the English public schools. The communal life was more intense, the atmosphere of moral endeavour more pervasive, than in the lycées. The word *virile* was as often on the lips of Catholic teachers as 'manly' on those of their English counterparts—perhaps in response to the allegation of critics of Catholic education that there was something effeminate and debilitating about education by priests.

Another parallel with the public schools was that older pupils were especially favoured: most schools had an 'Academy', a sort of literary and debating society, for senior pupils, who enjoyed an easier discipline, special privileges (though not usually authority over their juniors), and friendly relations with their head. The solicitude of Catholic teachers extended even beyond schooldays: they were always ready with advice to young men on their spiritual life, their moral conduct and their choice of a career, and some followed the lead of Dupanloup by establishing *cours supérieurs* in which older pupils were encouraged to stay on and read further under supervision. The sheltered nature of Catholic education posed special problems of transition from school to adult life; everything was done to postpone the loss of innocence for as long as possible.

The Catholic schools also resembled the public schools in their

[1] L. Marty, *Les Aumôniers dans l'Université* (1869), *passim*.

emphasis on physical education and health. These were matters which increasingly preoccupied French educational experts, especially after the publication of *L'Education homicide* by the Catholic poet Victor de Laprade in 1868. In this respect, the Catholic schools had great advantages over the lycées, for they frequently occupied new buildings in spacious grounds or rural settings. The lycées, on the other hand, were in cramped and insanitary premises in the centre of towns—often, ironically, old Jesuit colleges or monastic buildings taken over at the Revolution. The Catholic schools also had a reputation for greater comfort and better food. All these things, together with the paternal discipline and moral solicitude of the priests, were very attractive to parents —especially to mothers.

At their best, the Catholic schools could produce fervent Catholics and inspire an affection and loyalty which the lycées could not arouse. A parent might well feel that their claim to educate the character was justified, and that they gave a sounder preparation for the battle of life than the lycées. On the other hand, the heightened emotional atmosphere of the Catholic schools, and their insistence on religious conformity at an age when doubt is natural, must often have been oppressive, and produced unhappiness and bitterness. The lycées were formal, impersonal, tolerant: they inspired less enthusiasm than their Catholic rivals, but they gave their pupils more room to breathe and to develop in their own way.

The intellectual education given by the Catholic schools is less easy to assess, for there is little direct evidence of what was taught. There were 278 Catholic schools in 1865, but only ninety-six offered a complete secondary education,[1] as did the 137 *petits séminaires*. This was comparable with the seventy-seven lycées and the 131 municipal colleges with a complete series of classes. But the academic qualifications of the teachers were certainly inferior: the law required only that the head should have the baccalaureate. The teachers were products of the seminaries, whose backwardness in this period is notorious, and even the Catholic Laprade admitted the intellectual inadequacies of the

[1] *Statistique de l'enseignement secondaire en 1865* (1868), Table 26.

French clergy.[1] Some attempts were made to improve the situation—for example, the foundation of the *Ecole des Carmes* at Paris in 1845, which prepared priests for the degrees of the University; but real improvement had to await the introduction of Catholic universities in the seventies. It seems safe to say that the general level of intellectual education was lower in the Catholic schools than in the University.

The competition introduced by the loi Falloux did not lead to the variety and experiment which had been hoped for. Catholic teachers were more interested in re-establishing old traditions than in innovation, and none apart from the Christian Brothers showed an interest in working out new forms of education for the modern world. The Jesuits, for example, tried to restore their *Ratio studiorum* with as little change as possible. This was not always popular with parents: at Mende, the municipal college which the Jesuits had taken over was restored to the University in 1864 because of discontent at the Jesuits' introduction of textbooks written in Latin and their neglect of science and history.[2] The parents of Mende were no doubt thinking of the baccalaureate, whose demands were a powerful incentive to uniformity, here as elsewhere. In the Dominican schools, Lacordaire imposed the University's syllabus in place of older and more distinctive arrangements.[3]

Another important external pressure came from the entrance examinations of the *grandes écoles*—notably the Polytechnique, the officers' school at St Cyr, and the naval school at Brest. These examinations demanded scientific knowledge, and scientific education in the state schools was directed primarily towards their requirements. The Catholic schools could not afford to neglect them, for their own clientele was vitally interested in the careers for which they were essential: under the Second Empire, the

---

[1] V. de Laprade, *Le baccalauréat et les études classiques* (1869), 15-23. Cf. F. Garilhe, *Le clergé séculier français au XIXe siècle* (n.d.), 13 ff., E. Baudaire, 'La formation intellectuelle du clergé de France au XIXe siècle', *Annales de philosophie chrétienne*, 3rd series, v (1904), 158-69, 267-307.

[2] 1864 enquiry, IA Lozère.

[3] J. T. Foisset, *Vie du R. P. Lacordaire* (1870), ii. 253-4.

nobility was turning increasingly to careers in the army,[1] while the navy was a traditional career for the nobility of Brittany and the west.

In 1852, Fortoul introduced an important reform of scientific education in the lycées. Known as 'bifurcation', this involved the division of the higher forms into two sections, literary and scientific; the scientific section led to a new scientific baccalaureate, which became compulsory for entry to most of the *grandes écoles* and for other careers such as medicine. As has been mentioned, one aim of this reform was to help the lycées compete with the Catholic schools by concentrating on a side of education where the University was strong while the Catholic schools, lacking the necessary teachers and equipment, were backward and would be able to follow only with difficulty. Science was described by Fortoul himself as '*le seul enseignement du haut duquel nous puissions impunément défier la concurrence des établissements ecclésiastiques.*'[2]

The reform succeeded in embarrassing the Catholic schools and forcing them to follow suit. In 1853 Fortoul pointed out that, despite attacks on the reform by Catholic champions of the classics, it had been adopted in many schools, including eleven *petits séminaires*[3]. In 1855, it was noted with satisfaction that the reform had forced the Jesuits at Metz to spend half a million francs in order to compete with the lycée;[4] d'Alzon reluctantly introduced a scientific section at Nîmes,[5] and bifurcation was eventually applied in most of the larger schools, though in the smaller schools and the *petits séminaires* it was unusual.[6]

[1] R. Girardet, *La Société militaire dans la France contemporaine 1815-1939* (n.d.), 84, 195-6.

[2] AN 246 AP 16, Fortoul papers, Fortoul to Silvestre de Sacy, 16 September 1852.

[3] Report to Emperor, 19 September 1853.

[4] AN 246 AP 20, Fortoul papers, minutes of meeting of officials, 3 October 1855 (rector of Nancy).

[5] *Revue de l'enseignement chrétien*, i. 501-4 (September 1852). In 1854 the review began to include scientific problems in its pedagogic section.

[6] Scattered figures for individual schools and for departments in AN F^{17} 4342-4343, annual reports of *conseils académiques*, 1853-4, and F^{17} 4344-4359, annual reports of IAs, 1855-64.

Despite Catholic efforts at competition, the University's superiority in this field was maintained, and a form of specialization tended to develop where the Catholic schools were more 'literary' and the lycées more scientific. At Strasbourg, for example, the scientific section in the lycée far outnumbered the literary in 1855; but it was pointed out that this would not be true if all types of school in the area were taken into account—the lycée was preferred for science, because it was taught well there. Moreover, the *population sédentaire* of the department tended to use the *petit séminaire* or the Protestant *gymnase*; the lycée was left with the sons of officers and civil servants, who tended to follow their fathers' careers and hence to aim at the *grandes écoles*. In this way, the 'official' character of the lycées reinforced the tendency to scientific specialization, and such lycées as Brest, Rennes, Metz and Nancy were strongholds of scientific education. There is a sociological as well as an intellectual explanation for the connexion of science with the lay education of the state.[1]

The only serious challenge to the University in the scientific field came from the Jesuits. They did not adopt bifurcation, preferring to concentrate science at the end of the course in accordance with their own traditions. But they began to give an intensive and specialized preparation for the examinations of the *grandes écoles*, and developed their schools at Metz and Paris (Sainte-Geneviève, better known as the 'rue des Postes') for this purpose. In 1865, sixteen Catholic schools were giving special preparation of this kind, and their success was beginning to alarm the University. Sainte-Geneviève had one hundred successes in the examinations in 1865, against sixteen in 1858,[2] and in 1867 it was reported that some eighty of 350 pupils came from families of known liberal opinions. The success rate appealed even to 'Voltaireans, very well known as such', and one father was reported as 'caring no more about the religious and political

---

[1] On Strasbourg, AN 246 AP 21, Fortoul papers, minutes of meeting of officials, 6 October 1855 (rector of Strasbourg). See also 1864 enquiry, figures on application of bifurcation.

[2] Vincent, speech in Senate, 10 February 1866, reported in *Journal général de l'instruction publique*, xxxvi. 115.

question, where the Jesuit fathers are concerned, than he would have thought about the orthodoxy of his dentist in case of tooth-ache'.[1] This success led Duruy to study and imitate the Jesuits' methods in an attempt to improve the University's own prepara-tion for the examinations, but with limited success: the Catholic schools accounted for 127 of 836 admissions to the *grandes écoles* in 1867, 158 of 797 in 1868.[2]

Cramming for an examination, however, was rather different from giving a general scientific education, and the Catholics could not compete with the University on the broader front. The Catholic schools had to find their science teachers where they could—the Jesuits were fortunate in attracting mature converts, and the director of Sainte-Geneviève was a former mathematics teacher in the University.[3] The University, however, had special-ist teachers trained in the French scientific tradition, and many of the institutions which embodied that tradition—the faculties of science, the *Ecole normale*, the *agrégation*—were a part of the Uni-versity. It is significant that leading Catholic scientists, like Pasteur and Jean-Baptiste Dumas, remained loyal to the Univer-sity and did not encourage Catholic education.[4] Scientific culture, taught by men who believed in what they were teaching, was something generally available only in the University; most priests were at heart suspicious of science, which they associated with atheism and materialism, and hardly understood its spirit or appreciated its achievements.

If the University's scientific teaching was admitted to be super-ior, Catholics consoled themselves with the thought that only in their schools was the study of the classics maintained in its old purity. In this period, of course, the classics (French as well as

[1] AN F¹⁷ 8847, IA Toussenel to vice-rector of Paris, 25 February 1867.
[2] For 1867, figures in *L'Administration de l'instruction publique de 1863 à 1869. Ministère de S.E. M. Duruy* (n.d.), 573-4, for 1868 in *Bulletin adminis-tratif du ministère de l'instruction publique*, new series, xi. 54 (1869).
[3] 1864 enquiry, Paris, report of IA Delalleau.
[4] The chemist Dumas was the leading spirit in the 1852 reforms. Another scientist concerned with them, the astronomer Le Verrier, did give some support to the Catholic education movement.

Latin and Greek) were at the centre of secondary education in all types of school; indeed, in the early years of schooling especially, they left little time available for other subjects. *Universitaires* and Catholic teachers were at one in defending the dominant role of the classics, and they were equally conservative in their approach to teaching them. The same traditional methods, and often the same textbooks, were used in both types of school, and were inherited by both from the colleges of the ancien régime. The basic drills of grammar and composition gave little scope for variation. The choice of authors for reading, however, was a matter of controversy—but it was a controversy among Catholic teachers rather than between them and the University.

In 1851, the Abbé Gaume published his *Le ver rongeur des sociétés modernes, ou le paganisme dans l'éducation*. This was an attack on the teaching of the 'pagan' classics, to which Gaume attributed most of the evils of modern society. He claimed that in the Middle Ages, an age of faith, the classics had not been taught; their introduction at the Renaissance heralded the rise of Protestantism, rationalism, materialism and the spirit of the French Revolution. Gaume's recommendation for the salvation of society was the replacement of the pagan classics by the 'Christian classics', notably the writings of the Fathers.

Gaume's thesis was not new, but it caused a major controversy at this time because it was taken up by Veuillot and publicized in the *Univers*, so that the issue became entangled in the dispute between liberals and ultramontanes, and in particular between Dupanloup and Veuillot. Controversy raged in 1851 and 1852, in the pages of books, pamphlets, newspapers and pastoral letters, and was ended only by Papal intervention.

The arguments have little interest in themselves, and were easily won by Gaume's critics. But their intellectual links with other issues were significant: the effort to restore the Christian classics was analogous to the rejection of the Renaissance and the rediscovery of the Middle Ages in the fields of art, architecture and literature. Moreover, Gaume's attack on the Ranaissance was also an attack on the admiration for the seventeenth century, the *grand siècle*, which was at the centre of the French educational

82

tradition. The *grand siècle* was seen as the age in which the classical and Christian elements of French civilization were in perfect
balance, and was the symbol of a past in which the nation had not
been divided and which could yet form common ground between
Church and University. It was no coincidence that the Gallican
Dupanloup was a fervent admirer of the *grand siècle* and the chief
opponent of Gaume.

The immediate effect of this controversy was to distract and
divide Catholic teachers at the time when the opportunities given
by the loi Falloux were greatest. The Jesuits in particular were
embarrassed by it, as their teaching was the embodiment of the
traditions of Renaissance humanism. The dispute probably
did not delay the expansion of Catholic education, but it did
prevent it from presenting a united front. It was one reason for
the failure of d'Alzon's efforts to create unity, for d'Alzon was an
enthusiastic Gaumist, and the *Revue de l'enseignement chrétien*
became an organ of the cause (consequently devoting much space
to attacking fellow-Catholics). In 1852, a congress of Catholic
teachers proposed by the review was called off because of the
feelings aroused by the controversy.[1]

Gaume's principles seem to have been applied in full only in
the Assumptionist schools[2] and perhaps in some *petits séminaires*.
Elsewhere, his influence was confined to the addition of some of
the Fathers to the syllabus (this was also the case in the University). The two sides in the dispute were in fact less far apart than
the violence of their language indicated: Gaume admitted that, if
suitably expurgated, the classics might safely be taught in the
higher forms, while his opponents agreed that the pagan authors
could be dangerous if not taught with caution.

The model syllabus suggested by Dupanloup for Catholic
schools included some of the Fathers, but differed little in its
general outlines from the syllabuses of the University. The Latin
and Greek authors studied were essentially the same; where

---

[1] *Revue de l'enseignement chrétien*, i. 177-8 (March 1852), 500 (July 1852).
[2] AN F[17] 4345, report on private education to *conseil académique* of Paris,
1855: reported (as something of a curiosity) at the Assumptionist school at
Clichy.

French authors were concerned, however, prudery and intellectual timidity led Dupanloup to exclude anything which dealt with 'profane love' or encouraged scepticism. Dupanloup allowed only two plays of Racine (*Esther* and *Athalie*) and one of Corneille (*Polyeucte*), while Molière, Pascal and Voltaire were excluded entirely. Even La Fontaine was admitted only on tolerance.[1] Dupanloup's attitude may not have been typical of Catholic teachers, if only because of the demands of the baccalaureate, but it casts doubt on the Catholic claim to the guardianship of the classical literary tradition. Dupanloup's approach to classical teaching, with its emphasis on formal rhetoric and artificial exercises, was an old-fashioned one which the University was gradually abandoning.

The most sensitive subjects in the school curriculum were history and philosophy, and before 1850 the Catholics had often criticized the University for its teaching of them. What did they do with their freedom?

The Catholics had no ready-made philosophy to set against the much-criticized eclecticism of Cousin, for Catholic philosophy in France at this time was in a rather confused state. The old *philosophie de Lyon*, a mixture of Cartesian rationalism and scholasticism, had long held sway in the seminaries.[2] It was now discredited intellectually, but its eventual successor, neo-thomism, began to establish itself in France only in the sixties.[3] It took some time for current debates to be reflected in the teaching of the schools, and it seems unlikely that they were much influenced in this period either by neo-thomism or by the attempts of Gratry and others to work out new compromises between faith and reason. The pronouncements of Catholic teachers suggest that in practice the philosophy of the classroom was largely a matter of teaching

---

[1] F. Dupanloup, *De la haute éducation intellectuelle* (2nd edition 1866), i. 442-3, 513 ff. Cf. typical Jesuit syllabus in F. Butel, *L'Education des Jésuites autrefois et aujourd'hui. Un collège breton* (1890), 512-14.

[2] A. Cournot, *Des institutions d'instruction publique en France* (1864), 117-18.

[3] See L. Foucher, *La philosophie catholique en France au XIXe siècle avant la renaissance thomiste et dans son rapport avec elle (1800-1880)* (1955).

accepted truths dogmatically and in conventional form (as indeed was Cousinism). Its purpose was more pastoral than intellectual: to strengthen the pupil's faith and to prepare him to defend it against criticism. Both the Jesuits and Dupanloup favoured the old practice of teaching philosophy in Latin, for 'Latin is much more resistant than the vernacular to novelties and errors'.[1]

The evolution of a specifically Catholic philosophy in the schools was in any case hindered by the official programme laid down for the baccalaureate. This is illustrated by a philosophy 'manual' published in 1855 by Bensa, professor of philosophy at d'Alzon's school at Nîmes (a post also occupied for a time in the fifties by Emile Combes). Bensa seems to have been a Thomist as well as an ultramontane, and his aim was a fully Catholic philosophy which would rebuild what pagan rationalism since Descartes had destroyed—there is a close parallel with Gaume's attack on the Renaissance.

Bensa's book was meant for examination candidates, and it followed the headings of the official programme. Below them, however, Bensa expounded a highly controversial philosophy: he refuted in detail all the 'rationalists' down to Rosmini and Gioberti, and attacked the official philosophy syllabus introduced by Fortoul in 1852; he found room to condemn religious tolerance and the freedom of the press; he reached conclusions which were certainly not intended by Fortoul on the duty of governments to support the Pope's authority and maintain his temporal power. A short summary at the end, meant for examination revision, prudently omitted these divagations.[2]

This indicates how ultramontane and anti-liberal ideas must have been taught in some schools, and one wonders how a candidate who had used Bensa's manual would have fared before the University's examiners. The occasion probably arose rarely, for the manual—unlike the standard ones written by *universitaires*—ran to only one edition. We may suspect that most Catholic teachers preferred to keep more closely to the official programme,

---

[1] F. Dupanloup, *De la haute éducation intellectuelle* (1866), ii. 244.

[2] A. M. Bensa, *Manuel de logique pour le baccalauréat à l'usage des collèges catholiques* (1855), iii-vii, 83 ff., 453, 473 ff.

while giving an orthodox Catholic tone to the sections on religion.

Both ultramontanism and legitimism must have affected the teaching of history in many Catholic schools, though there is little evidence on this point apart from the occasional banning of textbooks by ministers of education and the 'exposures' published by anticlerical propagandists.[1] But if in the Catholic schools of Brittany 'the political questions of the day are more readily discussed with the children than are Cicero and Demosthenes',[2] most Catholic teachers seem to have shared the conservative idea of the time that recent history and controversial questions were unsuitable subjects for children—the more conservative, indeed, preferred to stop at 1789. However, in 1863 Duruy introduced 'contemporary history' in the programme of the lycées and the baccalaureate; the Second Empire's intervention in Italy was one of the subjects included, and since this was the most controversial political issue of the day this innovation must have widened the gap between Catholic and state schools.

Most Catholic teachers were instinctively suspicious of history as they were of science: they associated it with the anticlerical republicanism of Michelet and with the new German school of biblical criticism. As in other fields, it was the University which was more in touch with contemporary scholarship, and which formed (though reluctantly) the progressive sector of education.

We may now try to compare, necessarily in very general terms, the ideas and values which the lycées and the Catholic schools sought to impart, and to understand why the latter provoked so much hostility.

To some extent, it was less a case of two systems of values in competition than of the Catholic schools having a single ideal while the lycées did not. Catholic education had the unity and sense of purpose given by religious belief, and every aspect of the life of the school was directed to the same goal. In the lycées, intellectual education stood by itself (although it was claimed

[1] For example, *La politique et l'histoire contemporaines dans une école du clergé* (1864).

[2] 1864 enquiry, rector of Rennes.

that classical education had moral as well as intellectual benefits). There was no positive religious or moral aim: religious teaching was formal, with separate provision for Protestants and Jews, and the only provision made for moral education was the negative one of repression and surveillance. In the Catholic schools, the teachers intervened actively in the life of the community; in the lycées, the community consisted only of the pupils, and it was their 'underground' standards which had the most moral influence on a boy's development.

It was perhaps a logical result of the loi Falloux that the lycées should become centres of a secular ideology in competition with Catholicism, and such a development would have appealed to many teachers. But the Second Empire, by maintaining religious conformity in the lycées and restraining the radicalism of the teachers, held back this tendency. It chose instead to challenge the Catholic schools on ground where they were inevitably stronger —religious orthodoxy and social respectability. Teachers in the University, therefore, unlike their Catholic colleagues, had no clear definition of their own aims and beliefs; it was only later that a rationalism based on free philosophical enquiry became the orthodoxy of the University. Its real strength lay in its distrust of ideologies, and its cultivation of a tolerant and sceptical attitude; but this was rather felt as a weakness in this period, when men sought to base education on firm and dogmatic values.

The religious teaching of Catholic schools tended to produce an attitude towards modern society which was a compound of alienation, moral disapproval and self-righteousness. Many Catholic teachers had set their faces against the *siècle*, the modern world, and hoped to reverse the tendencies which they deplored by educating a new generation in sound principles. They taught their pupils that as Catholics they had special responsibilities, and that they were entering a society hostile to their faith and to the Church's claims. They would need all the strength of character which the schools claimed to develop if they were to resist the forces of materialism and decadence. The sense that militant Catholics were a minority fighting a losing but just battle against the odds was later intensified by the religious policy of the Third

Republic, but it was already well developed. It combined with the sheltered nature of Catholic education to produce the air of priggish purity which was characteristic of Catholic pupils, and which contrasted with the lycéen's affectation of cynicism and worldly wisdom.

If a Catholic education produced suspicion of many features of the contemporary world, it should not be supposed that the University inevitably fired its pupils with enthusiasm for science and progress. In the classical education common to both sorts of school, the emphasis was on imitation of the 'models' of both style and conduct provided by antiquity and by the French national tradition. The cultivation of style and elegance had its own dangers, and could lead in the University to a bellettrism as contemptuous of the modern world and as remote from its activities as any clericalism.

The social values taught by the schools resembled each other more than they differed. Both taught the conventional values of bourgeois society, though both also contained a certain mixture of classes and tried to discourage their pupils from thinking of themselves as a privileged caste. There was much emphasis on the responsibilities and duties of wealth, and in the Catholic schools, where the Société de St-Vincent-de-Paul was active, the practice of Christian charity was taught. But the leading Catholic schools were undoubtedly more socially exclusive than the lycées, and their principles were less sympathetic than those of the University to the idea of social mobility and personal ambition.

In neither type of school was there any stimulus to criticize the bases on which society rested—this was prevented by the University's optimistic belief in progress and by the Catholics' social conservatism. Nor did either type of school teach an ethic of public service in the style of the English public schools; we know that many Catholic pupils did have such an ethic, and were to serve France faithfully under the Republic, but this seems to have been a matter of family tradition rather than of education.[1]

Politically, the education given in both sorts of school was

[1] See the example of Lyautey in D. Thomson, *Democracy in France since 1870* (4th edition 1964), 61-2.

narrowly national and aimed at instilling patriotism. Interpretations of the past, of course, differed, as did attempts to mould specific political attitudes. In the lycées, attempts were made to inspire loyalty to the dynasty, while individual teachers might gain converts to the Republic. In the Catholic sector, legitimism was general in the schools run by the orders, but not necessarily elsewhere: the *petits séminaires* were controlled by the bishops, and most of the bishops supported the regime. The Catholic outlook on public affairs—favourable to the Empire in the fifties, hostile in the sixties—was no doubt passed on to the pupils.

The Italian war revealed the dangers created by the development of the Catholic schools, and sharpened the government's hostility towards them.[1] Most of the young 'Papal zouaves'who volunteered for Lamoricière's army were from Catholic schools: the Jesuit school at Vannes supplied over 100.[2] Their exploits were followed with enthusiasm in the schools, and money collected for their maintenance; those who were killed became the object of an intensely emotional cult.

The romantic heroism of the Papal zouaves perfectly expressed the moral atmosphere and idealism of the Catholic schools, and was in the tradition of Chateaubriand and Montalembert. But it embarrassed the government, and laid a foundation for the long-lasting and highly damaging charge that the Catholic schools put loyalty to the Pope before love of country. It was an element in the new attacks launched on them after 1870, when Renan, who felt that their education lacked both intellectual and moral rigour, declared that 'a pupil of the Jesuits will never make an officer capable of being set against a Prussian officer'.[3] Catholic resentment over this issue explains why the histories of Catholic schools put so much emphasis on the heroic record of their ex-pupils in

[1] The evolution of feeling in the University and of policy during the war can be followed quarter by quarter in AN F^{17} 2649-2650, quarterly reports of rectors.

[2] F. Butel, *L'Education des Jésuites autrefois et aujourd'hui. Un collège breton* (1890), 502-5. Of 115 names, 90 include 'de'.

[3] *Œuvres complètes de Ernest Renan* (ed. H. Psichari, n.d.), i. 392.

the war of 1870; indeed, complete books were devoted to this theme.

After the Italian war, the Second Empire pursued an overt policy of checking and reversing the progress of Catholic schools; these anticlerical tendencies had begun, though more discreetly, under Fortoul. There is no need here to retell the history of the Empire's conflicts with the Church,[1] but a few general comments are relevant.

The government's motives for keeping a watch on the Catholic schools were primarily political: they were suspected, with some justification, of being seedbeds of legitimist sentiment. For this reason, as well as because they were the most formidable rivals of the University, the Jesuits were seen as a special danger; as early as 1853, one of their schools had been temporarily closed down after a political incident.[2] For its part, the government tried to use the lycées to capture the younger generation for the Empire. Its policy of military glory was calculated to arouse the enthusiasm and patriotism of the young (another reason why the division sharpened in 1859), and even in 1856, when the troops returning from the Crimea marched into Rennes, it was noted that the acclamations of the pupils of the lycée contrasted with the absence of any demonstration on the part of the pupils of the Catholic schools.[3]

But the political interest of the government in education went beyond police supervision or the promotion of dynastic loyalty. The Second Empire claimed to be the heir of the principles of 1789, and it based its opposition to Catholic schools on similar arguments to those heard under the Third Republic. The *deux jeunesses* argument was used by Rouland when defining his policy in 1860,[4] and it was in the minds of many officials of the University. It is found expressed most clearly in the reports of Adolphe

[1] See J. Maurain, *La politique ecclésiastique du Second Empire de 1852 à 1869* (1930).

[2] At Saint-Etienne. J. Burnichon, *La Compagnie de Jésus en France. Histoire d'un siècle 1814-1914* (1914 ff.), iii. 402-6.

[3] AN F^{17} 1639, monthly reports of rectors, Rennes, 4 August 1856.

[4] J. Maurain, *La politique ecclésiastique du Second Empire de 1852 à 1869* (1930), 457-8, 470.

Mourier, successively rector of Rennes (a front-line post in the battle with the Catholics) and Bordeaux. Mourier is especially interesting because his views were conservative (and he was typical of the rectors appointed by Fortoul in 1854) and because he was a sincere Catholic of Gallican views. In his memoirs, he looked back to the 'old University' of this time, and contrasted it favourably with the sectarian University of the eighties. In the old University, religion had been accepted as the basis of educa-tion, yet it had been possible to combine this with liberalism and with the University's duty to serve the whole nation.[1] Mourier's opposition to clericalism and the orders was based not on hostility to religion but on the sense that they were disrupting a satisfactory compromise.

At Rennes in 1860, Mourier reported that 'in the University and in the majority of the private schools *on élève en présence deux Sociétés*'. At Bordeaux in 1861, he saw a special danger in the tendency of the liberal bourgeoisie to break with their traditions and to use the Catholic schools for reasons of snobbery: this was an attempt '*à reconstituer une espèce d'aristocratie au sein de cette société qui tient ses titres de 89, et dont le progrès et la force reposent sur le mérite personnel par l'ordre et le travail*'.[2] It was bad enough for the old nobility to cut itself off from the progressive tendencies of the age; that it should entice the active classes of the country to do the same was a grave political danger.

Other officials shared Mourier's concern at the emergence of 'two nations', and in this perspective trivial incidents took on an ominous significance. At Auxerre, fights between pupils of the college and of a private school had reached the point where their parents had joined in, 'striking each other in the streets with canes and umbrellas'; '*tout cela, . . . ce peut être un jour la guerre civile en France*'.[3]

[1] A. Mourier, *Notes et souvenirs d'un universitaire, 1827-1889* (Orleans, 1889), 156-7, 245-7.

[2] AN F^{17} 2649, quarterly reports of rectors, Rennes, 24 February 1860, and 2650, Bordeaux, 5 July 1861.

[3] 1864 enquiry, rector of Dijon; cf. rector of Rennes on similar incidents at Rennes and Saint-Brieuc.

To the Second Empire, then, the extension of state education meant extending the influence of liberal principles as well as of the regime. This is a reminder that anticlericalism was not necessarily connected with republicanism or with militant *laïcité*. Duruy was a freethinker, but Rouland was a Catholic of the same type as Mourier, and there were many others in the University. A priest, the Abbé Juste, was a rector from 1856 to 1862, and denounced the doings of the Jesuits as strongly as any of his colleagues.

All the ministers of education of the Second Empire insisted that the University should remain outwardly Catholic, and that its teaching should respect religion. This policy was designed to win back to the University the parents who had deserted it after 1850. For the great majority of parents had no sympathy with the freethinking or democratic ideas of the teachers: they wanted an education which stressed conventional values, including religion, and even those who lacked religious beliefs themselves thought that it did children no harm (except in excess, and for this reason they preferred the state schools to schools run by priests). Under the Second Empire, parents felt that their children were in safe hands; after 1880, when the University was free to develop according to its own instincts, they did not. One may suggest that this was one reason why, as the statistics have shown, the Empire's lycées competed more effectively with their rivals than those of the Republic.

Some supporters of the loi Falloux had hoped that it would reconcile liberals and Catholics and allow the two sectors of education to develop in harmony. On the side of the University, the possibility of cooperation still existed until the end of the Second Empire: the ideal of a Gallican, moderately Catholic University was not dead. But the gap had been made unbridgeable by the way in which the Catholic schools had evolved and by the new conflicts of the sixties—the Roman question, the Syllabus, and the disputes over the biblical criticism represented in France by Renan.

Could Catholic education have developed in a more liberal direction? Modern Catholic historians tend to see the association of the Church with conservative political and social forces as an unfortunate choice which might have been made differently. But in this case, there was no real choice. The only potential clientele for the Catholic secondary schools was the conservative one which they in fact attracted, and the only large source of teachers was the ultramontane orders. The Catholics might have acted with more prudence; the episode of the Papal zouaves was unfortunate, and the eagerness of the Jesuits to embrace legitimism and to appeal to the rich earned them the permanent hostility of republicans and democrats. But it is difficult to see that they could have acted in a radically different way. And if the content of their teaching may today seem backward and illiberal, it was nevertheless in conformity with the tendencies of contemporary Catholicism.

It may have been inevitable that Catholic education developed as it did, but it was perhaps less so that it should have caused acute political controversy. We have seen that, as might have been predicted in 1850, the two systems of schools had attracted different clienteles and developed divergent ideals. In many respects, they resembled each other more than they differed—in the teaching of the classics, in the details of daily life, in the assumptions about class and society which they took for granted. Nevertheless, it is true that 'two nations' were being formed with different political beliefs and different attitudes towards progress.

The situation in education only reflected the conflict within French bourgeois society. Education might have served to temper this conflict and provide a minimum of common beliefs and ideals. Instead, the effect of the loi Falloux was to aggravate the conflict, although hardly to the point—by 1870, at least—where the stability and cohesion of society itself were threatened. The Second Empire, despite its claim to represent the principles of 1789, did not see Catholic secondary education as a danger to the political bases on which the regime in fact relied, and it did not seriously consider challenging the Church on this issue. Why in later years men with different political aims thought such a challenge unavoidable, and were prepared to abandon the 'liberty of teaching' created in 1850 and to impose unity by force, and why in general the history of modern France did not conduce to pluralism in education, are questions which lie outside the scope of this essay.

CHAPTER III

THE CONFLICT IN POLITICS

BISHOP PIE'S CAMPAIGN AGAINST THE NINETEENTH
CENTURY: CATHOLIC LEGITIMISM AND LIBERAL BONAPARTISM
AT POITIERS DURING THE SECOND EMPIRE

AUSTIN GOUGH

1. *Mgr Pie and the legitimists*[1]

It is clear from the correspondence passing between the ministry of *cultes* and the French hierarchy in the year following the 1851 *coup d'état* that the government expected more opposition from the group of bishops—perhaps fifteen out of the eighty—who were known to be legitimists. In most cases, however, they seemed ready to accept the arguments which had convinced the rest of the episcopate, and the minister, Fortoul, and his senior officials were pleasantly surprised at the alacrity with which even the most extreme *ultras* declared their allegiance to Louis Napoleon. Where a legitimist bishop was thought to be particularly reluctant, or particularly influential, the full sunshine of official favour was turned on him: Brossais-St Marc of Rennes, for example, had his see raised to an archbishopric, and Mazenod of Marseilles received a grant to build a larger cathedral. The bishops of Moulins and Luçon rejected all approaches and remained irreducibly hostile, but they were unpleasant and

---

[1] I should like to express my appreciation of the unfailing and efficient assistance I received from the staff of the *Archives nationales* on many occasions during the years 1962-67. I must also thank M. Devos, *Conservateur* of the archives of the *Service historique de l'Armée* at Vincennes, for his valuable help; and the Director and staff of the *Archives départementales de la Vienne* for making my work at Poitiers so pleasant and for pointing out several interesting lines of enquiry.

94

eccentric personalities, unpopular in their own dioceses, and the government found it easy to isolate and discredit them. Only in the diocese of Poitiers did the new régime have to deal with a really troublesome opponent, an intelligent and dedicated man who set out to make his *évêché* the focal point of a national legitimist opposition.

Louis-Edouard Pie (1815-80)[1] was the son of a shoemaker of Pontgouin (Eure-et-Loire). As a child he had been placed in the care of the parish priest of Pontgouin, a survivor of the Vendéen wars, and had then passed from the *pétit-séminaire* of St Chéron to the *grand-séminaire* of Chartres with only the briefest contact with the secular world. St Chéron and Chartres were both unusually royalist in tone for the early years of the July Monarchy, being under the patronage of the bishop of Chartres, Mgr Clausel de Montals, a former chaplain to the duchesse d'Angoulême and an adviser to the court of Henry V in exile. Pie came to the bishop's notice by winning a prize for a poem on the birthday of Henry V, and by his brilliant work as a student of patristic literature. Clausel, seeing in this vigorous and intelligent seminarian a future leader of the Chambordist cause amongst the clergy, sent him for further studies at St Sulpice in Paris and then brought him back to Chartres as a junior administrator. When

---

[1] The main printed sources relating to Pie are his *Œuvres sacerdotales 1839-1849* (2 vols., 1891); *Œuvres de Mgr l'Eveque de Poitiers* (10 vols., Poitiers, 1858-94); most of the pastoral letters, *Instructions synodales* and addresses included in the *Œuvres* were published separately as pamphlets, and reference will usually be made to the individual publications. The principal biographical studies are L. Baunard, *Histoire du cardinal Pie* (2 vols., Poitiers, 1886-1887); Mqs de Moussac, 'Un évêque royaliste, le cardinal Pie', ten articles in the *Revue catholique et royaliste*, viii-ix (1908-9); E. Catta, *La doctrine politique et sociale du cardinal Pie* (1957). A valuable collection of Pie's correspondence, with some other useful material, was published as *Correspondance du cardinal Pie et de Mgr Cousseau* (Tours, 1896), and there is a great deal concerning his episcopate at Poitiers in the biography of his vicar-general: B. du Boisrouvray, *Mgr Gay, Evêque d'Anthédon* (2 vols., Tours, 1921).

Pie's personal file in the diocesan sub-series of the ministry of *cultes* archives is F.19.2561; other archival sources for his episcopate will be noted in the course of this article.

he was promoted later as vicar-general, Clausel appointed a second vicar-general to carry out the actual work of the diocese so that Pie could continue to study without interruption. His only duties were to act as spiritual director for some of the noble families of the region; in this milieu he acquired perfect manners and a distaste for the principles of 1789.

Pie's social and political doctrines, formed by years of reading in biblical, patristic and medieval sources and especially in the works of Aquinas and Maistre, began with the fundamental theocratic concept that 'Christ must reign also upon earth'. In all his later arguments the idea recurs again and again: France must found its public polity on the kingship of Christ with all its political consequences.[1] It followed that the Church was both the primary source of legislation and the final court of appeal. Rome must oversee the civil affairs of Europe: 'she has a certainty and precision of manoeuvre which allows her to guide humanity through all dangers, taking account both of the principles which never vary and of the circumstances to which those principles must be applied';[2] on a lower level the clergy, trained in correct theory in the seminaries, were best fitted to act as arbiters of public life. The role of the state was to 'recognize the fact of Original Sin' and to act on the direct advice of the Church. France would recover its political health only in the rule of 'a divinely ordained monarchy detached from the abuses of gallican alliances, and finding in its total union with the Holy See of Rome its real spirit and tradition'. He saw Henry V as the true ultramontane king, *le restaurateur futur du règne de Jésus-Christ*, and wrote declaring his allegiance:

'God has given me the grace of being one of those Frenchmen for whom the religion of 'the second Majesty' and devotion to the race of Saint Louis occupy the first place. . . . Thus I have never ceased to pronounce in my prayers the name of the eldest son of the Church, and I pray each day that he may be given the

[1] Catta, *La doctrine . . . du cardinal Pie*, 90, 137-8, 156.
[2] Pie, *Troisième Instruction synodale . . . sur les principales erreurs du temps présent* (Poitiers, 1864), 283.

gifts which he will need to accomplish the most important and most difficult mission ever confided to a Prince since the beginning of the Christian era.'[1]

In 1844 Pie was invited to deliver the annual sermon on Joan of Arc at Orléans, and turned it into a panegyric on the ancient French monarchy which made his own sympathies quite plain.[2] There was some official criticism but he received messages of congratulation from the comte de Chambord himself, from Alfred de Falloux and from many priests. After several more such addresses, notably a sermon on Saint Louis at Blois in 1846, he was established as the leading *henricinquiste* of his generation.

Although he shared the common dislike of churchmen for the July Monarchy, Pie was not one of those priests who welcomed the Revolution of 1848. Called upon to bless a tree of liberty at Chartres, he quoted Matthew 15.13: 'Every plant which my heavenly Father hath not planted shall be rooted up', and then spoke sourly of revolutionary principles: true liberty was the conquest of sin; equality—'yes, before the same Redeemer and Judge'; fraternity extended to sincere Christians, but not much further.[3] In May 1849 his friend and admirer Falloux, now minister of *cultes*, offered Pie a more active counter-revolutionary role by nominating him for the see of Poitiers, *en pleine Vendée royaliste* as another of his patrons remarked rather enviously.[4] He was thirty-four; his opinions on theology and politics were fully matured and were to remain unchanged until his death in 1880.

Poitiers had not really been considered a centre of Catholic legitimism for many years; the phrase *en pleine Vendée royaliste* had almost an antiquarian flavour. This part of the west was usually described as a peaceful region where the left was feeble and the right quiescent. It was predominantly agricultural, and prosperous in good seasons. Industry was small and scattered—a

[1] Baunard, *Histoire du cardinal Pie*, i. 340.

[2] *Eloge de Jeanne d'Arc*, 8 May 1844, in *Œuvres*, i. 17 ff.

[3] Catta, *op. cit.*, pp. 281-2.

[4] Cousseau, bishop of Angoulême, to Pie, 30 December 1851: *Correspondance Pie/Cousseau*. Mgr Cousseau, an ardent legitimist, was languishing in one of the most dechristianized and Bonapartist dioceses in France.

tannery at Niort, cutlery and small-arms factories at Châtellerault —and there was very little socialism or political unrest amongst the working class. In the *chef-lieu* of Poitiers itself several factors had encouraged the growth of a substantial educated middle class: the city controlled much of the administrative and intellectual life of the western region through being the seat of the criminal and appeal courts, and of the academy with its faculties of law, letters and medicine and its supervision over the schools in the west; there were flourishing historical and musical societies, several banks and a considerable volume of publishing. In the last years of the July Monarchy the representatives of *les classes éclairées* at Poitiers were said to be politically liberal and socially conservative; prefectoral reports mentioned that legitimism persisted amongst the nobility and clergy, but usually went on to repeat a number of common phrases about the legitimists' extreme conservatism and the deeply ingrained habit of seclusion which kept them out of public affairs. But perceptive observers, like Falloux himself, had noted the way the legitimists had come to life in the provinces since the Revolution of 1848; their 'seclusion' was mainly social, and did not mean political nullity. In 1848 they had emerged from the 'emigration of the interior' to accept official posts and contest elections, in the belief that the restoration of Henry V was imminent.

In the Vienne and the Deux-Sèvres the legitimist revival had a particular historical momentum. To the Catholic clergy at the *évêché* and in the religious houses of Poitiers, and to the aristocrats whose châteaux dominated the countryside and whose town houses with their blank shuttered façades filled the old quarter of the city, the word 'Poitou' evoked the entire mythology of royalist France. The magnificent Romanesque churches of Poitiers were encrusted with monuments recalling the Crusades, the resistance to the Muslim invaders, the rise of the great families of Valois and Bourbon, the wars against England. The King in exile, the comte de Chambord, was all the more highly regarded for his ostentatious medievalism, and at any time after 1848 the uncertainty of politics seemed to hold out hope of a restoration in which the historically conscious legitimists of the west might play a leading part. The apparent leader of legitimist opinion in Poitiers was the vicomte Emmanuel de Curzon, proprietor and editor of the newspaper *L'Abeille* in which the case for a Bourbon monarchy was argued with the most extreme violence and intransigence. Curzon's legitimism was in the romantic style of 1832. He was the local correspondent of the comte de Chambord, and agreed with the view then current in the exiled court at Fröhsdorf that Henry V would be restored by a military *coup* rather than by political action; he had raised a troop of vigilantes called the 'Friends of Order' to be ready when the time came. Summing up his impressions of local politics during the Second Republic, however, the *procureur-général*, M. Damay,[1] noted that the more substantial legitimists of Poitiers were inclined to deprecate Curzon as a hothead, and that the real problem was the potential force the right could exert through social, religious and educational pressure. All over the region magistrates, police commissioners, taxation officials and schoolmasters were hindered by a subtle network of 'local influence'; the legitimists of Poitiers were unable to bring this influence fully to bear, Damay thought, because of their lack of really effective leadership.[2]

Pie's nomination was thus a considerable event. He arrived in Poitiers on 8 December 1849, to find the older part of the city decorated with crosses and fleurs-de-lis, and clergy and legitimists waiting impatiently to welcome him. '*Benedictus qui venit*', wrote Curzon in the *Abeille*; 'Enter the walls which saw the birth and death of Hilary and which guard the tomb of Radegonde. . . . This ancient soil of Poitou, which once gave birth to giants who knew how to fight and die for their altars, is ready to flower again at your voice and your blessing.'[3]

[1] Natalis Damay (1795-1872). Damay's background and his political ideas are described later in the present article. Citations hereafter as 'Damay (date)' will refer to his regular reports to the minister of justice, in the *Archives nationales* sub-series BB.30.385.

[2] Damay, 31 November and 31 December 1849, 31 August and 15 November 1850, 15 April and 9 November 1851; and retrospective notes on the Vienne department addressed to Persigny by Claudius Gallix, Inspector-General of *Colportage*, 20 October 1861: F.18.297.

[3] *L'Abeille*, 8 December 1849.

The new bishop devoted his first year at Poitiers to ecclesiastical controversies bordering on politics. Throughout his career he was to fight on two fronts, upholding the royal cause against the governments of the Republic and the Empire, and within the Church fighting tirelessly against liberalism and gallicanism; in 1850 he was the most outspoken defender of Veuillot's flamboyantly ultramontane paper *L'Univers* when the liberal archbishop of Paris, Sibour, tried to tone down its violence or have it suppressed, and he attacked the loi Falloux as an unworthy compromise which left some elements of the state educational system still intact. In July 1851 he appeared for the first time in an overtly political situation. Louis Napoleon and a group of cabinet ministers came to Poitiers on July 1st to open the new railway station, and were received with tremendous enthusiasm; the middle classes especially, who had been made acutely aware in 1848 that the number of qualified electors at Poitiers had risen from 900 to over 30,000, now welcomed Louis Napoleon as the man who would tame the capricious energy of the mass vote.[1] The diehard legitimists closed their shutters and remained indoors, but Pie himself was compelled by his position to give an address at the opening ceremony. He began with a prayer, and noted that of all the official party on the platform only the president made the sign of the cross; he went on to commiserate ironically with the ministers for having to manage French society, which since 1789 had behaved like a runaway train.[2] How much easier it had been to control this fiery engine, he said, under the ancien régime when the monarchy had enjoyed the guidance and support of the Church. It had made a very bad impression, Damay reported, for Pie to have said nothing about the services already rendered by Louis Napoleon, but instead 'to have read him a lecture full of theocratic affect-

---

[1] Damay, 9 July 1851; cf. analysis of electoral and plebiscitary figures 1849-52, by the prefect, December 1852, F.1.c.III Vienne 4; and *Annuaire du départment de la Vienne*, 1846, p. 95.

[2] Baunard, *Pie*, i, 339. The cabinet ministers present were Boulay de la Meurthe, Léon Faucher, Baroche, Randon, Admiral Chasseloup-Laubat, and Pierre Magne—not a noticeably *dévot* group.

ations'.[1] At the same time Pie was writing to a friend that he had tried to avoid anything really theocratic: 'there were ears not capable of hearing'.[2]

The *coup d'état* was generally welcomed by French legitimists, in spite of their coolness towards the president beforehand, as a blow struck against the forces of disorder, a defeat for parliamentarism, and the beginning of an interregnum which could lead to the return of Henry V. Encouraged by Louis Veuillot, whose editorials in the *Univers* carried considerable weight in royalist circles, and by Falloux who campaigned openly in favour of Louis Napoleon, legitimists either voted 'Yes' in the plebiscite of 21 December 1851 or abstained;[3] and the abstainers often took the trouble to explain that they did not mean to imply disapproval.[4] At Poitiers the legitimists came out in large numbers and voted 'Yes', a fact which both Damay and the prefect, baron Jeanin, attributed to the advice of the bishop.[5] Pie's view of the *coup d'état* had been influenced by a letter from his old patron Clausel de Montals in June 1851. Clausel had seen Louis Napoleon and urged him to seize power so that he could 'play the role of Monk'.[6] After the *coup* Pie wrote to Veuillot, who had spoken in the *Univers* of the dilemma of royalists at such a time:

[1] Damay, 9 July 1851. Louis Napoleon already regretted having signed Pie's nomination papers, and blamed Falloux for a bad choice: Falloux, *Mémoires d'un royaliste* (2 vols., 1888), i, 492.

[2] Baunard, *Pie*, i, 338.

[3] The reports to this effect from the *Gendarmerie* who supervised the plebiscite, *Archives historiques de la Guerre* (AHG), *Correspondance générale*, F.1.54, are borne out by the correspondence Veuillot received during December 1851 and January 1852 from legitimists and Catholic journalists: Veuillot papers (VP), *Bibliothèque nationale: Nouvelles acquisitions françaises* 24225.

[4] A legitimist landowner of Mayenne, asked why he and his friends had stayed away from the polls, replied that 'we know quite well that the President will get enough votes without ours, otherwise we should abandon everything to go and vote for him': Lieutenant of Gendarmerie, Sainte-Suzanne (Mayenne), 23 December 1851: AHG F.1.54.

[5] Prefect Vienne, 28 November 1852: F.1.c.III Vienne 4; Damay, 10 February 1852.

[6] Clausel to Pie, 10 July 1851, in Baunard, *Pie*, i, 370-1.

'Yes, you are right. We are between the sabre and the revolutionary's dagger. . . . In view of the hereditary repugnance of the Vendée for the name of Napoleon, I must exercise great care; nevertheless my clergy know that I regard every "No" vote as giving direct support to the party which wants to burn the churches and assassinate the priests. This is why all those who do not vote "Yes" will abstain, in my opinion.'[1]

Eventually, he thought, 'the régime of force will give way to the régime of right'. He encouraged his clergy to recommend a 'Yes' vote, but then conspicuously abstained himself; when Jeanin complained that the bishop should have voted to set a good example, Pie replied that it would have been an equally good example if the prefect and his staff had attended mass after the polling 'and voted "Yes" for Jesus Christ'.[2] Clausel wrote again after the plebiscite stressing the significance of Louis Napoleon as a transitional ruler who would purify France and prepare it for the monarchy, and Pie grudgingly agreed.[3]

The unconcealed movement towards the hereditary Empire during the year 1852 confronted legitimists with an awkward decision. In general they favoured co-operating with Louis Napoleon's government so long as it could be looked upon as an interregnum, but should they continue to support a régime which now claimed to have supplanted the monarchy altogether? Pie interpreted the rapid development of Bonapartism and the official favour for Saint-Simonian ideas in 1852 as a revival of the bourgeois and Voltairean spirit: 'to my mind we are being plunged straight back into the régime of July. The things we see are in open contradiction of all the religious promises.'[4] When Louis Napoleon came in October 1852 to open another railway station, this time at Niort, Pie greeted him with guarded courtesy; in his address of welcome he reminded the prince-president of his duty to bring civil society into harmony with Christian law, and added that this mission was not yet fully accomplished.

[1] Pie to Veuillot, 13 December 1851: VP 24225:308.
[2] Barnard, *Pie*, i.
[3] E. Sevrin, *Mgr Clausel de Montals* (2 vols., 1955), ii. 647.
[4] Baunard, *Pie*, i. 371.

Louis Napoleon replied cryptically: 'I agree, Monseigneur, that my mission is not yet fully accomplished'. Pie was convinced by this time that the prince-president was not capable of 'applying a firm hand to a nation drunk with the excesses and abuses of liberty', and he wrote to Dom Guéranger: 'Believe me, this régime is not viable'.[1]

At the end of October 1852, a few weeks before the re-establishment of the Empire, Chambord issued his celebrated manifesto: 'Frenchmen, you want the monarchy . . . all the genius and glory of Napoleon could not establish anything stable; his name and his memory can suffice still less'. The *Bureau du Roi* in Paris sent out a circular: if there should be a plebiscite on the question of the Empire, legitimists were to dissuade as many people as possible from voting. Pie announced from the pulpit that he personally would abstain. Jeanin sent a worried circular to sub-prefects and mayors urging them to eliminate the names of the dead and the incapable from their lists of qualified voters; prompted by the bishop, the legitimists would claim every non-appearance of a voter as a hostile abstention. But even allowing for 'torrential rain and a furious wind 'on polling day Jeanin was surprised at the number of abstentions. Eight thousand fewer voted than in December 1851, and legitimists probably accounted for at least half of this figure. They had seen the plebiscite of 1851 as 'Order against Chaos', Jeanin commented, but in 1852 it was 'the Bonapartes against the Bourbons'.[2]

As the Empire entered its first confident phase after 1852, Pie set to work to turn Poitiers into the capital of French legitimism. He saw the restoration of Henry V both as highly desirable in itself and as a necessary step towards destroying the legacy of 1789 and reconquering France for Christianity; in the meantime Poitiers was to return to the role it had played in the fourth century when its bishop had been the great Hilary, the scourge of Arianism. Pie assumed the mantle of Hilary with fierce conviction. Almost single handed Hilary had fought the Arian heresy which denied that Christ's nature had been fully divine; the new Hilary

[1] Baunard, *Pie*, i. 376-8.
[2] Prefect, 7 November and 28 November 1852, F.i.c.III Vienne 4.

was to confront the modern Arianism according to which 'Christianity was no more than a philosophy, an elevated one no doubt, but essentially human', and on whose principles the State claimed to be exempt from the sanctions of Divine Law.[1]

'To say that Christ is God of individuals and families but not of peoples and societies . . . to say that Christianity is the law of the individual but not of men collectively . . . to say that the Church is judge of private and domestic morality but not of public and political morality. . . .'

this was Arianism reborn;[2] the duty of any bishop, and *a fortiori* the successor of Hilary, was to fight it and to insist on the full kingship of Christ. He was encouraged by the many examples of Hilary's utter intransigence in the face of criticism from prudent churchmen and secular authorities who complained of his disturbing the settled Church-State relations of the Roman Empire. 'The whole world woke up Arian', but Hilary, according to Sulpicius Severus, stood alone 'and delivered Truth from her captivity'.[3] Pie told the bishop of Nantes that their colleagues in the episcopate 'will all die from good behaviour; our predecessors were not so devoted to a quiet life'.[4] A bishop had no business admitting, for example, that manifest error deserved any freedom of expression, or that the Church could endorse any system of government which claimed to base its authority on the principles of 1789. *Condescendre, c'est descendre,* he quoted Pope Gelasius: churchmen and Christian statesmen must stand by the theocratic ideal in its fullest integrity, 'even when it is temporarily not applicable for want of a Christian prince'.[5]

[1] P. Martain, 'Saint Hilaire et le cardinal Pie', *Revue augustinienne,* vii (15 October 1905), 399. Priests of the diocese said that Pie 'hardly ever advanced a point of doctrine without putting it under the patronage of Hilary': *ibid.,* 406.

[2] *Œuvres de Mgr l'Evêque de Poitiers,* vii. 537.

[3] Martain, *op. cit.,* 403.

[4] Pie to Mgr Jacquemet of Nantes, undated (early Empire): *Correspondance Pie/Cousseau,* p. 110.

[5] *Deuxième Instruction synodale,* 1855, in *Œuvres,* iii. 261; *Œuvres,* ix. 217-18; Catta, *op. cit.,* 32.

His apparent immunity from censure heartened his supporters. In 1854 he felt able to issue a pastoral full of veiled suggestions that the Crimean War was the beginning of a European struggle which could restore the Bourbons,[1] and to tell his friends openly that the casualties at Sebastopol were 'a divinely inflicted punishment on apostate France';[2] on his advice the legitimists refused in a body to subscribe to the war loan.[3] He managed each year to disguise the official Bonapartist festival of August 15th as 'the feast of Saint Radegonde, Queen of France', 'the feast of the Assumption', or 'a special mass for the Pope'; on 15 August 1854 he had the cathedral decorated with fleurs-de-lis and said from the pulpit that 'certain public necessities' compelled him to speak favourably of Napoleon III.[4] In sermons he referred to 'the King my master' without making clear whether he meant Jesus Christ or Henry V.[5] But gestures like these were trivial compared with Pie's success in using the social power of the *évêché*, a success which emphasized the inherent superiority of bishops over laymen as directors of local legitimism. The comte de Chambord's correspondents in the French provinces were for the most part aristocratic amateurs without toughness or dexterity, and in any case Chambord's futile policy of 'abstention' had forced them to give up the very positions in public life which they might have used to rally support for the royal cause. A bishop, on the other hand, had official status, wide publicity for his opinions, and in a reasonably Catholic diocese hundreds of obedient subordinates and a wide network of influence. In the case of Poitiers the government had unwittingly contributed to the growth of Pie's influence by suppressing his main rival in the legitimist party. One of the prefect's first actions after the *coup d'état* had been to close Emmanuel de Curzon's newspaper

---

[1] Pastoral of 26 April 1854, and comments by the minister of *cultes* (Fortoul), 8 June 1854: F.19.2561.

[2] Prefect Vienne (Rogniat), 21 May 1854: F.19.2561.

[3] Damay, 14 August 1854.

[4] Damay, 7 September 1853, 31 January and 7 September 1854, 28 January 1855.

[5] Damay, 6 January 1852; Martain, *op. cit.*, p. 389.

L'Abeille and to dissolve his private army[1]; the result, which Jeanin should have foreseen, was to leave the bishop with the undisputed leadership of legitimist opinion. Curzon's contacts deserted him at once. The legitimists read the diocesan paper, the *Courrier de la Vienne*, and did not miss the *Abeille*. Pie now began to receive visits from the travelling representatives of the exiled court of Henry V; they no longer bothered to call on Curzon, and in return Curzon refused to attend these meetings at the *évêché*, thus cutting himself off from the main Chambordist current. Pie and the diocesan publisher, Henri Oudin, offered him a deputy editorship of the *Courrier*, but he soon fell out with Oudin and left, to relapse into ineffectual grumbling and dreams of armed risings; the legitimism of 1832 had been replaced by a more doctrinally coherent theocratic variety in which 'the Altar took upon itself the task of restoring the Throne'.[2] The great royalist figures of the west, Des Cars, Villeneuve-Bargemont, Rohan-Chabot, Quatrebarbes, who found their own bishops 'feeble and unsatisfactory', came from all the Vendéen departments to revolve around the *évêché* of Poitiers.[3] Their wives, many of whom had come under Pie's guidance as a preacher and confessor in the forties, worked to raise money to help him build a Christian society. The diocesan revenues in any case were enormous, quite apart from the official *budget des cultes*. The profits of Oudin's publishing business, which employed sixty men, were 200,000 francs a year, of which he gave half to the bishop in return for a monopoly of ecclesiastical printing in the diocese. Pie received another 100,000 francs a year in gifts and legacies, from the resources of the thirty-three religious communities under his control, and from the workshop of monumental masons conducted by the Oblates, who had also secured a monopoly.[4] The ramifications of a diocese provided an absolutely legal framework for the collection and channelling of legitimist funds.

[1] Damay, notes on the Curzon correspondence, 9 October 1858: BB.30. 385; Gallix, 20 October 1861: F.18.297.

[2] Gallix, F.18.297.

[3] BB.30.421: (P.1625).   [4] Gallix, F.18.297.

A substantial part of the resources at Pie's disposal went towards the expenses of the St Vincent-de-Paul Society which was to be one of his chief weapons in establishing a legitimist ascendancy. The Society, founded by Ozanam in 1833 for purely charitable ends, had been taken over during the July Monarchy by legitimist aristocrats whose aim was to embarrass the Orléanist government by creating a political alliance of both ends of the social spectrum against the middle. Paternal nobles and Catholic workers were to combine to checkmate the liberal bourgeoisie: 'Ministers of liberalism, we will defend the people against you'.[1] The Society with its affiliated clubs had some success in the forties but lost much of its credit amongst the working classes in 1848 by siding with the authorities and providing a large number of recruits for the *Garde Mobile* in the June Days.[2] The St Vincent-de-Paul Society was active in several clandestine attempts during the Republic to raise irregular troops for the Chambordist cause, distributing alms in the name of Henry V and enrolling 'sergeants' and 'corporals' for battalions which never materialized;[3] the lower ranks of Curzon's 'Friends of Order' appear to have been collected in this way.[4] In 1852 Armand de Melun persuaded Louis Napoleon that the Society should be allowed to take part in the administration of the new *sociétés de secours mutuel*, and from this point its provincial branches enjoyed a conspicuous revival. Under a president and a secretary-general who were

[1] The *Gazette de France*, quoted in Duroselle, *Les débuts du catholicisme social en France 1822-1870* (1951), 201. See also the remarks by the legitimist deputy Béchard in A. Tudesq. *Les grands notables en France 1840-1849* (2 vols., 1964), i. 199-201, 223.

[2] On the part played by the Society under the Second Republic, J. Schall, *Adolphe Baudon* (1900), Ch. 10; M. Lescoët, *Le comte Gaston du Plessis de Grenadan* (Rennes, 1861); G. Baguenault de Puchesse, 'Le vicomte de Melun: souvenirs et correspondance', *Le Correspondant*, 10 February to 25 March 1882.

[3] A legitimist agent, M. Hulard, reporting to Pastoret, secretary of the *Bureau du Roi* in Paris, 26 August 1848: in Pastoret papers, Bibliothèque nationale, *N.a.f.* 12946: 524/5. The most highly organized of these attempts, although in the end totally abortive, was in the Northern departments in 1850: BB.18.1484: (8560).

[4] Damay, 9 November 1851.

both enthusiastic legitimists and regular visitors to Fröhsdorf new branches sprang up all over France presided over by local Chambordists and organized by legitimist youth groups. By 1859 there were 1,300 branches with over 30,000 members; it provided the manpower for other subsidiary *œuvres*, the Society of St Francis Xavier for skilled artisans, the St Joseph Society for apprentices, and the Sunday Observance Society. The amount of tangible social work done, however, was disproportionately small in relation to the resources available, as official critics were not slow to point out. The provision of clothing and free meals was slight compared to the effort expended in using the Society as an employment agency with strong elements of coercion and exclusiveness, and in recruiting its members for various legitimist projects including electoral campaigning.[1] By 1855 the government recognized 'a potential embarrassment if not yet an actual peril'.[2] While most of the bishops adopted a hesitant attitude towards the St Vincent-de-Paul Society, Pie was one of the few to give it an unreserved welcome. He set up a branch as 'the advance-guard of the apostolate' under the presidency of the comte de Bigemont, a former cavalry officer *démissionnaire de 1830*, and in the inaugural address gave very much less emphasis to charity than to the Society's role in 'resisting liberal ideas' and preserving Catholics from compromise in religion and politics.[3] Addressing a general congress of St Vincent-de-Paul branches at Poitiers in 1853, Pie turned the concept of charity into 'a struggle by a young militia against error, lies . . . evil public morals and pleasures forbidden by the Christian law', ending with a torrent of metaphors about fidelity to a sacred flag and the Maccabees who stood firm 'while others capitulated to the army of Antiochus'.[4] The Society extended its operations

---

[1] F.19.6427 (*Associations diverses*); examples of detailed reports from *procureur-général* Toulouse, 17 July 1855, 14 January and 14 July 1856: BB.30.388; *procureur-général* Aix, retrospective report of 7 July 1860: BB.30.370; J. Maurain, *La politique ecclésiastique du Second Empire* (1930), Ch. 6; Duroselle, *op. cit.*, 209-27, 501-7, 550-2.

[2] *Extrait des rapports politiques*, January-June 1855, BB.30.368.

[3] Baunard, *Pie*, i. 333-4.

[4] *Ibid.*, i. 391-2.

throughout the Vienne and the Deux-Sèvres under Pie's general direction and with the full support of his parish clergy.[1] Each branch had its *œuvre des bons livres*, distributing handbooks for apprentices, soldiers, farmers and mothers of families, and historical novels by bitter legitimists like the Abbé Chantrel whose heroes were pious Vendéen dukes, defenders of Throne and Altar, and saintly villagers of the revolutionary period who organized resistance against Jacobinism and the Cult of the Supreme Being. Members of this group volunteered also to buy and destroy booksellers' stocks of indecent and Protestant literature. At Poitiers the *œuvre* was staffed by members of the aristocracy who imported royalist books from Belgium to escape official surveillance.[2]

The legitimists' campaign for the conquest of Poitiers made continual use of this machinery of the St Vincent-de-Paul Society. Their social pressure operated principally through their salons, into which members of the official class could penetrate only at the cost of shedding all traces of Bonapartism or 'governmentalism'. This exclusiveness began with the prefect; by cutting him dead and refusing his invitations they succeeded in socially devaluing the prefecture to the point where three successive prefects, despairing of ever establishing their own salon as the centre of Poitevin public life, asked to be replaced.[3] 'In this region', wrote Emmanuel de Curzon in 1856,

'the royalists have held themselves aloof, and maintained a very firm and hostile attitude towards the present state of affairs. At Paris they have no idea of the persistence and animosity of the political struggles in our provinces. There are some who regret this; for my part I am glad, because it is a proof of the vitality of patriotism in the departments. The situation imposes privations and sacrifices on us, undoubtedly, but this is the very thing which will save us from great perils, one day soon. Here the

[1] Damay, 28 October 1859; also F.19.6253 (Poitiers).

[2] Gallix, F.18.297; cf. P. Pierrard, *La vie ouvrière à Lille sous le Second Empire* (1965), 268-76.

[3] Notes by Gallix on the rapid succession of prefects in the Vienne department between 1852 and 1860: F.18.297.

public functionary is not considered as a fellow-citizen. He is part of an army of occupation, who lives apart and with whom most people will have nothing to do unless it is to talk scandal about him.'[1]

But conversely, even minor civil servants or barely successful businessmen were made welcome in the salons if they held office in the St Vincent-de-Paul Society and spoke respectfully of Henry V. A *percepteur* or a bookseller could sit on a St Vincent-de-Paul committee beside barons and vicars-general; if he displayed particular zeal he might rise still higher to the circle of the *évêché* where he (and his wife) could have the heady experience of being introduced by the bishop to Vendéen celebrities like the duc de Rohan-Chabot and Théodore de Quatrebarbes, privileges denied to the prefect himself.

Rogniat, who took over the prefecture from Jeanin in April 1853, began bravely by promising to make of the administration of the Vienne 'a veritable army corps with its hierarchy, ranks and special unity'.[2] He had little hope of success. There had always been a tendency for local officials to succumb to the allure of the salons; now, with the legitimist party galvanized by the bishop and reinforced by the charity committees, there was a steady and embarrassing drift towards the opposition. The St Vincent-de-Paul Society encouraged recruitment to the local offices of the Ministry of Finance; legitimist salons were then observed to be full of taxation officials. After several hints from Damay, Rogniat moved or dismissed a number of them, but the basic problem remained.[3] There was a disappointing erosion of support also amongst the commercial middle class. Virtually all of the private

[1] Curzon, writing to one of his former schoolmasters in June 1856: this is one of the copies of correspondence seized when Curzon was arrested in 1858: BB.30.421: P.1625.

[2] Quoted by Howard Payne, *The Police State of L-N. Bonaparte* (Seattle, 1966), 169.

[3] Damay, 31 January 1854; Rogniat, reports of July 1854, F.I.c.III Vienne 6; December 1854, F.I.c.III Vienne 8. Rogniat's situation was better than that of the prefect of the Haute-Garonne, where a check of the *fonctionnaires* in 1853 revealed 53 supporters of the régime, 629 legitimists, 241 Orleanists and 53 Republicans; but Toulouse did not have a legitimist bishop.

banks and insurance companies of Poitiers were directed by Catholic *dévots* who had ignored legitimism under the July Monarchy but found the new ultramontane legitimism harder to resist. Shopkeepers and small businessmen were subjected to cruder pressure from the Sunday Observance Society, which arranged boycotts of firms which displayed decorations on August 15th or declined to advertise in the *Courrier*, and from the *Société des Blandines*, an espionage agency of domestic servants controlled by one of Pie's subordinates.[1]

Pie and the legitimist notables had reservations about this influx of support from the middle class. They were always delighted to see the slightest evidence of support from peasants or workers, but to admit too many civil servants, lawyers and businessmen to the party might have been to open the gates to a Trojan Horse of Orleanism. Middle-class recruits had a tendency to take charge of legitimist affairs by virtue of their superior energy and capability, the outstanding local example being the council-general where the two middle-class legitimist councillors, a lawyer and a merchant, easily led and dominated the other five legitimists who were all aristocratic proprietors.[2] But more fundamentally there was a feeling, fostered by right-wing journalists like Lourdoueix and Laurentie in eighteen years of pamphlet warfare against the prevailing tone of the July Monarchy, that the very nature of his occupation and his style of life prevented the bourgeois from being fully Catholic. The true social peril of the day, Pie wrote, came 'not from the uncouth greed of the lower classes, but from irreligion in that so-called conservative category which in each town is represented by the mayor, the school-teacher, the notary, the doctor . . .' who distrusted the priest and refused to recognize the Church's vital importance as the only real guarantee of the institution of property itself.[3] The high-minded bourgeois was as bad as the

---

[1] Darnis, *premier avocat-général*, report of enquiry, 1859: F.19.6253; Gallix, F.18.297.

[2] Prefect's assessment of the councillors-general elected in 1852: F.1.c.V Vienne 2.

[3] Baunard, *Pie*, i. 334-5.

outright anticlerical, Pie thought; on Sundays, instead of coming to mass, he 'shut himself in his study and wrote gravely on questions of social reform'.[1] At Poitiers Pie hoped to inaugurate a national process by which the control of society was handed back to a class more suited to exercise it, the aristocracy. The men 'obstinately faithful to their king' were also those most faithful to the Church's ideal social order:

'The only rich men who fulfil their religious duties, in nine-tenths of France; the only men in whose hands fortunes are put at the disposal of Catholic works. . . . Do you wish me to place in the same rank as these the bourgeoisie now grown rich? Their only merit is to give me a fine dinner when I visit their parishes, and to come to church on that day only; you cannot wish me to give them the same consideration as the true Christians whom one meets every day before the altar, who sustain our seminaries, who respond to our appeals'.[2]

Pie, however, was always ready to welcome any member of the middle class who had experienced a whole-hearted conversion and wanted to cut himself off from the entire ambience of the bourgeoisie. Some were attracted by the example of Jules Richard, president of the charity committees of the Deux-Sèvres and a great favourite of the salons. Richard was a substantial business-man who had been a republican deputy in 1848 and had voted against sending a French army to the assistance of the Pope; he had undergone a religious conversion at the time of the *coup d'état*, and later gave away much of his property and worked so hard for the St Vincent-de-Paul Society that after his death Pie actually proposed him for canonization.[3]

It was no wonder that the Poitiers region contributed so largely to the boom in the assumption of false titles which began in the west during the early fifties. The social climber whose name

---

[1] Pie, *Instruction pastorale*, Easter 1850, *Œuvres*, i. 138.

[2] Pie to Guéranger, 3 January 1852: Delatte, *Dom Guéranger, Abbé de Solesmes* (2 vols., 1910), ii. 52.

[3] Baunard, *Pie*, i. 397-400. Richard founded more than thirty branches of the Society in the Poitiers diocese.

had acquired the particle almost overnight usually adopted legitimism as an insurance; his new status was more likely to be tacitly accepted in the salons. The prefect of Maine-et-Loire wrote:

'Every day I observe the most peculiar transformations of name, followed immediately by equally peculiar transformations of opinion. The real nobles mock these people but cannot help welcoming them as recruits to the legitimist cause, often very ardent ones. Naturally, each time this happens the government loses a supporter, and this from the very class we rely on so much, the men of order, the educated classes.'[1]

In 1858 the government tried to check this widespread movement with legislation under which genuine nobles had to register their claims with the local courts, and the *conseil du sceau* was revived to adjudicate in doubtful cases.[2] The law of 1858 only redoubled the efforts of the *arrivistes* of Poitiers; they would not approach the *conseil du sceau*, Damay reported, because its scrutiny was too rigorous, but instead applied to the local courts in a deliberately casual and indifferent manner designed to give the impression that their titles went back at least to the Crusades, and that they could afford to put up with a brief ceremony of formal recognition. Unfortunately, although the prosecutors were determined to apply the strict letter of the new law, claims of nobility too often came before magistrates who were themselves the worst offenders; in one typical case the request of a M. Merland to add 'de la Guichardière' to his name was heard and allowed by two notorious climbers, M. Girard *de Vasson* and M. Merveilleux *du Vignaux* (Damay's italics).[3]

The courts, in fact, represented a serious problem for the

---

[1] Prefect Maine-et-Loire, 21 January 1858, BB.30.371.

[2] *Exposé des motifs* and discussions of the law of May 1858, in N. Batjin, *Histoire complète de la noblesse de France* (1862); see also Pol de Courcy, *De la noblesse et des usurpations nobiliaires* (1858).

[3] Damay, commenting retrospectively on several similar cases, report of 7 May 1863. The text of the circular of the Poitiers *parquet* inviting nobles to apply for recognition was printed in the *Annuaire de la noblesse* for 1861.

administration. Damay could rely on his own subordinates, the *procureurs-impériaux*, and on most of the police commissioners and *juges de paix* in the countryside, but the senior members of the bench seemed to be either old-fashioned Bonapartists of an unpleasantly authoritarian stamp or legitimists; some of the latter had attended the comte de Chambord's rally at Wiesbaden in 1850, and had electioneered or even stood themselves in legitimist campaigns for the local councils, a most undesirable practice 'which led them to solicit votes from people who might one day appear before them in court'.[1] Piquant situations arose quite often when magistrate and prisoner both belonged to the St Vincent-de-Paul Society, or when the accused made a point of mentioning his legitimism; the police found themselves powerless in such cases.[2] In the middle of the fifties the courts provided the most notable of many bitter struggles between the *évêché* and the administration for the allegiance of men in official positions. Casimir de Sèze, president of the *cour impériale* of Poitiers, was a nephew of the *avocat* who had defended Louis XVI, a brother of the former legitimist deputy Aurélien de Sèze, and probably the most influential legitimist layman in the department. In 1854 Persigny decided to try and recruit him for the presidency of the council-general—'the support of such an eminent man could be very useful in this region'.[3] There were, however, three main difficulties. The prefect had significant doubts: a man

---

[1] Damay, 17 July 1851.

[2] This was a problem throughout the west: cf. a report of the *procureur-général* of Angers, 21 January 1858, BB.30.371. In 1852, when the government's main concern was to conciliate 'men of order', the prefect of the Ille-et-Vilaine asked Persigny if he was contemplating a purge of hostile legitimists in the judiciary. Persigny replied: 'Your ideas on the extent of the obligations of the magistrates, as regards the degree of support which they ought to give the government, seem to me to be exaggerated. The members of the judicial order cannot be equated completely, in this respect, with administrative civil servants, who ought certainly to display full and active cooperation whatever may have been their previous affiliations or their personal sympathies.' Minister of Interior (Persigny) to prefect, 24 August 1852: F.1.c.III Ille-et-Vilaine 12.

[3] Persigny to prefect Vienne, 20 April 1854: F.1.c.V Vienne 2.

uniting the two presidencies of the court and the council-general 'might neutralize the influence of the prefect himself.[1] Secondly, an excellent Bonapartist, M. Evariste Robert-Beauchamp, had strong claims to the presidency of the council. Thirdly, it was probable that there would be some difficulty in having de Sèze elected.

The government brushed aside these objections in one of the clearest demonstrations of the policy already established of ignoring provincial Bonapartists for the sake of winning over legitimist notables.[2] The prefect managed to obtain the resignation of a M. Bazille from the council, and de Sèze appeared as the official candidate for a by-election in the canton of Loudun in July 1854. Pie thought his acceptance of official patronage a disgrace; the diehard abstentionists regarded him as a traitor. They put up M. de Lavau, 'a rich and honorable proprietor' and a friend of the bishop, to oppose him:

'A committee was organized at Loudun; the communes were heavily canvassed, voters were visited in their houses, the mayors were harassed, voting papers distributed in large numbers. . . . M. de Sèze was represented as an apostate, a La Rochejacquelein, a Pastoret. . . . Outside the poll yesterday voting papers were torn out of the voters' hands.'[3]

The prefect rallied his forces, applied unashamed pressure to 'all

[1] Prefect Vienne, 28 June 1854: F.i.c.V Vienne 2.

[2] Robert-Beauchamp's supporters were furious at his being passed over for a legitimist. He was a forge-master and also owned land in four of the five cantons of the Vienne; he had been secretary of the council-general for five years and had recently married the daughter of another Bonapartist councillor, de Soubeyran. His cousin, the baronne de Serlay, was dame of honour to the princesse Mathilde and had written to the emperor supporting Robert-Beauchamp's candidature: letter of 1 July 1854, in F.i.c.V Vienne 2; also notes on Robert-Beauchamp prepared for the Emperor's secretary, F.i.c.III Vienne 4.

[3] Prefect Vienne, 17 July 1854, F.i.c.V Vienne 2. La Rochejaquelein, whose name stood for the purest Vendéen tradition, had allowed himself to be made a senator and president of the council-general of the Deux-Sèvres; Pastoret, head of the *Bureau du Roi* in Paris until the *coup*, had given up his legitimism for a seat in the Senate.

those who owe some support to the government', and suspended two mayors who refused to electioneer for de Sèze. The result was 1352 votes for the official candidate and 685 for Lavau, and de Sèze was duly appointed president of the council by decree— 'but it augurs ill for the future, with the legitimist party stirred up like this'.[1]

For about three years de Sèze remained an ally of the government, working actively for official candidates in the elections of 1855 and 1857, rallying support in the courts and amongst the civil servants[2]—and was rudely shunned by legitimist society.[3] At the beginning of 1858 Damay thought him fairly reliable;[4] but in the course of that year, a year of revived hopes for the legitimist cause, the bishop made a determined and successful attempt to win him back from the government camp. He consulted de Sèze more and more frequently on the appointment of young men to legal posts, and absorbed him smoothly into the network of the St Vincent-de-Paul Society. When the government made de Sèze an Officer of the Legion of Honour, Pie arranged (as no layman could have done, not even Chambord himself) for the Roman Curia to make him a Grand officer of a Papal order, and acted as intermediary for an exchange of letters between de Sèze and the Pope. He asked the president's help in some educational matters which came under the jurisdiction of the council-general, and then thanked him in a public address in which he called de Sèze 'the defender of religion' and spoke also of his part in 'placing good men in key positions', adding many other compliments 'at which the magistrate was obviously pleased'.[5] De Sèze succumbed to this campaign and attached himself once again to the évêché. The legitimists realized that instead of losing the president of the court to the official machine, they had in effect captured the presidency of both court and council for themselves; they went

[1] Prefect Vienne, 17 July 1854, F.1.c.V Vienne 2.
[2] Report by de Sèze on his efforts in the elections, 18 June 1857: BB.18. 1567.
[3] Damay, 28 January 1855, 18 June 1857.
[4] Damay, 29 January 1858.
[5] Gallix: F.18.297.

out of their way to emphasize the power and prestige of the dual office, and, as he had feared, the prefect found himself walking in processions three paces behind M. de Sèze.

As Pie's power increased he became more combative, and it was impossible to predict how widely or how deeply his influence would have permeated after another five or ten years in the diocese. From the fastness of Poitiers he made regular forays in imitation of Hilary against the heretics, denouncing the corruption of French society, the lukewarmness of Catholics, the licence allowed to agnostics and liberals, and the irrational public prejudice against the cause of the Bourbons. The Catholic press, hypnotized, seldom mentioned his name without adding *le nouveau Hilaire*. He adopted an Olympian attitude towards the civil power, and a semi-Papal mode of address. His pastorals read like encyclicals.[1] Damay, observing the situation in 1858, thought that it would be only a matter of time before Pie began to sign himself *Servus servorum Dei*, or tried to depose the prefect—and in fact Paulze d'Ivoy, who had succeeded Rogniat in 1857, was half deposed already. Paulze was a grand-nephew of an eighteenth-century bishop of Poitiers, and had begun his term of office by establishing close relations with the *évêché* and asking Pie to be godfather to his son. After six months he was in a very weak position, patronized by de Sèze, and limply accepting the dozens of nominees Pie put forward as mayors, notaries, postal officials and land surveyors.[2]

ii. *M. Damay and official resistance to the bishop*

M. Natalis Damay had not been long in his post before coming to the conclusion that the *procureur-général*, rather than the prefect, was the man best fitted to act as the embodiment of the Empire

---

[1] Where other bishops began with preamble, Pie always began: 'Louis-François-Désiré-Edouard Pie, par la grace de Dieu et du Siège Apostolique, Evêque de la Sainte Eglise de Poitiers, Assistant au Trône Pontifical. . . . Au clergé et aux fidèles de notre diocèse, salut et bénédiction. . . .' The phrasing asserted Pie's autonomy, his ultramontanism, and his contempt for the workings of the Concordat.

[2] Damay, reports of January, April and June 1858.

and to stamp his own particular image of Bonapartism on the region. The prefect's apparently greater importance was an illusion, at least in the west. As head of the *magistrature debout*, and thus controlling the machinery of courts and prosecutions, the *procureur-général* could nullify the work of an unsatisfactory prefect; his territory covered four departments to the prefect's one, and he dealt with three bishops;[1] his network of information was both much wider in extent than the prefect's and better in quality. Above all, he was immune to the social pressures which the legitimists could apply to the prefecture; working in his less public sphere, the *procureur-général* enjoyed comparative security of tenure while prefects came and went. It is clear from Damay's assessments of western politics in the early years of the Empire, and from his disparaging and evidently well-justified comments on the abilities of the prefects Jeanin, Rogniat and Paulze d'Ivoy, that he knew he must project himself into the front line to struggle with the legitimists and their champion the bishop. His qualifications were well suited to the task. Damay was one of the men of liberal background who had entered the magistracy immediately after the Revolution of July 1830. He spent several years as *procureur du roi* at Abbeville and later at Amiens, and was *premier avocat-général* at Amiens when the July Monarchy fell in 1848. As a progressive whose opinions had caused some comment amongst the conservative Orleanists of the Amiens bar he had felt no need to resign at the advent of the Republic, and was rewarded by being made *procureur-général* of Poitiers in June 1848; his appointment was gazetted during the June days. When he arrived in January 1849 to be installed in the post which he was to hold until 1870, through the terms of office of six prefects, Damay was already fifty-four years old and an experienced administrator. The impression arising from the trenchant and widely ranging reports which he submitted to the Ministry of Justice and from the many references to him in other sources is of an urbane and witty radical, with the rather

---

[1] Damay's *ressort* included the departments of the Vienne, the Deux-Sèvres, the Charente-Inférieure and the Vendée, and the dioceses of Poitiers, La Rochelle and Luçon.

exalted concept of law natural to his profession, but with a sense also of the limits of authority which led him on many occasions to invoke the principles of 1789 in assessing a situation or in making a practical decision.[1]

Damay's installation at Poitiers took place six weeks after the election of Louis Napoleon as president of the republic; he at once made it clear that he was a supporter of the new régime, but one for whom Bonapartism was essentially a liberal creed. The senior magistrate, M. Vincent-Molinière, who had been trained under the Empire and had presided over one of the courts at Poitiers since 1811, welcomed Damay with a speech which equated the Bonapartist idea with the purest authoritarianism. Damay replied only with some formal compliments to Poitiers, 'city of studies and science', and went on to stress the need for the legal system to act with care in a politically explosive situation: 'the régime of universal suffrage requires a spirit of moderation and mutual concessions';[2] He ended with a polite bow to 'the great name of Bonaparte', but Vincent-Molinière's address had not been at all to his taste. Looking back later on the events of his first few months at Poitiers he wrote that Vincent-Molinière had perhaps held his job for too long; these old Bonapartists who remembered nothing of the Napoleonic Empire but its unity and its power must give place to men who recognized Louis Napoleon both as his uncle's heir and as 'the standard-bearer of 1789'.[3]

Damay's first circulars in 1849, defining the scope of political police work, were drafted on the assumption that if there was

[1] Apart from his reports to the Minister of Justice, in the *Archives nationales* sub-series BB.30.385, there is a considerable amount of Damay's correspondence in the archives of other ministries, especially in the series BB.18 (Justice) and F.19 (Cultes), and in the *Archives départementales de la Vienne* (ADV). Other sources relating to Damay are his personal file in the series BB.6.II, the *Procès-verbaux* of the installation of Damay in 1849 and of his successor in 1871, and the texts of his addresses at the annual opening ceremonies of the courts at Poitiers.

[2] *Cour d'Appel de Poitiers: Procès-verbal de l'installation de M. Damay, le 24 janvier 1849* (Poitiers, 1849).

[3] Damay, reports of 30 November 1849, 15 November 1850.

going to be any trouble it was likely to come from the left. They were careful and pragmatic documents without any of the characteristic feverishness of provincial officials under the Second Republic. The eighteen *procureurs* and the judiciary police under their control were to observe the political clubs; they must, however, 'avoid any inquisitorial measures which might go beyond our proper judicial duties . . . and disregard sincere differences of opinion and interest'. The correct approach to the problem of the working classes was to study their resources, their grievances and their political ideas. Quite apart from considerations of humanity, Damay remarked, the cause of order was best served by serious investigation; the police official who knew the interests and motives of the working classes most intimately was the one best able to divert them from 'the dangerous promises of utopians' and the seductions of the more violent political clubs.[1] But from the day in 1851 when he had seen the confrontation between Mgr Pie and Louis Napoleon's ministers at the opening of the Poitiers railway station, and noted its political overtones, Damay concentrated his attention on the right and mounted a continuous campaign against the *évêché*.

One of the most important weapons at his disposal was the opportunity to deliver each year a reasoned statement of principle in the form of an address at the inaugural session of the courts. When prefects spoke, for example at the official *fêtes* of August 15th, they were usually addressing the general public and did not attempt to explore the constitutional theory of the Empire. At least until the arrival of Levert as prefect in 1861, prefectoral speeches were more or less ceremonial and without political interest. The *procureur-général* spoke before a more sophisticated audience of magistrates, *avocats* and professors of the faculty of law; his annual addresses reflected on the one hand the professional interest taken by this circle in constitutional matters, and on the other hand Damay's own ideas and his rather optimistic interpretation of the direction the Empire was taking. The councillors-general, the bishop and a group of senior clergy were invited to

[1] Damay, Circular to the *procureurs de la République*, 27 November 1849: BB.30.385.

the opening of the courts, and for one day in the year had to listen while Damay expounded a liberal Bonapartist message with overtones of deism. His addresses were literary performances in a style familiar to old lycéens, studded with classical quotations and arguments from Montesquiou, and clearly echoing the religious radicalism of the thirties and forties when the *Débats* and the *Deux Mondes* had followed each step in the search of Quinet and Cousin for a nineteenth-century religion which would be free of the doctrinal rigidity and theocratic pretensions of Catholicism. Opening the first session of the courts under the Empire in 1853, Damay spent some time describing the many parallels between Christianity and 'the primitive religions of ancient Scandinavia'; no doubt Christianity was the true religion in a general sense, but final and absolute truth eluded men of religion, as it sometimes eluded magistrates.[1] Catholicism, he said in another address filled for Pie's benefit with quotations from Bossuet, Augustine and Aquinas, 'must shake off the dust of ages and ally itself with the progress of enlightened opinion'.[2] On each occasion he made some direct or implied reference to the bishop in order to strike a contrast between Pie's absolutist millennium of 'the reign of Christ on earth' and an ideal picture of the ultimate aims of Bonapartism; as in 1815, he said, to rally to the Emperor was to declare oneself against a static and repressive ancien régime, and for a system whose possibilities for development were limitless.[3] Bonapartism was the only possible framework for French culture and French politics. Its cultural side was expressed by the essentially Bonapartist institution of the *université* which Napoleon I had founded to be the instrument for reconciling the France of 1572 with the France of the Revolution.[4] Reconciliation in intellectual affairs, Damay said in his address of 1856, meant recognizing the power and competence of man's reason, and defending the freedom of philosophical enquiry

---

[1] *De la vérité considérée notamment dans les fonctions judiciaires: discours prononcé à l'audience solonnelle de rentrée de la Cour d'appel de Poitiers, le 3 Novembre 1853* (Poitiers, 1853).

[2] *De la modération: discours prononcé … le 4 novembre 1861* (Poitiers, 1861).

[3] *Ibid.*

[4] *De la conciliation: discours prononcé … le 4 novembre 1856* (Poitiers, 1856).

against extremists who said flatly, in the manner of 1572 or of 1793, that one view was entirely right and all other views entirely wrong. What could be a more effective contrast to the theocratic programme of censorship and hostility to free enquiry than the *université*, under whose tolerant patronage 'religion and philosophy could advance like two sisters, hand in hand?'—Damay quoted this catch-phrase of the eclectic school in his address of 1856 to annoy Pie, who had spent much of that year in well-publicized efforts to have the works of Victor Cousin placed on the Index, and he compounded his offence in the eyes of the clergy present by referring to recent writings of Cousin and Jules Simon which suggested that of the 'two sisters' philosophy probably had the greater power of survival. It was to be through state education, especially scientific education, that the Saint-Simonian aspects of Bonapartism which Damay obviously found most congenial would reach their fullest development; he quoted the most Saint-Simonian passages from the *Idées napoléoniennes* of 1839—the Napoleonic idea 'inspires agriculture, invents new manufactures... levels mountains, crosses streams, facilitates communications, and obliges all nations to be at peace'—and made a valiant attempt to see something of this in the first decade of the Empire. Science and technology could flourish only under stable centralized government; encouraged by the Napoleonic State, electricity and steam would 'make one family of the human race' and thus do more than generations of diplomacy to prevent war; in the future, Damay remarked, people would be astonished that anyone could ever have been so barbaric as to resort to arms.[1] Universal scientific education would reconcile the classes divided by hostile and untenable creeds; it was a poor civilization that was afraid of the light. The *université* must extend its activity further into the social fabric, Damay said, conscious that part of his audience would have preferred to see the *université* disappear altogether.[2] Education for the masses must be both free and obligatory; he rejected any

---

[1] *De la modération* . . . (1861). This was perhaps not the best date for recalling the theme of '*L'Empire, c'est la paix*'.

[2] *Ibid.* This article will not deal with the conflict between the state and ecclesiastical school systems at Poitiers.

argument based on a supposed right of parents to keep their children ignorant. Let France imitate her neighbours who were just as much concerned with liberty but saw that on this matter the state had a right to insist. Most particularly, state education must be made available to the farmer. The real remedy for the drift to the cities was to educate the farmers, not just vocationally but deliberately 'above their station . . . to make the profession of *agriculteur* dignified and attractive'. Let them learn to understand the soil, botany, meteorology; let the farmer's leisure be filled with reading, science, even poetry and the arts, instead of the 'inert repose' that was so often the case.[1]

In Damay's later addresses, delivered under titles like 'Conciliation' and 'Moderation', the conventional praise of the régime expected on official occasions always led him to the theme of Bonapartism and liberty. The Napoleonic system, not socialism nor any of the other programmes of the left, was the road to freedom. Order and liberty could be reconciled only by 'handing the reins of authority to a liberal prince': Damay spoke always of 'the liberal government of the emperor', 'Napoleon III and his liberal régime', 'his liberal and progressive policies'.[2] The fact that virtually all sections of society had voted in his favour, Damay argued, conferred on Napoleon III a unique authority but also implied a duty of the Imperial government to deal fairly with all groups and classes. The more massive the electoral endorsement, the more binding was the government's duty of magnanimity and reconciliation. In his address of 1861 he described the transition of the régime from its first authoritarian phase of 'military justice' to its later and more liberal reliance on the civil courts. The *commissions mixtes* of 1851 had applied their repressive justice only to one group, the working-class radicals; the lawyers may have applauded the repression of 1852 as men of order, but their professional pride had been hurt by this intrusion of military law into matters which could have been dealt with by

[1] *De la parole: discours prononcé . . . le 3 novembre 1866* (Poitiers, 1866).
[2] There are signs in his addresses that he may have read Emile de Girardin, articles on the Empire in *La Liberté*, later reprinted as *L'Empire avec la liberté* (1859).

the courts. Damay had protested at the absurd severity of the *commission* in the Vienne department which had 'exiled the heads of families, leaving starving children behind', for having demonstrated against the *coup d'état*;[1] when the exiles had been pardoned in 1854 he reported an excellent effect on local opinion.[2] The Empire, he said in 1861, was now able to rely with confidence on the civil courts which treated all sections of the community alike, and in political cases acted only when there was a clear incitement to disorder; even those whose opinions were by official standards futile and misguided 'deserve their place in the sun'.[3] Damay thought that the law ought, in fact, to show a degree of compensating favour to those who were at a social disadvantage. Occasionally in his addresses he referred obliquely to his own efforts to use the legal machinery for the benefit of the working classes and the poorer farmers; in 1853 his office initiated several prosecutions for usury—'since the introduction of the *Crédit foncier* there is no excuse for it'[4]—and throughout the fifties he made repeated efforts, ultimately with success, to find enough hard evidence to prosecute a group of bakers in the Vienne who were operating a price ring which caused a great deal of misery and resentment, and to act against small-scale monopolists in the fisheries and salt works of the coastal departments.[5]

Damay's general theme, embroidered with many variations, and with examples like the innovation by which the government began later in the sixties to send out pamphlets explaining and justifying new laws and decrees,[6] was that every sign pointed in

[1] Damay, 9 May 1852, BB.30.385: he suggested in this report that the *garde des sceaux* ask Marshal Canrobert to revise the sentences in the Vienne.

[2] Damay, 31 January 1854.

[3] *De la modération* . . . (1861).

[4] Damay, 31 January 1854.

[5] Damay, 31 January 1854, 28 January 1855. The *Caisse de boulangerie* set up in Paris by a decree of 27 December 1853 to equalize the price of bread does not seem to have applied to the western provinces at this stage.

[6] Regarding the government's *Exposé succint de la loi militaire de 1868*, sent out with instructions that it was to be circulated amongst men of influence, Damay reported on 15 April 1868 that the gesture was better appreciated than the arguments contained in the pamphlet itself.

the same direction; the Empire stood for toleration and a spirit of reason, most particularly in the two fields of religion and the law. In 1856 he was able to mention the Empire's greatly improved taste in bishops: Landriot, recently appointed to the neighbouring see of La Rochelle, was one of the most outstanding liberals in the French clergy, a protégé of Maret and Montalembert and a formidable opponent of the *veuillotistes*. His first pastoral as bishop of La Rochelle had been an appeal for friendship with the city's large and historic Protestant minority; it made a significant contrast, Damay said, with Richelieu who had declared himself a lieutenant-general in order to reduce La Rochelle to submission; he made the comparison in such a way that his listeners could hardly miss the implied reference to a recent pastoral in which Pie had tried to enlist the secular arm to subdue the remains of the *Petite Eglise* in the Deux-Sèvres.[1] With regard to the law, having noted the transition from the neo-military rigour of 1852 to the confident security of the sixties, Damay felt able to predict in 1861 that eventually in some final idyllic condition of Bonapartism the coercive apparatus of the state would 'disarm itself', and leave only a society of free men.[2]

Pie's reaction to these annual addresses was to try to have the *procureur-général* removed. On his way back from a visit to Italy in 1855 during which he had seen both the Pope and the comte de

[1] *De la conciliation . . . (1856)*. The schism of the *Petite Eglise* had begun under the First Empire when a group of royalist bishops had refused to accept the provisions of the Napoleonic Concordat under which they were asked to resign their sees; their followers still survived in parts of the west, almost without clergy. Damay on an earlier request from Pie for government action to suppress them: 'They are peaceful, honest and charitable, and the Emperor's government ought to treat them as well as previous governments have done. Mgr Pie may take whatever ecclesiastical action he likes—from his point of view the schism is regrettable. But he and the priests of the Deux-Sèvres must recognize the need for prudent moderation. *Le bras seculier* especially must act prudently because the *Petite Eglise* are legitimists by principle and we do not want to appear to be persecuting them. . . . [They have no clergy except] Father Bernier, an unfrocked priest; he is a sodomite and if we ever wished we could prosecute him with sound evidence, but his congregations are worthy of our tolerance': report of 31 January 1854.

[2] *De la modération . . . (1861)*

Chambord, Pie had an audience with Napoleon III and complained that Damay was spreading sceptical and radical ideas throughout the Catholic west.[1] At the *rentrée de la cour* of 1856 he was so visibly annoyed at Damay's remarks about eclecticism and philosophical neutrality and his praise of Landriot that Casimir de Sèze and another senior magistrate went afterwards to the *évêché* to tender an apology.[2] 'As at the time of Hilary,' said Pie sarcastically, 'we see once again the Arian coalition: so many great minds, and fortified by the support of the magistrature of the Empire.'[3] He invited the celebrated Jesuit preacher Fr Felix to give a series of addresses in the cathedral on 'pseudo-Christianity' and the errors of Cousin, as a direct reply to Damay, and lost no opportunities himself. At the opening of the new Market of St Hilary in 1857 he told the businessmen of Poitiers that the so-called progress of the Empire was in reality a descent into materialism, luxury and indecency;[4] his *Instructions synodales sur les principales erreurs du temps présent* of 1855 and 1858 rebuked Catholics who accepted the secular view of religion as a private matter and declined to fight for a Christian society. He was most eloquent, and most disquieting to the government, when he countered Bonapartist liberalism by emphasizing the theme of *la Vendée catholique et militaire*. Since the fiasco of 1832 nobody in the ministries seriously believed that a revolt in the west could succeed, but it was possible at the very least that a revival of Vendéen fanaticism at some moment of crisis could embarrass the government and disturb the careful equilibrium of the Empire. In departments where the duchesse de Berry's rising twenty years earlier had left its mark, prefects and *procureurs* worried over the most trivial incidents. When he was made president of the Agricultural Society of the Deux-Sèvres, the marquis de La Rochejacquelein expressed the hope 'that the farmers of the west would rally to his name in time of peace, just as they had rallied

[1] J. Maurain, *La politique ecclésiastique du Second Empire* (1930), 245; Baunard, *Pie*, i. 591 f.

[2] Baunard, *Pie*, i. 616-19.

[3] Martain, *op. cit.*, 400.

[4] Baunard, *Pie*, i. 641-2.

to his father's name in time of war'; Damay thought it 'a joke in poor taste' but some of the local officials were thrown into a panic.[1] For Pie the Vendéen tradition, or an idealized version of it, was the perfect antithesis of Damay's idealized Bonapartism: when La Rochejacquelein's mother, a heroine of the *guerre des géants*, died in February 1857, Pie delivered a funeral oration which presented the Vendée as an untainted source of counter-revolution:

'There is no other province in France where the gentleman and the peasant have enjoyed more points of contact and agreement than in this country of the Gâtine and the Bocage. In this *pays* the nobility had enough faith in themselves not to seek any factitious grandeur . . . and a religious faith lively and practical enough to understand that as between Christians, between Frenchmen, between free men, disparity of rank should reveal itself only in a superiority of education and material benefits. For their part the people knew by experience that their masters never sought to humiliate them or to enslave them. . . . From this springs this phenomenon hardly known elsewhere: a friendly and honoured nobility, supported by a proud and submissive people . . . from this proceeded the magnanimous war of the peoples of the west, a war impossible wherever mistrust and separation between castes prevented the people from giving themselves to their leaders, and prevented the lords from finding soldiers.'[2]

For the moment, however, the idea of the Vendée could be no more than a reserve of psychological strength for the legitimists, without any immediate political importance. As for Damay, the over-optimism of his theory did not affect his practical efforts to encourage the growth of a Bonapartist circle as an alternative to the legitimist salons. For the time being, Bonapartist society at Poitiers was to have its nucleus not in a salon, since the prefecture never succeeded in forming one and Damay himself lived austerely and did little entertaining, but amongst the staff of the faculty of

[1] Damay, 28 January 1855.
[2] *Eloge funèbre . . . la marquise de La Rochejacquelein . . . le 28 février 1857*: in *Œuvres*, ii. 684 ff. Pie delivered a similar *éloge* at the funeral of the dowager marquise de Dreux-Brézé in 1861: Gallix, F.18.297.

law and the academy, many of whom were conscious of the steady tidal progress of the professional middle classes in France and saw no advantage in making humble approaches to the aristocracy. This group was strengthened by a new element in the courts, younger lawyers elevated to the bench when elderly magistrates retired—Emmanuel de Curzon said of these new men, perhaps with a little truth, that when they were presiding no legitimist *avocat* could possibly win his case[1]—and also by those doctors and notaries whose practices did not take them into fashionable society. Damay's reliance on *les classes éclairées* matched Pie's detestation of them. In 1855 the faculty of law supplied Poitiers with a mayor after the office had been vacant for more than a year, the assumption being that nobody of any consequence would accept it for fear of being ostracized by the salons. The prefect thought that the only solution would lie in the virtual surrender of the mayoralty to the *évêché*, by appointing a mayor 'from the upper reaches of legitimist society'; finally, with Damay's support, M. Grellaud, professor of the Code Napoléon at the faculty, was nominated and held office for several years with a fair degree of success. Another lecturer at the faculty of law, M. Bourbeau, was mayor during the last five years of the Empire.[2]

The Bonapartist circle was further consolidated when Damay, after repeatedly complaining that the rector of the academy of Poitiers, Audinet, was a clerical-legitimist, succeeded in having him replaced by a very able governmental priest, the abbé Juste, formerly dean of the theological faculty of Rouen. Juste, like Landriot a gallican-liberal of the school of Maret, was appointed primarily as a counterweight to the bishop and told to engage Pie in public debate whenever his more outrageous statements seemed open to challenge on theological grounds.[3] Since his appointment

[1] Undated letter: copy in Curzon's correspondence seized in 1858: BB.30.421 (P.1625).

[2] Prefect (Rogniat) to Minister of Interior, 19 May 1855; and other documents relating to the mayoralty of Poitiers, in F.i.b.II Vienne 6.

[3] Reports and correspondence of the abbé Juste on ecclesiastical politics in the Poitiers diocese, in F.19.2561; Damay, reports of January and April 1858, 29 June 1861; also, G. Vauthier, 'Mgr Pie et le gouvernement de Napoleon III', *La Révolution de 1848*, xx (1923-24).

coincided with the revision of the loi Falloux in 1854 which, amongst other changes, greatly increased the powers of the rectors *vis-à-vis* the municipal authorities and the clergy, Juste was in a strong position to resist Pie's attempts to influence the faculties or the schools; in educational matters he outranked Pie, as his jurisdiction covered eight departments.

Damay pointed out on many occasions, with supporting evidence from the sub-prefects and police commissioners of the region, that the government was neglecting opportunities of creating a body of support in the middle range of society, councillors-general, mayors, professional men and civil servants. The situation called for a middle-class Bonapartist party, perhaps without formal organization but with at least sufficient cohesiveness to be able to resist the pressures of theocratic legitimism, and ultimately to break the power of the right-wing opposition in the west; it was all the more necessary because in the lower echelons, at the level of gendarmes and minor *fonctionnaires*, the instruments at the government's disposal tended to be crude and unpopular. One of the tax collectors at Poitiers, for example, had annoyed a number of businessmen, and this just before an election, 'by the impolite and even brutal manner with which he interviews people calling to pay their contributions'.[1] Dealing with legitimism was increasingly going to mean dealing with the *évêché* and the clergy, and 'our usual agents of surveillance are the *gendarmerie*', wrote the sub-prefect of Châtellerault; 'I wonder if they are not perhaps a little rough and ready for such delicate assignments'.[2] Only men of education and status could manage the subtleties of what was essentially a warfare of concepts. The way to build this Bonapartist party was to reverse the government's feeble policy of conciliating the supposedly *rallié* legitimists and to stop endorsing them for public office and government posts. 'The government treats with the legitimists as one power to another', wrote Damay

'but nothing is gained by the system of affability and concessions. They remain in a state of expectation, the *purs* refusing all offers

[1] Commissioner of Police, Poitiers, 28 June 1857: ADV M.4.103.
[2] Sub-prefect Châtellerault, 29 April 1959: ADV V.25.

so as to remain free, the clever ones accepting everything and believing themselves for this reason better agents of their king. The more we give them, the more they come to exaggerate their own power and importance.'[1]

The electoral situation of the legitimists at Poitiers was ambiguous. Some of them were inclined to obey the comte de Chambord's instruction that they should resign from all public offices and take no part in elections; it was well known that Chambord had refused to reconsider even when told by *politiques* like Falloux and Resseguier that abstention would lead to the decay of the legitimist party.[2] On the other hand Pie, a field commander where Chambord was an armchair strategist, believed that legitimists should try at least to win local elections. He and the legitimist notables of the region knew from the experience of 1852 that nothing could be done on the level of the elections for the *corps législatif*; the official candidates always beat the right-wing opposition, even in the most *chouan* departments. Prosperity had persuaded the farmers of the west that they should vote for a Bonapartist in preference to any candidate supported by the nobles and the clergy.[3] Within a few days after the death of the deputy for the Poitiers electoral district in July 1854, the ministry of the interior received applications from no less than five prospective candidates with the most impeccable Bonapartist credentials; any one of them could have carried the by-election. The emperor took the opportunity to reward M. Robert-Beauchamp, who had been passed over for the presidency of the council-general only a few weeks earlier.[4] He was endorsed, and his victory was such a

[1] Damay, 18 July 1859.

[2] Falloux, *Mémoires d'un royaliste*, vol. ii.

[3] Damay, 28 January 1855, 31 January 1859; cf. *procureur-général* Angers 11 July 1857, BB.18.1567, and 21 January 1858, BB.30.371; *procureur-général* Rennes, 11 December 1859, BB.18.1567.

[4] The papers on the by-election at Poitiers, prepared for Napoleon III by his secretary, contain the applications of Bourgnon de Layre, supported by the Minister of Justice, Abbatucci; De Voyer d'Argenson, supported by Rodolphe d'Ornano, Imperial Chamberlain; the Baron de Brion, supported (half-heartedly) by Albert de Dalmas, *Chef de Cabinet* to the

foregone conclusion that some of his own closest friends did not bother to vote.[1] In the *corps législatif* elections of 1857 the legitimists of Poitiers, on Pie's advice, abstained completely.[2] In the elections for the councils-general of the departments in 1852, however, and in the subsequent *renouvellements* of 1855 and 1858 the government continued to endorse legitimist candidates, regarding them as 'men of order' and potential allies in local affairs, and Pie saw no reason to disturb this useful arrangement. The councils-general, in any case, were an important factor in legitimist-decentralist theory. Whatever the political complexion of the central government, legitimist notables had a reasonable chance of succeeding on the department level where elections were often fought on local issues, and could then make an attempt to use the structure of local government for a program of 'national regeneration'; before the revision of the loi Falloux in 1854 they had hoped, for example, to take advantage of the clause which required four members of each council-general, chosen by their colleagues, to sit on the committee which supervised school inspection in the department. And electoral campaigning, even when unsuccessful, offered great opportunities for embarrassing the régime and creating an atmosphere of ferment and crisis.

The government endorsed seven legitimists for the council-general of the Vienne in the election of 1852, and these men sat throughout the fifties beside twenty-eight 'Bonapartists' of various kinds; all seven were in close contact with the *évêché*, and once elected made no secret of their fundamental allegiance to Henry V and their coherence as an opposition group. The government took no action, although reports from Damay and the prefects made it clear that, like other *prétendus ralliés* in the provinces, 'they remained faithful [to the Bourbon cause] in their inmost hearts, and that it was in the interests of the legitimist party that they

Emperor; M. Desvarannes, a former officer of the Empire; and Robert-Beauchamp, whose nomination is endorsed: 'recommended very warmly by M. Pelletier on behalf of M. Fould'. The emperor was already aware of Robert-Beauchamp's claim to attention. F.1.c.III Vienne 4.

[1] Prefect, 29 September 1854: F.1.c.III Vienne 4.
[2] Casimir de Sèze to *garde des sceaux*, 18 June 1857: BB.18.1567.

should occupy all the posts with an eye to some future happening'.[1] The attempt by Orsini to assassinate Napoleon III on 14 January 1858 made local authorities more acutely aware of the danger created by this conciliatory approach to the right. Already at the time of the Crimean War the legitimists had talked so openly of their expectation that the emperor would be killed in battle or overthrown by international diplomacy that some army garrison commanders had become alarmed at the possibility of a royalist rising in the west or the south.[2] Orsini's attempt threatened the disintegration of the Empire almost overnight: 'the possibility of the emperor's sudden death keeps alive the illusions of the legitimists', Damay reported;[3] if he were to be killed, and Henry V disputed the throne, 'how many of our *prétendus ralliés* would be loyal to the infant prince imperial and a regency?'[4]

Whatever the legitimists who held public office may have thought about the Orsini affair, there was no doubt at all about the views of the *réfractaire* group. A large number of them, led by Mme de Rohan-Chabot, came to the *Te Deum* for the emperor so that they could ostentatiously walk out of the cathedral when it began.[5] Pie wrote privately: 'Napoleon's fate will be that of all governments which do not proclaim divine law. God will make use of him for a time and then break him. . . . For the past seventy years it has been like this.'[6] He issued a perfunctory pastoral of half a page on the emperor's escape, and was thought to have encouraged the parish priests to avoid celebrating the *Te Deum*

[1] F.1.c.IV: 8 (Councils-general); prefectoral reports on the successful candidates in July 1852, in F.1.c.V (by departments); prefect Vienne, 6 November 1852, F.1.c.V Vienne 2; Damay, 9 May, 31 July 1852, BB.30.385. The quotation is from a report by the *procureur-général* Agen, 21 July 1854, BB.30.370.

[2] Prefect Vendée, 2 March 1854, F.1.c.III Vendée 5; and cf. the opinion of Marshal Castellane at Lyon that the prospect of the Emperor's death had temporarily united the legitimists and the left-wing secret societies: 10 March 1855, AHG G.8.19.

[3] Damay, 19 July 1858.

[4] Damay, 9 October 1858.

[5] Damay, 19 July 1858.

[6] Baunard, *Pie*, i. 648.

on various pretexts: the curé of St Hilaire told his congregation that he would say the *Te Deum* 'although no doubt it will be as little to your taste as to mine', and two other priests delayed it until January 21st and then announced that it was really in honour of the martyred Louis XVI.[1]

Throughout 1858 the 'forward party' of the legitimists gave signs of renewed activity, duly reported by the police of several departments. If Orsini had failed, another might succeed. In July the comte de Chambord came from Fröhsdorf to Cologne, perhaps expecting some development in the affairs of the Empire.[2] His presence near the Rhine frontier had a curious sequel at Poitiers: in August Emmanuel de Curzon was suddenly arrested for sedition. The unusual behaviour of a messenger led the police to seize Curzon's correspondence, which revealed that he had drawn up a petition to Chambord to the effect that 'there are many brave hearts and many strong arms in the west, waiting with faith and with impatience'; he had collected signatures from amongst the members of the *Cercle Gorini*, a club affiliated with the St Vincent-de-Paul Society and frequented by artisans and tradesmen who had leanings towards legitimism.[3] The original of the petition had been taken to Cologne by two of Curzon's fellow *réfractaires*, Henri de Maillé of Poitiers and a Vendéen noble, Alphonse de la Rousselière; they had been received with great benevolence and had been granted several audiences with Chambord. On 27 July 1858 Maillé had written to Théodore de Quatrebarbes:

'Why did you not come with us? I would tell you more if my head

---

[1] Political reports on the clergy, July 1858: F.19.5605 (Poitiers).

[2] There is evidence to suggest that some legitimists had known in advance of Orsini's *attentat: gendarmerie* reports of January 1858, AHG G.8.46; Damay, reports of 28 October 1859 and April 1860. During 1858 the police and *gendarmerie* discovered several conspiracies to assassinate Napoleon III; one of these, to be carried out at Plombières in July, was better organized and equipped than Orsini had been: *gendarmerie* report of 17 July 1858, AHG G.8.49.

[3] The correspondence seized from Curzon and from various members of the *Cercle Gorini*, and reports relating to the affair, are distributed between the following files: AHG G.8 50-51; BB.24.548-561; BB.30.385; BB.30.421 (P.1625).

were clearer, but I am still a little drunk with exhilaration. [The King said to me] "Never would I bring civil war to France, but at the first crisis I shall arrive immediately. . . . I shall sacrifice my own person if need be. Make this perfectly clear to all my friends. Let them count on me, as I count on them. Let them be ready and organized. In the meantime their *politique* should always be one of conciliation."'

There had been many visitors at Cologne; some of those not hitherto completely on the royalist side had been won over, Maillé wrote, by Chambord's charm. 'I should mention one amongst others, who on coming out from his audience gave us to understand that he now believed himself destined to play the part of General Monk'.[1] Chambord told Maillé at the end of their conversations:

'Since January 14th many mistakes have been made. Napoleon might disappear from one moment to the next. I am ready, let it be known. . . . I have made this voyage to Cologne to show that I have not lost hope.'[2]

When the delegation returned to Poitiers Curzon called a meeting of sympathizers at the *Cercle Gorini* so that Maillé could read a message from Chambord, but the police raided the building before the meeting was due to begin.

The patrons of the *Cercle* brought to trial for collecting signatures to the petition were absolutely typical of the lower-class legitimists concerned in similar affairs during the Republic and the Empire; their backgrounds recall the complaint sometimes heard from senior members of the St Vincent-de-Paul Society

[1] This may have been the Breton general Lamoricière, a former Saint-Simonian who was later to take command of the Papal army in 1860; his biographers describe him as wholeheartedly Chambordist from 1858 onwards. After Lamoricière's unexpected death in 1865 Chambord wrote to his widow: 'We had hoped that the hour would strike soon when, emerging from his enforced inaction, he would draw his noble sword . . . to hasten the triumph of the great principles which are the only true and solid basis for social order. But God had other designs for him' : *Lettres d'Henry V* (ed. A. Peladan), (Avignon, 1874), p. 179.

[2] Maillé to Quatrebarbes, 27 July 1858: BB.30.421 (P.1625).

that the charity organizations had been able to attract men from the lower middle class, 'model employees', clerks and pious shopkeepers, but very few actual workers.[1] Just as the recruits for the 'secret battalions of Henry V' in the northern departments in 1850 had been tailors, shopkeepers, waiters and cab-drivers,[2] the men arrested at the *Cercle Gorini* were artisans, small businessmen, employees of the public administration, and domestic servants. One was 'a retired baker, very well thought of in the *Cercle*, who has received from the comte de Chambord a signed print of the royal arms for his work in the cause'; in his house the police found a number of rifles and an unusual amount of ammunition for a private citizen, although he denied any plans for a rising.[3] Another was 'a poor grocer with a legitimist clientèle'; others were a clerk employed by the municipal council of Poitiers, and 'the concierge of the *Cercle*, who would have lost his job if he had not obeyed orders by making copies of the petition'.[4] One man, Simon-Bardoux, was a perfect embodiment of the *gardemobile* type. He was a blacksmith, 'formerly known as a republican and a hater of the rich and noble ... with a house full of atheist and socialist pamphlets'; lately, however, he had begun to invite a dozen friends to his house each year on July 15th to celebrate the Feast of St Henry, and to collect signatures for legitimist addresses and petitions.[5] These were all 'men with limited ideas', Damay thought; none of them would know enough even to appeal against

[1] After many years of work in this field Fr Marquigny S.J. wrote that 'our workers' circles never attracted the real workers . . . (but only) the laggards of industry, the dunces of the factory . . . employees of clerical bookshops, *des bedeaux en rupture de hallebarde*, retired sacristans, concierges of religious houses, and the office-boys of our own organizations': quoted by E. Barbier, *Histoire du catholicisme libéral et social* (5 vols., Bordeaux, 1924), i. 367n. Cf. P. Pierrard, *La vie ovurière a Lille sous le Second Empire*, 389-91.

[2] *Procureur-général* Amiens, 16 February 1850, BB.18.1484 (8560).

[3] Damay, 11 August 1858: BB.30.421.

[4] Damay, 29 September 1858: BB.24.528 (S.58.8515).

[5] Damay, 31 January 1859: BB.30.385. Compare Victor Prospert, one of the legitimist recruiting officers at Rouen in 1850: 'a former tailor and *éxalté* demagogue who has deserted the socialists to join the legitimists': *Procureur-général* Amiens, 18 February 1850: BB.18.1484 (8560).

a prison sentence. He recommended that they be prosecuted but then released as 'a spontaneous act of clemency' which would have a good effect on public opinion. But the cases of Curzon and Maillé called for stronger measures. Curzon was defiant: he told the *procureur impérial* that the police would do better to concentrate on the reds, but added that 'of course the reds in this district are in small numbers. We legitimists are stronger than they are; we will crush them easily at a given moment . . . we will protect you from them.'[1] He had not abandoned his military ambitions of 1848, and believed deeply in the impermanence of the Empire and the imminence of a socialist revolution. In 1856 he had written to M. de Rohan-Chabot: 'The people here do not believe that the régime will last; they are convinced that any serious attempt to overthrow it will be crowned with success'.[2] To Belleval, the secretary of the *Bureau du Roi* in Paris, he wrote that 'all is not lost so long as the emperor goes on reviewing troops in public'.[3] In several other letters Curzon expressed his distrust of Pie and of the men like Laurenceau and de Sèze whom Pie encouraged to continue in official positions under the Empire; he thought that the legitimist cause would gain nothing from this strategy of compromise and political action.

The prefect, Paulze d'Ivoy, was almost entirely under the spell of the bishop, and was inclined now on Pie's advice to let the Curzon affair blow over without a prosecution. In Damay's opinion this would have been fatal. The prefect seemed to think that dropping the case would appease the *rallié* legitimists. 'But who are our *ralliés* at Poitiers?' Damay asked bitterly; 'I would be very embarrassed if asked to produce more than four names.' The legitimists in the courts and on the council-general would take a pardon for Curzon as a sign that anyone could collect signatures for a petition calling for Chambord to return by a military *coup*.[4] Eventually, after the *avocat-général*, Darnis, had advised that it

[1] Conversation reported by Damay, 11 August 1858: BB.30.421.
[2] Curzon to comte de Rohan-Chabot, 27 April 1856: BB.30.421 (P.1625).
[3] Curzon to M. de Belleval, 19 October 1856: BB.30.421 (P.1625).
[4] Damay, 11 August 1858: BB.30.421; 29 December 1858: BB.24.548 (S.8515).

would be hard to obtain convictions because of the number of St Vincent-de-Paul members and legitimists on the bench, and had been attacked by Casimir de Sèze for slandering the judges,[1] a trial took place; after a protracted series of hearings and appeals, Curzon received a fine of 500 francs and two months' imprisonment, Maillé a fine of 500 francs and one month, and four of the lesser accused received fines of 100 francs and one month's imprisonment each. Their confinement became a joke. They were given special lodgings by prison officials who belonged themselves to the *Cercle* and the St Vincent-de-Paul Society. Their meals were served by a *maitre d'hôtel*. Each of them received a gift of 1,000 francs from Poitevin legitimist sources. Visitors were allowed at all hours, and the courtyard outside the prison was filled from morning to night with carriages, often as many as forty at a time. The case, according to Damay, consolidated legitimist opinion in Poitiers and resolved several factors of disunity; Curzon was even reconciled with Pie. The legitimists became more refractory than ever, and appeared to have agreed to ostracize all officials and anyone compromised in any way with the administration. The zealots ceased to frequent the *Cercle Gorini* and found another meeting-place, 'difficult to discover'.

III. *The Poitevin clergy*

The Curzon case was unusual in being entirely an affair of the laity. Almost every other enterprise of Poitevin legitimism in this period had its origin and its base of operations at the *évêché*, and Mgr Pie profited more directly from the occasional success than did the comte de Chambord. His influence as leader of the right-wing opposition would have been much more extensive, however, if there had not been one serious flaw in his plan of campaign. He had applied religious and social pressure to weaken the fabric of the official bureaucracy, and had been at least partly successful; but since his first year as bishop, Pie had seen that it would be necessary also to turn his diocesan clergy into a legitimist civil service in its own right—and here he had encountered some of the peculiar weaknesses of nineteenth-century French Catholicism.

[1] Darnis to *garde des sceaux*, undated (September 1858): BB.30.421.

In the immediate circle of the *évêché* he had inherited fairly promising material; the older clergy of Poitiers mostly owed their nominations to an earlier bishop, Mgr de Bouillé, who had once been chaplain to Marie Antoinette and appointed only legitimists to clerical posts in the diocese. Pie had been able to build on this foundation with surprisingly little hindrance from the Concordatory system, which in theory subjected the bishop's nominations to the criticism of the prefect, the *procureur-général*, and the sub-prefects and police officials concerned before sending them for approval by the ministry of *cultes*. In practice the agents of the government usually accepted the fact that Pie always nominated a legitimist if one could be found, and objected only when the candidate was thought to have other defects besides his legitimism. By the end of the fifties Pie had managed to surround himself with congenial colleagues: his secretary, his vicar-general, all eight of the canons of the cathedral of St Pierre and the curés of the five major churches of Poitiers were legitimists. In each individual case the government acquiesced in the appointment: the mayor of Poitiers wrote concerning one of Pie's candidates that his ideas were 'ultramontane-legitimist, and hard to reconcile with the principles which rule our civil society . . . he will do nothing to discourage the spirit of sacerdotal supremacy amongst the local clergy'; but on the other hand the man was friendly and conciliatory in his manner, and had no taste for the strenuous life of public controversy.[1] Another nominee was 'a good sound man, very learned . . . who sometimes lets his political opinions carry him too far in the pulpit', but was incapable of provoking real trouble.[2] Another priest nominated as a canon of the cathedral was a very hostile legitimist, but 'we may as well present his nomination to the emperor for signature, because anyone else proposed by Mgr Pie will be just as bad'.[3] When the elderly vicar-general de Rochemonteix died in 1861 Pie replaced him with a talented and formidable priest of his own age, the abbé Charles Gay. The abbé Gay belonged to the '*Cercle de la rue Cassette*',

[1] Mayor (Professor Bourbeau) to prefect, 5 October 1867, ADV V.25.
[2] File on the abbé Charbonneau, ADV V.25.
[3] Prefect, 27 October 1865, ADV V.25.

a group of young clergy with royalist backgrounds and private fortunes—Louis Gaston de Ségur, Emmanuel d'Alzon, and the abbés de Conny and Combalot were amongst the members—who met regularly in Paris to organize various ultramontane and legitimist *œuvres* during the Second Empire. Pie invited several of this group to preach at Poitiers, and was particularly attracted by Gay, who had all the fascination of the reformed worldling. He had been trained as a concert pianist and was a close friend of Liszt and of Gounod; as a rich and irreligious student in Paris he had begun also to write novels, including an autobiographical sketch in imitation of Sainte-Beuve's *Volupté*. In 1835 he had been one of the fashionable young men who had crowded Notre-Dame to hear Lacordaire's celebrated *Conférences*, and shortly afterwards he had been received into the Church by that most aristocratic of confessors, Xavier de Ravignan S.J. Gay studied for the priesthood at the French seminary in Rome, and emerged a vigorous ultramontane and a passionate legitimist; at Poitiers, as vicar-general and later as auxiliary bishop, he was to be Pie's most constant companion and adviser, always an advocate of stronger measures and greater defiance.[1]

But when Mgr Pie tried to marshal the diocesan clergy beyond his own immediate circle he had to recognize that the task was not easy. Men like Pie himself, Clausel de Montals, Ségur and Gay might have been legitimists by family background or by reasoned conviction, but the royalism of the average parish priest was based on a simpler instinct for survival and advantage. After the unhappy experience of the July Monarchy, country priests tended to have a nostalgic and exaggerated idea of the extent to which the Bourbons had been champions of religion and friends of the clergy. But in this respect the Bourbon cause was completely overshadowed by the immense effect of the year 1852: parish priests opened the *Univers* and found editorials by Louis Veuillot, whom they trusted and admired almost more than the Pope, to the effect

---

[1] Notes on Charles Gay by the mayor of Poitiers, 10 October 1868, ADV V.25; also B. du Boisrouvray, *Mgr Gay* (2 vols., Tours, 1921); *Correspondance de Mgr Gay* (2 vols., Poitiers, 1880). Gay was born on the same day as Pie, 1 October 1815.

that the *coup d'état* had brought to power a Christian prince who had destroyed socialism and liberal parliamentarism. Louis Napoleon would be 'greater than Charlemagne'; and throughout 1852 the *Univers* reported each sign of the new era, increases in the *budget des cultes*, grants of money for churches and seminaries, gestures of favour to bishops, the closing of Protestant libraries. In the west many priests deserted the traditional politics of their regions. The *coup*, wrote one, offered a tremendous opportunity to Christianize France,

'to combat evil in all its forms and to extend the reign of good. To this end I hope that there will be a *ralliement* of the élite of the legitimist party; God has given them a clear sign to dissolve, and they will learn wisdom at the excellent school of humiliation.'[1]

The clergy of the west, wrote the Catholic journalist Gustave de la Tour,

'believe, with Rome, that God alone gives and takes away crowns and that the designs of Providence are fulfilled when the hand which possesses the force protects the truth. . . . Even the priest who has little love for the Emperor hopes that he will come to equal Charlemagne and Saint Louis.'[2]

The parish clergy remained convinced so long as Veuillot continued to support the Empire, which he did at least until the end of 1858; and the *Univers* was only echoing the high opinion of the Second Empire which prevailed at that time in Rome, at the Papal court and in the offices of the *Civiltà Cattolica*. Mgr Pie complained in 1855 that 'one dare not go to Rome these days branded with the colours of opposition [to the Empire], because one will succeed in nothing'.[3] The stricter legitimists were angry and disappointed with Veuillot, and some of his oldest friends

---

[1] The Abbé Chesnel to Gustave de la Tour, 12 December 1851, in Veuillot papers, *N.a.f.* 24225: 247.

[2] La Tour to Veuillot, 27 September 1854, Veuillot papers 24226: 146.

[3] *Louis Veuillot*, iii. 71.

broke off relations with him;[1] Clausel de Montals and Falloux attacked him for his apparent treachery to the Bourbon cause. Emmanuel de Curzon, who under the Second Republic had seen Veuillot as the hope of pure Catholic royalism,[2] told the *Bureau du roi* in 1856 that the *Univers* was seriously dividing and weakening the legitimists in the clergy.[3] In 1858 the legitimist historian Crétineau-Joly went to Rome to try to have Veuillot silenced, but as one official of the Curia remarked: 'Poor fellow! He little knows where he is treading'.[4] The emperor's tour of Brittany and the Vendée in 1858 was 'the last straw for our poor legitimists';[5] 'already sulking at their inability to check the élan of the people of the countryside', they were infuriated to find the parish priests as enthusiastic as their flocks.[6] Fulsome reports of the tour in the *Univers* were read from pulpits in Pie's own diocese.

Even without the advent of a Christian prince to replace the Bourbon kings there were many signs, by the middle of the century, that the traditional alliance of château and presbytery on which legitimist leaders placed so much reliance was no longer viable. Behind the common phrase of official reports that 'the clergy here are dominated by the châteaux' lay a great deal of ambiguity and tension. The Abbé Aguettand, who wrote a manual for country priests called *Le curé instruit par*

---

[1] See the sarcastic account of a Veuillot family wedding in *L'Union de l'Ouest*, 12 October 1858; the editor, Poinsel, had been a fervent admirer of Veuillot before the *coup d'état*.

[2] Curzon to Veuillot, 8 September 1850, VP.24225: 107-8; and Sevrin, *Clausel de Montals*, ii. 603.

[3] Curzon to Belleval, 30 October 1856 (copy): BB.30.421.

[4] Abbé Baseredon, secretary to Cardinal de Villecourt, to Abbé André Dust, Rome, 20 November 1858: letter forwarded to Veuillot, VP.24227: 131.

[5] Mgr Brossais-St Marc, Archbishop of Rennes, to minister of *cultes* (Rouland), September 1858: F.19.2567.

[6] Reports of the *gendarmerie* of the Vienne and the Deux-Sèvres, August-September 1858: AHG G.8.50; and reports of the *procureur-généraux* of western departments, July-September 1858, in the series BB.30. Falloux has some brilliant and bitter pages in his *Mémoires*, ii. 287-97, about Vendéen priests greeting their Majesties 'with perfumed phrases mixed pell-mell with Biblical texts'.

l'expérience,[1] said that although a young priest 'could not help feeling a secret joy cross his heart' when he arrived in a new parish and saw in the distance a large château, and would look forward to rising in the world and increasing the range and power of his apostolate, disillusion followed swiftly when he was exposed to the *morgue* of the aristocracy. 'They have a thousand little ways of making him feel socially inferior.' He is expected to consider himself lucky to be invited to dinner once a year; and if he comes simply on a visit,

'when the curé enters the salon not only does nobody come forward to greet him, but he scarcely receives so much as a brief nod by way of salute. He is not asked to sit down; in conversation they pay scant attention to what he says, and are all too eager to turn rudely from him to talk to somebody else. When the time comes he is allowed to leave as he came, without any marks of friendliness or regard.'

Even the most sincerely religious aristocrats tended to treat the curé as a servant, to expect their 'advice' on the running of the parish to be taken as a command, and to cut off the flow of gifts, donations, support or even common courtesy if the priest showed signs of 'independence'.[2]

Parish priests found little in their dealings with the other ranks of society to console them for the arrogance of the nobles. The situation in most parishes of the west was a long way from the ideal picture presented by royalist writers who described docile congregations listening with respect, while their curé expounded ultramontane and legitimist doctrines from the pulpit. The clergy of the Poitiers diocese seem to have been engaged in an endless warfare for which they were very badly equipped. Sceptical and ill-disposed parishioners complained about the obvious ignorance of country priests, and laughed at their naïve puritanism. Even quite good priests had to put up with public ridicule over the truly extraordinary number of clerical scandals in the western depart-

[1] *Le curé instruit par l'expérience, ou vingt ans de ministère dans une paroisse de campagne* (2 vols., 1856).

[2] *Ibid.*, ii. 452-7.

ments in this period. The many cases of 'moral outrage' or *attentats contre la pudeur* by members of the clergy had their origin in the perennial crises of clerical recruitment during the July Monarchy, when diocesan seminaries and the novitiates of the various orders of teaching Brothers had accepted too many young men who had no real vocation; they were vowed to celibacy, Damay wrote, 'but award themselves the most monstrous compensations'.[1] Considering Pie's own rigorous standards of morality, his behaviour in these cases was curious: when asked to move or suspend the most flagrant offenders he offered all kinds of obstruction, on the grounds that civil society ought not to interfere in clerical discipline. Compelled after much resistance to move one priest convicted of indecent exposure, Pie defiantly appointed him chaplain of a girls' college; but the bishop's apparent condoning of immorality was widely quoted as a point against the legitimist party.[2]

The *police des cultes*, investigating reports that a particular curé or *desservant* was preaching legitimism, found in the majority of cases only fresh evidence of the helplessness of the parish clergy. The *desservant* of Cisse, the Abbé Delcroix, was reported to be a legitimist: when the mayor asked him in July 1860 to say a mass for the late King Jerome Bonaparte he scribbled a curt refusal on the back of the mayor's letter and returned it.[3] Delcroix had been quarrelling for ten years with the municipal councillors of Cisse—he referred to them sarcastically in his sermons as *le corps législatif*—and appeared to be conducting a vendetta against the entire middle class, of which he took the councillors to be representative. The complaint was referred to Pie, who visited Cisse and wrote to the minister explaining Delcroix' impossible situation. The government had granted funds several years earlier for repairs to the presbytery, but the council, dominated by anti-clericals, had voted to use the money instead to enlarge the church

[1] Damay, 6 November 1863. On the Brothers of Saint Gabriel, whose many prosecutions prompted this remark, sub-prefect of Montmorillon to prefect, 10 April 1862, ADV V.25; and Damay, 7 May 1863, BB.30.385.

[2] Damay, 6 November 1863, 14 June 1864.

[3] Original in file on the Abbé Delcroix, ADV V.25.

steeple, a local landmark. When Delcroix attacked the mayor in a sermon, the council pretended to agree to his repairs; they began by demolishing the staircase to the upper storey of the presbytery and then ordered the work to be stopped. 'The poor man lives in an abandoned building-site', Pie wrote, 'the only access to his bedroom being a vertical ladder which I myself was not brave enough to climb'. Delcroix lost this battle and had to be moved to another parish; nine years later his successor was still writing furious letters threatening the mayor with divine vengeance if the presbytery was not made habitable.[1] In another case a curé accused of preaching against the Second Empire turned out to be a choleric man driven completely mad by years of fighting with his local council over repairs, and by the casual anticlericalism and loose morals of his parishioners; he had begun to reveal the secrets of the confessional, to throw money back at people who put only a few centimes in the collection, and to tell outrageously dirty jokes from the pulpit.[2]

Damay's attitude illustrates the absolutely Voltairean (and Napoleonic) assumptions behind official policy: although the educated classes were gradually emancipating themselves from religious belief, anything that eroded popular respect for religion was a threat to social stability; and in this respect fanaticism amongst the clergy, especially if it had a political flavour, was worse than immorality. The clergy represented a problem for the government, not because of any fear that they might challenge the state by acquiring too much popular influence, but because of the real possibility that by too many displays of ineptitude and too many errors of judgement they might destroy the credit of the established religion itself, with disastrous effects on the social fabric.[3] In the early years of the Empire the government had been inclined to give free rein to the zealots in the provinces; Damay

[1] Minister of *cultes* (Rouland) to prefect Vienne, 28 July 1860; Pie to Rouland, 4 September 1860; curé of Cisse to mayor, 25 July 1869: ADV V.25.
[2] File on the curé of Andillé, ADV V.25.
[3] Damay's attitude is made clear in his reports of 31 January 1850, 18 February 1851, 10 December 1852, and on several occasions later in the Empire: BB.30.385.

noted one case in 1855 where a curé, with support from the local bench, had been able to have a Methodist missionary imprisoned, and he wrote that the politically tinged sermons and processions of the Catholic clergy in this region were far worse than anything done by a solitary Methodist; they were likely to destroy all respect for Christianity.[1] After the hardening of the government's ecclesiastical policy in 1856 local officials were told to bear down heavily on the symptoms of excessive zeal,[2] and from this point onwards, although the Catholic laymen who organized legitimist affairs in country towns continued to take their lead from the bishop and the aristocratic circle of the *évêché* of Poitiers, they found their own parish priests almost useless as allies because of the intense official surveillance. The parish clergy faced a dilemma: to keep the bishop's favour one had to be a legitimist, or at least an opponent of the Empire; to have any chance of promotion to a more interesting and dignified post close to the *évêché*, legitimism was indispensable. On the other hand, a priest who gave a political sermon or took part in an election campaign was likely to be denounced to the authorities. Parishioners grumbled even about priests who had acquired local influence quite naturally and legitimately, and wielded it with tact. The curé of one parish, for example, was an intelligent and able legitimist; the mayor came to rely on him for advice in administrative matters, and ended by giving him virtual control over the municipality. The result was a great increase in local anticlericalism, and a complaint to the prefect.[3] Legitimist judges and civil servants in country towns could easily shield one another from official censure but they could not protect their curés, harassed as the latter were by political police, *police des cultes*, *gendarmerie* and special agents.[4] In 1858 a ministerial report said, not surprisingly, that the clergy of the

[1] Damay, 28 January 1855.
[2] Ministerial circular of 24 December 1858, recapitulating the instructions in previous orders: ADV V.25.
[3] *Juge de paix*, St Georges, report of 27 September 1867: ADV V.25.
[4] A typical case is reported in the file on the Abbé Jourdain and the *juge de paix* Dupleix: BB.18.1607: 2583. A3.

Vienne and the Deux-Sèvres were '*légitimiste au fond* but well-behaved'.[1]

Towards the end of 1854 Mgr Pie invited the Jesuit Order to open a college for boys at Poitiers. This was a very effective stroke of policy which almost made up for the impotence of his parish clergy, because the Jesuits who came to Poitiers, most of them from the Belgian establishment of Brugelette, now dissolved, were intelligent and capable men and deeply committed to legitimism. The middle of the nineteenth century marked a reactionary phase in the history of the great Order during which it lent its support to a number of causes already lost, and with the exception of the group in Paris directed by Fr Matignon S.J., who were resolutely non-political and were suspected at Rome of being liberals, the French Jesuits at the time of the Second Empire belonged to the *ultra* party in both ecclesiology and politics. Their leading *brochuriers* and teachers came from families of the old nobility, with unbroken records of counter-revolution.[2] The colleges of Blois, Metz, Lyon and Toulouse were directed by men who had succeeded in overcoming the prejudice of an older generation of legitimists against the Order, and had made their schools socially irresistible, enrolling not only the nobility but also the sons of prefects, chiefs of police, magistrates, engineers and bankers. Young future businessmen, lawyers and civil servants grew up alongside the sons of landed proprietors, and climbed socially through the Old Boys' Associations. At Vannes the new Jesuit college of St Francis Xavier was so successful that after five years it had forced out of existence a distinguished state college which had produced pupils like Billault and Jules Simon.[3] Jesuit

[1] *Personnel et esprit du clergé*, 1857/8: F.19.5605.

[2] The provincials at Toulouse and Lyon were Fathers de Blacas and de Jocas, and French Jesuit writing in this period was dominated by Fathers Marin de Boylesve, de Damas, de Foresta, de Caqueray, du Coëtlosquet, de Pontlevoy, de Regnon, Elesban de Guilhermy, de Ravignan and prince Jean Gagarine: all of these had links with Fröhsdorf: F.19.6288; *Les établissements de jésuites en France depuis quatre siècles* (in progress) (Enghien, 1949-); J. Burnichon, *La Compagnie de Jésus en France: Histoire d'un siècle 1814-1914* (4 vols., 1914-22).

[3] F.19.6288 (Vannes); J. Allanic, '*Histoire du Collège de Vannes*', *Annales*

schooling, although excellent in some respects, emphasized the pure *ultracisme* of Maistre and Taparelli; students of history were taught to admire 'the real France' of the Bourbons and to believe that there was no need to be enthusiastic about the France of Morny and Rothschild, Renan and Rachel. The mathematics and physics studied by senior pupils were 'balanced', or submerged, by heavy doses of moral philosophy which led to 'conclusions unfavourable to the general movement of French society in the nineteenth century'.[1]

Pie had no trouble in raising 80,000 francs by private collections amongst the nobility to build the College of St Vincent-de-Paul at Poitiers. Paulze d'Ivoy was persuaded to lay the foundation stone, and later received a reprimand for sitting on the platform while Pie made a speech to the effect that with the arrival of the Jesuits it could not be long before the state college of Poitiers also 'fell once again into the hands of the Church'. The Jesuit college immediately took its place in the structure of political opposition; the St Vincent-de-Paul Society met in its classrooms, and on royalist feast-days the chapel was decorated with fleurs-de-lis for masses in honour of Louis XVI and St Henry; an invitation to attend one of these became an index of one's social success. At a school debate presided over by Pie in 1858 the winning team, all young nobles, said that they did not intend to be like their parents and allow a sacred cause to fail by default.[2]

IV. *The Roman Question and the decline of Mgr Pie's influence*
From 1859 onwards, however, the political balance at Poitiers was altered in the government's favour by the events arising out

de Bretagne, xviii (1902-3); R. P. Orhand S.J., *Le R. P. Pillon de la Compagnie de Jésus* (Lille, 1888).

[1] F. Butel, *L'éducation des jésuites: un collège breton* (1890); recollections of Th. de Regnon S.J. in *Etablissements de jésuites*, i. 953-4; 'Ch. de ***', *Brugelette: souvenir de l'enseignement chez les jésuites* (Toulouse, 1879). See also Montalembert's remarks on Jesuit education, in Lecanuet, *Montalembert* (3 vols., 1904), ii. 273-4.

[2] On the College of St Vincent de Paul, Damay, 29 September and 2 October 1854, 28 January 1855, 29 January and 9 October 1858: BB.30.385; Prefect Vienne to Minister of *Cultes*, 17 July 1861: F.19.6288; report by Cl.Gallix, F.18.297.

of French intervention in Italy; a series of conflicts over the Roman question resulted in defeats for Pie and qualified victories for the official régime in the west. The Italian war united the right-wing opposition, reconciling differences between legitimists who were not quite ultramontane and ultramontanes who were not quite legitimist. The pulpit, the ecclesiastical press and what remained of the royalist press were mobilized to persuade French Catholics of the apocalyptic nature of the struggle between Cavour's Piedmont, industrial, parliamentary, secular, the quintessence of everything the Catholic right meant by the phrase *la Révolution*, and the Papal States, representing the old theocratic ideal of monarchy standing against the political and social forces of the nineteenth century. In ultramontane rhetoric their confrontation took on a symbolic force: it was 'Revelation against revolution'. By assisting Piedmont in 1859 and thus giving a fatal impetus to the Italian national movement which was about to swallow the Papal States, Napoleon III, according to the ultramontanes, had placed himself in the revolutionary camp. At the end of 1859, after the Romagna province had seceded from the Papal States and asked to be annexed by Piedmont, the emperor issued the semi-official pamphlet *Le Pape et le Congrès* in which he advised the Papacy to accept the *fait accompli* and to be content with a temporal power of much smaller extent; after this, hints and even flat declarations began to be heard from the pulpit that Catholics should transfer their allegiance to that sworn defender of the Papacy, Henry V.

Mgr Pie threw himself into the campaign, preaching, writing and organizing with tremendous verve. He was passionately French, but France had 'forgotten her traditional role'; what is patriotism, he asked, if it merely enlists our support for a cause which can turn to the disadvantage of the Church? 'I say with St Augustine: Oh God, *Thou* art my King, my party, my fatherland, my life!'[1] Where most Catholic apologists had to admit that the Papal government was far from perfect by modern standards, and that revolt had been simmering in the States of the Church for

---

[1] Private note quoted in Catta, *Doctrine du card. Pie*, 332.

at least a decade before the secession of the Romagna, Pie had no reservations:

'The temporal government of the Vicar of Christ is today the only real refuge of an orthodox polity. What a triumph for Hell if this last fortress of Christian public law should be overthrown!.... It is a supreme effort of the Revolution to introduce the principles of '89 into the States of the Church....'[1]

Who, he asked, could fail to see 'the manifest superiority of the institutions of the Roman State over the utterly unsettled, wavering, tottering institutions of modern times?'[2] In the margin of his copy of *Le Pape et le Congrès* he wrote a phrase from Hilary, *stylo antichristi compositum*, and immediately began a refutation in the form of an attack on Napoleon III's Italian policy. He announced that this would be read aloud in the cathedral; the ministers of the interior and *cultes* both telegraphed the prefect, asking him to prevent any public reading on the grounds that a statement 'which erected the inviolability of the Papal States into a dogma' would be 'subversive of religion and public order'.[3] The prefect woke Pie at 3.30 in the morning to deliver this message, but without success; the *Mandement portant condemnation des erreurs . . . dans la brochure Le Pape et le Congrès* was read at high mass in the cathedral on that day, January 15th, and then from pulpits throughout the diocese.

The parish clergy hardly needed Pie's encouragement to join the agitation over the Roman question. The tangible threat to the Papacy, and the news which went round quickly at the beginning of 1860 that Louis Veuillot and the *Univers* had gone over to the opposition were enough; they emerged from their habitual caution and did everything possible to spread alarm and despondency amongst their parishioners. Sermons rose to extraordinary heights: Napoleon III had embraced the doctrines of Garibaldian revolution, and the collapse of all civil order in Europe was imminent;

---

[1] *Lettre adressée au Souverain Pontife . . . juillet* 1860.
[2] Baunard, *Pie*, ii. 7.
[3] Telegrams of 14 January 1860: F.19.2561.

the Pope would be murdered; 1793 was coming again, priests would be assassinated and the churches burned; private property and marriage would be abolished; Catholics should prepare themselves for another Vendéen war in which the clergy would lead them against 'Jews, Protestants and Socialists'; ultimately Russia and Austria would invade France and restore Henry V, and Napoleon III would 'follow his uncle to a deserted rock in the Atlantic'. It was time to 'paint out the eagles on the public buildings and to 'throw away the worthless tinsel decorations of the Empire'.[1] In every part of the Poitiers diocese there were incidents like that of the curé who offered to bet the mayor 100 francs that Napoleon III would be replaced by a legitimate sovereign within two years, or the priest who began a sermon: 'The kingdom of France . . . (murmurs from the congregation) . . . well, the Empire, if you insist'.[2]

Pie was most conspicuous in his advocacy of the 'Crusade' of 1860. Shortly after the appearance of *Le Pape et le Congrès* the Papal government decided to try and recover the Romagna province by military force; since no Italians would enrol in the existing Papal army, the idea arose of an international Catholic volunteer force which would re-create the ancient orders of chivalry, the Templars and the Knights of Malta. The Breton general Lamoricière, appointed by the Pope in March 1860 to command these *Volontaires pontificaux*, announced that 'the Revolution, like Islam in former times, menaces Europe today';[3] it was expected at Rome that at least 100,000 men would respond and would save the Papacy by invading the Romagna and defeating the Piedmontese and Garibaldians at a new Lepanto. 'For the triumph of a sacred cause', Pie said in a special address,

---

[1] These examples are drawn from *gendarmerie* reports in AHG G.8.64-68, and reports of *procureurs-généraux* on the Roman question, BB.30.451.

[2] Damay, 3 March 1860: BB.30.451; April 1860: BB.30.385.

[3] Emile Keller, *Le général de Lamoricière* (2 vols., Paris, 1880), ii. 318. Mgr Pie seems to have been the first to use the analogy with Islam, in a sermon on St Emilien at Rennes in November 1859; Madame de Lamoricière was in the congregation: *procureur-général* Rennes, 9 November 1859: F.19.2561.

'it is not too much that the Spiritual Sword and the Temporal Sword should be drawn together, and that each should glitter in the hands of the one who should bear it ... Gladius Domini et Gedeonis! ... Against the Revolution, the Crusade! Never will this great word have a more exact application.'[1]

Members of the St Vincent-de-Paul Society, already busy distributing copies of Pie's *Mandement*, and collecting signatures for addresses to the Pope and to the French senate whose wording made their legitimist origins unmistakeable,[2] applied their energies to a recruiting drive for the volunteer force. Their efforts were coordinated by M. Bain de la Cocquerie, a prominent member of the Poitiers *fausse noblesse*, and by M. Bardy, a legitimist magistrate and councillor.[3] To stimulate enrolment, thousands of copies of the pamphlet *Le Pape* by Mgr L-G. de Ségur were distributed through the Christian Brothers' schools for the children to pass on to their families; *Le Pape* argued that as a legitimate king Pius IX had a perfect right to raise armies and to suppress rebellions.[4]

In order to pay for the new military programme the Roman authorities in 1860 revived the *Denier de St Pierre* as a system of voluntary monthly contributions from Catholics. *Comités de St Pierre* were set up in each French diocese; the minister of *cultes*,

---

[1] Address in Poitiers cathedral, 26 June 1860: BB.30.385 and F.19.2561. Mgr Baunard omitted some of Pie's remarks on the Crusade from the first edition of his *Histoire du cardinal Pie*, but had to restore them in the second edition (1887) after complaints from the *ultras* of Poitiers: see L. Mahieu, *Vie de Mgr Baunard* (1924), 329-338.

[2] The addresses to Pius IX from various French dioceses are reported in BB.30.450, and their texts printed in the collection *La Sovranità temporale dei Romani Pontefici ... dal suffragio dell'Orbe cattolico* (6 vols., Rome 1860-4). The Poitiers address, signed by eighty-six men and 515 women, was presented to the Nuncio by the legitimist pamphleteer Grimouard de St Laurent: *Carteggio Antonelli-Sacconi 1858-1860*, ed. G. Mariano (2 vols., Rome, 1962), ii. 449.

[3] Damay, 25 July 1860: BB.30.385; prefect Vienne, 28 December 1863: F.19.2561.

[4] *Le Pape* (1860), Chapter 12. On the distribution of Ségur's pamphlet, BB.30.450-51; Damay, April 1860 and 25 July 1860: BB.30.385.

Rouland, warned the bishops not to have anything to do with them, since their literature implied that Catholics should obey the temporal commands of the Pope before those of their own governments, and the funds of the *Denier* were going directly towards the expenses of recruiting Frenchmen to serve in a foreign army.[1] Pie replied by announcing his fullest support and setting up sub-committees of St Vincent-de-Paul members and *Dames royalistes* to collect contributions.[2]

His confidence was shaken, however, by the timid response from the rest of the episcopate. While the parish clergy throughout France preached with increasing fury on the Roman question, and sustained so many prosecutions that it seemed at times as if the entire work of the ministry of justice was concerned with *paroles tenues en chaire*, the bishops generally kept a prudent reserve. Even amongst those who had been legitimists before the Empire only a few followed Pie into public criticism of the government's Italian policy; fearing that an open revolt might provoke Napoleon III to abrogate the Concordat, most of the *ultras* confined themselves to circulars in Latin to their clergy and a discreet display of fleurs-de-lis on their episcopal vestments. Jacquemet of Nantes, urged by Pie, consulted three other Breton bishops about the *Denier*:

'All are hesitant; they believe the moment inopportune or fear an outright failure. Even in my own good region I can foresee great difficulties. . . . People are half persuaded that the problems of Rome are a matter only of temporal interest and money.'[3]

---

[1] Rouland's circular to the bishops, 1 July 1860: F.19.5631.

[2] Damay, 25 July 1860. Provincial army commanders reported that 'ladies of the best local society' had asked the officers of some garrisons to help in collecting for the *Denier*: AHG G.8.67.

[3] Baunard, *Pie*, ii. 74. Pallu du Parc of Blois wrote to Pie: 'Shall we not risk wounding or irritating those whom we must not flatter, certainly, but equally ought not to provoke? There is reason to fear that such reflections will occur to a number of French bishops, and that the *Denier* will not enjoy that unanimous support without which it will appear as the idea of a single party': *ibid.*, ii. 73.

Some of the legitimist *ralliés* in the courts and the civil service did come out in displays of opposition, appearing at rallies of the St Vincent-de-Paul Society and helping to distribute copies of Pie's *Mandement*, Ségur's *Le Pape*, and a selection of pamphlets about the Vendéen wars and the approaching fall of the Bonaparte dynasty.[1] But rather to the government's relief the ebullience of clergy and legitimists in the west had no effect on the mass of the population, who were completely apathetic towards the fortunes of the Papacy. Congregations grew restive during sermons on the temporal power and sometimes walked out, or sent deputations to ask the priest not to preach on this subject: *'le curé nous ennuie avec son pape'*.[2] Many farmers and townspeople in the west had sons or relatives serving with the French occupation force in Rome whose letters gave a highly realistic picture of the Papal States; they turned a deaf ear to the version presented by their curés, and burned the copies of *Le Pape* brought home by school-children or distributed outside the churches.[3] In Poitiers itself, Damay reported, 'the great majority of educated opinion consists of various shades of liberalism'[4]; the sympathies of the middle class were with Cavour, and often took the form of investment in Piedmontese government bonds. Sermons about Piedmont being 'the spearhead of the revolution' cut little ice with Catholic investors and businessmen, and the clerical campaign aroused nothing but resentment. The Italian war had been a success; French influence was now predominant in Italy, and after the annexation of Nice and Savoy in 1860 the emperor's prestige was at its highest point. Pie's attack on *Le Pape et le Congrès* trebled its sales and the booksellers had to send to Paris for extra copies.[5]

---

[1] Damay, retrospective report of 29 June 1861: BB.30.385; prefect Vienne, 20 August 1861: F.19.2561.

[2] Complaint of a congregation in Brittany: *procureur-général* Rennes, 7 March 1860: BB.30.451.

[3] Damay, 26 October 1860; cf. *procureur-général* Rennes, 18 January 1860: BB.18.1567.

[4] Damay, 30 January 1861.

[5] Lynn M. Case has examined press comment and the reports of the *procureurs-généraux* in 1859-60 in *French Opinion on War and Diplomacy*

Those *bien-pensant* Catholics of the middle class who had allowed themselves to become entangled in the network of clerical legitimism found that the Roman question confronted them with an unpleasantly direct challenge. During the fifties they had been able to enjoy the superior social attractions of the *évêché*, and had been called upon only to take part in a surreptitious and amusing war of pin-pricks against the sober representatives of the government; but in 1860 it had become a more serious matter of declaring oneself openly for the bishop and against Napoleon III. For all but a handful of ultramontane zealots, such a decision was impossible. The Empire, after all, had protected them from jacobinism and revolution. The 'collapse of civil order in Europe' that was supposed to follow the fall of the Pope's temporal power was understood to be a more or less geological process of decay which might become evident after several centuries; but the danger of social upheaval in France was more immediate. To undermine the authority of the Empire, to risk plunging France into another 1848, to expose oneself to prosecution—this called for a revolutionary temper which very few of the *frondeurs de l'évêché* possessed. When it came to the point, 'moderate' views prevailed. The insubstantiality of the right-wing opposition was revealed in the fiasco of recruiting for the Papal army. From the whole of France only 781 volunteers went to fight under Lamoricière in the first year of the *corps des volontaires pontificaux*; of these almost half were young nobles, principally from the Breton and far-western departments and belonging to families with *émigré* and Vendéen traditions. The extravagantly Chambordist flavour of the enterprise was too much for some Catholics who might have been willing to fight for the Pope but were not ready to commit themselves to the cause of Henry V. Although

during the Second Empire (Philadelphia, 1954), Chapters 3-4. From the immense pamphlet literature on the Roman question, three very interesting statements of the Catholic middle-class view: Arnaud de l'Ariège, *La Papauté temporelle et la Nation italienne* (Paris, 1860); *Les défenseurs du Pouvoir temporel, par un Lyonnais* (1860); and H. Castille, *Napoléon III et le clergé* (1860). The Roman question converted Castille, the editor of the *Globe*, from absolutist to liberal Bonapartism.

Pie was one of the few bishops to give open support to Papal recruiting, the Poitiers diocese supplied no more than twenty-five volunteers between March 1860 and March 1861; during the same period 149 volunteers went from the department of the Loire-Inférieure alone, and 124 from the thinly populated departments of the Côtes-du-Nord, Morbihan and Finistère. Of the twenty-five Poitevins, six belonged to the genuine nobility (including Emmanuel de Curzon's son André), four probably to the *fausse noblesse*, and the rest were workers or lads from the villages.[1] Reports in the French press of the comic-opera adventures of the Papal army contributed to the failure of the *Denier de St Pierre*; it received large single donations from landed proprietors, but the stony resistance encountered amongst the middle classes and the farmers was frankly recognized in two remarkable handbooks issued for parish priests, *Le Pape devant un Maire de Village*, by the Abbé Poplineau of Niort, and *Trois Gascons causent avec leur curé sur le Denier de St Pierre*, written by the Abbé Poussou of Montauban and circulated through all the western dioceses. These were imaginary dialogues with refractory parishioners who claimed not to see why the citizens of the Papal States should not enjoy the free institutions of Piedmont, or why French Catholics had a religious duty to take up arms for the Pope. 'You have convinced me by a sequence of arguments better aligned than a platoon of grenadiers', says the sceptical mayor at

---

[1] For an anlysis of material on the Papal army, drawn from the *Matricule . . . des Zouaves pontificaux 1860-1870*, the records of Papal recruitment (*Amministrazione Pontificia Riformata: Ministero delle Armi: Archivio di Stato*, Rome), and the intelligence reports of the French Army of Occupation in Rome, AHG G.6, see A. G. Gough, *French Legitimism and Catholicism 1851-1865* (D. Phil. thesis, Oxford, 1966), Chapter 10.

The volunteers from the departments of the Vienne and the Deux-Sèvres in the first year of Papal recruitment: Augustin and Joseph Bertrand, Thomas Brondois, (?) Carteau de Trallebeau, Charles Champtoiseau, Jean-Louis Chapalay, Adolphe Charpentier, Georges de Chergé, André de Curzon, Paul Dupré de Puget, E. Ferdinand, Paul Frotier de la Messelière, Elie Gabilliet, Louis Gicquel, Henri Gilbert, Adrien Juiteau, Henri de la Rochethulon, Jean Marcel, Antonin de Morin de Senneville, Arthur Nouveau de la Carte, Edouard Palmier, Léopold Poncin de Casaquy, Paul Raison, Pierre Sandillon, Victor de Vigier de Mirabal.

the end of one of these discussions[1]; but in hundreds of parishes the entire collection for the *Denier* amounted to only a few centimes.[2]

Throughout the period of the Roman question the repressive machinery created after Orsini's *attentat* in 1858 to crush the extreme left was employed by the government to deal with the extreme right. Suspected sedition by legitimists, especially legitimist clergy, was punished harshly and immediately; in one case a deaf-mute, a pupil of the disreputable Brothers of St Gabriel, was imprisoned for having 'signified by gestures his preference for Henry V'.[3] But there was always the possibility that the government's own weapons of law enforcement might prove unreliable in a religious crisis. The *procureurs-généraux* were satisfied with the loyalty of the police, but in 1860 some of the metropolitan press hinted that the army could be particularly susceptible to disaffection because of the large number of officers with Catholic and royalist backgrounds. This was quickly shown to be an illusion; but the Christian Brothers and the St Vincent-de-Paul Society, who conducted evening classes and charities for soldiers in every military district, worked hard to distribute Ségur's *Le Pape* amongst the rank and file and to persuade soldiers to desert and join the Papal army.[4] This campaign generally failed because of the vigilance of senior officers and the irreligion of the troops.[5] The commanding officer of the garrison at Poitiers,

[1] Poussou, *Trois Gascons causent* . . . p. 281.

[2] A Papal Loan floated on the Paris Stock Exchange at this time fared little better; once again Pie was almost the only bishop to give it full and open support: F.30.309; *Journal des économistes*, xxvii (1860), p. 154, 'L'Emprunt militaire papal'; and J. Lorette, 'Aspects financiers de l'aide au Saint-Siège: les emprunts pontificaux de 1860, 1864, 1866', *Risorgimento*, iii (2), (1960).

[3] Damay, digest of *délits politiques*, June 1861; report of January 1862: BB.30.385; and several cases in ADV V.25.

[4] Marshal Randon to Prefect of Police, Paris, 8 February 1860, AHG G.8.64; other correspondence concerning attempts by 'guest speakers' to address evening classes of soldiers on political questions, in AHG G.8.64-67.

[5] The St Vincent-de-Paul Society's *Œuvre des militaires* managed to send to Rome only a few dozen deserters, described by General Schmid of the Papal army as 'drunken and useless': Schmid to G.O.C. French Army of Occupation, Rome, 9 August 1860: AHG G.6.8.

however, was on good terms with Pie, and was thought to have encouraged a group of young officers who publicly insulted the prefect when the civil authorities banned a royalist pageant in May 1860. Marshal Baraguey d'Hilliers came from headquarters at Tours to investigate, and found that the incident had arisen from an entirely non-political dispute over horses and carriages. At Poitiers he heard complaints that many officers of the garrison belonged to the circle of the legitimist aristocracy: of course they do, he reported:

'But in the legitimist party there are many nuances, and it is not surprising that young officers with a taste for the pleasures of the world have accepted invitations from families whom one certainly does not meet, it is true, at the prefecture, but who are represented in the army by their sons and close relatives ... These young officers give way to the temptations natural to their age, they join the hunting parties of the best society, but they remain strangers to all the petty political obsessions in the midst of which they move.'[1]

The Poitevin clergy fought the local elections of 1860 and 1861 with great bitterness, haranguing their congregations in support of legitimist candidates whom a few years earlier they had dismissed as 'a petulant faction'. Government mayors retaliated by harassing the priests, 'forgetting', for example, to sign the form necessary for the local curé to receive his monthly salary.[2] The government, sensing the public mood, endorsed a number of liberal lawyers and some 'moderate democrats, men of 1848', and obtained almost a clean sweep of the places up for renewal, even defeating Pie's principal nominee, M. Bardy.[3] After this the parish clergy relapsed into an angry and disappointed silence; but Pie himself came into renewed conflict with the government when the news reached France at the end of September 1860 that the Papal army had been overwhelmed by the Piedmontese at

[1] Baraguey d'Hilliers to Minister of War, 7 June 1860, AHG G.8.67.
[2] Damay, 30 January 1861.
[3] BB.18.1607: 2583 A3 (Elections of 1860); Damay, 25 July and 26 October 1860; and AHG G.8.69.

Castelfidardo, and that twenty of the French volunteers had been killed. It seemed to the *ultras* that this was surely the moment for a united protest from the hierarchy; but once again 'how many silent voices!' wrote Jacquemet; 'why do the archbishops and bishops refrain from speaking out? Is this the time for reserve? Should they leave us to appear before public opinion as a handful of malcontents in the midst of a satisfied and complacent episcopate?'[1] In Pie's opinion their spinelessness could be explained, though not justified, 'by certain currents of debilitating doctrines which enervate their characters and enfeeble their principles'.[2] Théodore de Quatrebarbes, who had commanded part of the Papal force at Castelfidardo, came to Poitiers and gave Pie an account of the battle which provoked him to flights of sybilline rhetoric. It was 'the hour of the combat of Michael and Lucifer . . . the Mystery of Iniquity is abroad'.[3] Earthly governments, he told the congregation at a service for the 'Martyrs of Castelfidardo', had a right to exist only if they provided the Church with its normal conditions of action and development; French Catholics should therefore 'be ready to draw their swords in the face of a manifestly unjust order of things. . . . We fight against a persecutor who wins by deceit and seduction.' As a rival of the Church Napoleon III was no more than 'an insignificant Caesar of the *Bas-Empire*' who imagined himself a Nero.[4] At the mass for the anniversary of his consecration the choir began the *Domine salvum*; Pie brusquely ordered them to stop.[5]

In February 1861 another semi-official pamphlet, *La France, Rome et l'Italie*, suggested that the disasters experienced by the Papal government in 1860 were partly its own fault, and that Catholics should not blame Napoleon III for the consequences of the Italian national movement. Pie replied with a biting pastoral: 'Wash thy hands, Pilate; declare thyself innocent of the death of

---

[1] Jacquemet to Pie, October 1860, in Baunard, *Pie*, ii. 99.

[2] Baunard, *Pie*, ii. 92.

[3] Circular to the clergy of Poitiers, quoted by Damay, 26 October 1860: BB.30.385.

[4] Pie's address of October 11th, in *Courrier de la Vienne*, 16 October 1860.

[5] Damay, 30 January 1861.

Christ!'[1] This, at last, was too much. The ministry of *cultes* decided to have Pie proceeded against by the *conseil d'État* for a breach of the Organic Articles, and although he was defended by Cornudet and a team of Catholic lawyers from the *conseil* itself, his condemnation was inevitable.[2] At the same time Damay prosecuted Pie's publisher Henri Oudin for his failure to lodge the statutory advance copies of the bishop's pastorals with the *parquet*, and made sure that the courts went on fining him every time he committed the slightest technical infringement; the unfortunate Oudin became so hyper-cautious that he refused to print Pie's next Easter message to the diocesan clergy.[3] To emphasize Pie's disgrace the government cut off funds for the repairs currently in progress on the cathedral, and sent instructions that the bishop was to receive the bare minimum of co-operation required by the Concordat. Most importantly, he was to be isolated as far as possible from all direct contact; no *fonctionnaire*, magistrate, teacher, military officer or employee of any branch of the government service was to be allowed to call at the *évêché*, and Pie himself was not to be invited to any public function.

This tactic could never have been put into practice effectively by the conciliatory men who had been prefects of Poitiers in the fifties; but in December 1860, to Damay's surprise and pleasure, the government had replaced the timid Paulze d'Ivoy with a new prefect who shared some of Damay's own views and was prepared to deal forcefully with the clerical opposition. The new appointee was Charles-Alphonse Levert, a tough Bonapartist who had just completed a term as prefect of Algiers and had a reputation for equal severity towards left and right. One of his first actions at Poitiers was to import an experienced journalist from the staff of *La Presse* in Paris to turn the feeble *Journal de la Vienne* into an

---

[1] In the first draft of the pastoral Pie had added a sentence about Pilate's wife pleading with her husband to act justly towards Christ. Pie's mother, who lived at the *évêché*, persuaded him to leave this out, as the reference to the Empress Eugénie was too obvious: B. du Boisrouvray, *Vie de Mgr Gay*, i. 226.

[2] Correspondence on the proceedings, February-March 1861, in F.19.2561.

[3] Damay, 29 June 1861; and subsequent report of January 1863: BB.30.385.

organ of the government.[1] Damay's reports began to include unaccustomed compliments to 'the clever and energetic prefect' and 'the new spirit at the prefecture'. Levert and Damay clashed at once with Casimir de Sèze over the matter of Pie's isolation. The President of the Court was asked to compose a circular instructing magistrates to break off relations with the bishop. De Sèze, protesting a devotion to the government which had not been very noticeable during the Italian crisis, said that several magistrates with legitimist opinions had already left their cards at the *évêché*, and that he preferred to approach them individually in private conversation. Damay insisted that De Sèze write a formal instruction like the one sent by the rector, Juste, to all academic staff; the minister of justice endorsed the file: 'I agree with the opinion of the *procureur-général*', and De Sèze had to submit.[2] Surely, he suggested, the bishop should at least be asked to the ceremony of the *Rentrée de la Cour?* Damay replied that enough concessions had been made already, and was supported in his refusal by the new prefect.[3]

Pie seemed unrepentant. He wrote a special pastoral on the *conseil d'État*—'As you know, my dear colleagues, condemnations by bodies of this kind have no canonical value'—and travelled through the diocese preaching to the effect that Catholics should obey the instructions of the Church rather than those of 'transitory governments doomed to disappear in a few years more or less'.[4] The mayors were warned not to give him a welcome, and he found himself speaking mostly to congregations of schoolchildren. He knew, privately, that the cause of ultramontane legitimism had been set back many years by the failure of the campaign over the Roman question. In a rare moment of self-analysis he explained in a long letter to the minister of *cultes* that he sometimes grew weary of having to strike defiant attitudes in public, for the benefit of his supporters. He was not a blind *éxalté*, he told Rouland; he understood the great changes that had taken place in the west since the

[1] Cl. Gallix on the press of Poitiers: F.18.297.
[2] Damay to Minister of Justice (Delangle), 8 March 1861: BB.18.1606.
[3] Correspondence in F.1.c.III Vienne 9.
[4] Damay, 29 June 1861.

Vendéen wars, and knew that many men of sincere religious feeling disagreed with his principles and rejected his methods:

'and do not imagine that I am not conscious of ambition. It would have been possible for me, as much as for others and perhaps more, to reach certain brilliant and lucrative dignities which on several occasions have been conferred on men who are my juniors in the episcopate.'

As a private citizen he could have been more accommodating in political matters; but he was a bishop, and the urgent duty of the episcopate in France was to instil zeal and enthusiasm, to wake up 'the men of good will who are honest enough but timid, flabby, irresolute, afraid of all bold declarations'. A bishop, once convinced that Christ should reign on earth by the instrument of the hereditary monarchy, had no choice but to be fanatical; and he quoted Hilary: 'I cannot stifle the zeal which the faith has put into my soul beneath a calculating and ambitious silence, or a tolerance injurious to truth'.[1]

A fortnight after writing this letter Pie gave a singular example of what he meant, in a sermon on the persecution of St Peter by Herod; each time he mentioned the Jewish king he called him 'Herod III'. The French ambassador in Rome asked Pius IX to reprimand Pie, but the Pope replied that 'this was an historical citation which anyone may interpret as he likes'.[2] After making sure that there was no such king as 'Herod III' the government decided on another prosecution; but Damay found it impossible to collect evidence and had to drop the case. In the atmosphere of 1861 to have been present at Pie's sermon was almost in itself a sign of clericalism, and nobody from the congregation would agree to testify against the bishop. The assistant secretary of the prefecture had been at mass but said that he was 'a little hard of hearing'; another civil servant claimed to have fallen asleep and missed Pie's remarks on Herod.[3] Evidently the official policy of

[1] Pie to Rouland, 16 June 1861: F.19.2561.

[2] Maurain, *Politique ecclésiastique* . . ., 521-23. Pie had been in the highest favour at Rome since 1859, and was in close touch with Pius IX and the Curia over the preparation of the *Syllabus errorum*.

[3] Damay, 21 July and 12 August 1861: BB.18.1606; 7 May 1863: BB.30.385.

isolation had not completely broken the social power of the *évêché*. Amongst the general public, however, there was no doubt that Pie's implacable opposition and his efforts to keep the Roman question alive were becoming very unpopular. At high mass on the official feast-day of 15 August 1861 the legitimists made their usual demonstration, overturning their chairs in unison when the celebrant began the *Te Deum* for the Bonaparte dynasty, and walking out of the cathedral. When they reached the doors they found their way blocked by a crowd of about 10,000 people who pushed the legitimists back into the cathedral and cheered for Napoleon III and the Empire.[1]

In September 1861 the St Vincent-de-Paul Society held a rally under Pie's chairmanship at Lusignan, chosen for its associations with the medieval crusades. Hundreds of Breton and Vendéen legitimists attended, including a number of returned volunteers from the Papal army, and there were inflammatory speeches full of military metaphor.[2] Persigny, then minister of the interior, had just finished reading a special report on the Society by Claudius Gallix, and a dossier on its activities in 1860—apart from election-eering and recruiting for the Papal army, the Society had been concerned in plans to assassinate Napoleon III, and one of its clandestine presses had been printing instructions for the home manufacture of gunpowder[3]—and the Lusignan rally decided the issue. Persigny sent out a circular which had the effect of dissolving the Society, as the provincial branches disbanded rather than accept the government's terms for remaining in existence. This was a heavy blow to legitimist and ultramontane influence at Poitiers; but at about this time also the power of the *évêché* was undermined more subtly by the fact of Mgr Pie's becoming entangled in a number of unintentional comedies.

[1] Prefect (Levert), 20 August 1861: F.19.2561. The incident may not have been completely spontaneous, but after 1860 government agents had no trouble in arranging demonstrations against the *évêché*: see Commissioner of Police to prefect, 1 and 3 March 1861, on popular feeling in Poitiers: ADV V.25.

[2] Pie to Rouland, 11 November 1861: F.19.2561; A. Foucault, *La Société de St Vincent-de-Paul* (1933), pp. 180-86.

[3] F.7.12.389; AHG G.8.67; BB.30.423.

One of the few working-class volunteers for the Papal army to enrol at Poitiers, a certain Louis Gicquel, had been reported killed at the battle of Castelfidardo, and Pie, who had blessed Gicquel before he set off for Rome, gave a special memorial address in which he described him as a martyr and a model for Christian youth. Gicquel, inconveniently restored to life, turned up in October 1861 in a courtroom at Laval where he was sentenced to gaol for fraud and robbery; he had a long criminal record. The *affaire Gicquel* became a national joke, particularly enjoyed in Poitiers.[1] A sense of humour might have preserved Pie from the even more piquant *affaire* of the Sacred Prepuce. A peculiar object found in a box at the Ursuline convent of Charroux was declared by the Mother Superior, with Pie's express approval, to be the Sacred Prepuce removed at the Circumcision. Pie raised funds to build a sanctuary for this precious relic, and founded a sub-order of nuns to keep perpetual vigil over it. In 1862 he attended an elaborate festival at Charroux, when every part of the convent, Damay reported, was decorated with fleurs-de-lis;[2] Pie gave an address in which he derived the name Charroux from *Chair rouge* and congratulated the nuns on having preserved 'the only part of Christ's body left behind when He ascended into heaven'.[3] The more serious friends of the *évêché* would have preferred the whole matter to have faded quietly into oblivion, but pious local antiquaries insisted on publishing articles every few months describing the very characteristic miracles wrought by the Sacred Prepuce during the Middle Ages; the sceptical middle classes of Poitiers were still reading these avidly when the campaigning began for the national elections of 1863. Miracles and processions of sacred relics only accelerated the strong trend in the western electorate towards liberalism, and everything done by the ultramontane-legitimist party in their campaign seemed designed to

[1] There are two separate dossiers on Gicquel, in BB.18.1618 and F.19.2561.
[2] The nuns innocently explained that the fleurs-de-lis were 'not political, but simply Monseigneur's favourite flower': Damay, 17 May 1863: BB.30.385.
[3] Damay, 13 November 1862, and Levert, 15 November 1862: F.19.2561. Pie's biographer Baunard, although convinced of the genuineness of the relic, cannot bring himself to say what it was: Baunard, *Pie*, ii. 184-85.

amuse or annoy the greatest possible number of voters. The clergy electioneered for legitimist candidates 'with a violence not seen since the introduction of universal suffrage', and were openly heckled during sermons. The St Vincent-de-Paul Society, officially disbanded, went from house to house distributing pamphlets and voting papers, and were very active in defacing government posters. The *évêché* gave wide publicity to recent decisions by the Sacred Penitentiary in Rome confirming that Catholics who invested in Italian government bonds were automatically excommunicated.[1] Mgr Pie mishandled the election in the Deux-Sèvres, endorsing a legitimist candidate without making enough enquiries about him. The man, Dr Morin, was a curiously eighteenth-century figure, a legitimist-Voltairean, and the local clergy refused to campaign for him.[2] On polling day the right-wing opposition was wiped out, in spite of having received some support from extreme left-wing voters who had no candidates of their own; at Poitiers Pie's candidate Bardy, whose campaign had emphasized the Roman question and the moral decay of modern France, got only 150 votes.[3]

Within eighteen months of the elections of 1863 two events convinced the supporters of the government that the ultramontane-legitimist party had no more real force in the Poitiers region. As a protest both against the election results and against the government's refusal to suppress the publication of Renan's *Vie de Jésus* in June 1863, Pie arranged a pageant to commemorate the 'Miracle of the Keys': in the year 1262 the keys of Poitiers, traitorously delivered to a besieging force by 'an apostate cleric' (nobody missed the reference to Renan), had miraculously been recovered by the Virgin Mary. Every prominent legitimist in the region attended, and special trains brought thousands of priests and nuns. Official isolation was applied strictly, and Pie had to do without the usual party from the prefecture and detachment of

---

[1] Damay, 7 May 1863, and *Premier avocat-général* Gast (substituting for Damay, who was on leave in June and July), 10 July 1863: BB.30.385; F.19.5607; and *Civiltà Cattolica*, Series V, vol. vi (18 May 1863).

[2] *P. avocat-général* Gast, 10 July 1863: BB.30.385.

[3] Gast, 10 July 1863; Damay, 6 November 1863: BB.30.385.

troops.[1] The banners and decorations cost the diocese 20,000 francs; the procession contained tableaux representing the highly political miracle of La Salette of 1846 and others in which the Virgin Mary was identified with Marie Antoinette and Marie-Caroline de Berry—'although for real connoisseurs of bad taste', Damay remarked, 'the festival of the Sacred Prepuce at Charroux last year was worse'.[2] If the demeanour of the crowds lining the streets was any indication, the pageant was entirely counter-productive as a political gesture.

The second event was the publication in France in January 1865 of the Papal *Syllabus of Errors*, which was to be taken by the extreme right in Europe during the next half-century as a banner of counter-revolution, 'the Declaration of the Rights of God'. Pie, who had played a large part in the composition of the *Syllabus*,[3] was determined that it should make a resounding impact on the Poitiers diocese. He wrote a pastoral to the effect that the *Syllabus* had revealed the essential falsity of the principles on which Napoleon III's government claimed to rest, in particular the 'consent of the majority', and ordered this to be read in all the churches but not published. The parish clergy were encouraged to add their own embellishments: one of them organized a school play in which the godless French government collapsed and the Catholic monarchs returned, bearing copies of the *Syllabus*. Legitimists ran through village streets on Sunday mornings shouting 'Long live Henry V, long live the Syllabus!'[4] But once again excess led to failure. The educated classes took the sardonic

[1] Levert, 2 December 1863: F.19.2561. Pie's comment on the *Vie de Jésus*: 'I occupy the see of Hilary, and here is Arius himself!' *Correspondance Pie/Cousseau*, 406.

[2] Damay, 6 December 1863: F.19.2561.

[3] On the Encyclical *Quanta cura* and the *Syllabus errorum*, R. Aubert, *Le pontificat de Pie IX* (Paris, 1963), Chapter 8; G. Martina S.J., *Il liberalismo cattolico ed il Sillabo* (Rome, 1959); Martina, 'Sulle varie redazioni del Sillabo', in *Chiesa e Stato nell'Ottocento: miscellanea in onore di Pietro Pirri* (2 vols., Padua, 1962). The extent of Pie's contribution is indicated in his *Instruction synodale ... sur les principales erreurs du temps présent* (Poitiers, 1864).

[4] Prefect (Tourangin), 26 February 1865, and other correspondence on the *Syllabus* agitation: F.19.1935.

view of Papal condemnations expressed in the *Revue des Deux Mondes*, the *Siècle* and the *Opinion nationale*, and there was hardly a ripple of interest in the mass of the population; even some legitimists began to complain that Mgr Pie and the Pope seemed determined to make Catholicism repellent.[1]

After 1865 the government's position at Poitiers was reasonably secure. Damay thought that the bishop had so weakened his own position that there was no longer any point in prosecuting him for his occasional outbursts.[2] The low political credit of the clergy made it easier for the Government to satisfy liberal opinion, which was becoming increasingly radical and anticlerical. The *parquet* acted several times against priests who promoted spurious miracles, or who called in missionaries noted for their fiery eloquence to attack local citizens who had been lukewarm over the Roman question or the *Syllabus*.[3] Damay launched frequent prosecutions to emphasize the classic anticlerical point that the clergy, while preaching a grimly puritanical code of morals, often failed to practise it themselves; and at the same time he intervened in favour of the accused in certain cases where the clergy were calling for severe penalties. Women were driven to the common crime of infanticide, he reported, by the public opprobrium roused by priests against unmarried mothers, and by the lack of any proper legal machinery to compel men to pay adequate maintenance. In cases of homosexuality he pointed out that French law was kinder than Canon law: there were no prosecutions if the acts were 'in private, without coercion, and did not concern minors'. He went out of his way to be conciliatory to the Protestants in the Vienne and the Deux-Sèvres. Besides being models of decorum in religious matters, they always voted for the official candidates; Damay and the prefect rewarded them by protecting them from attacks by religious extremists, and by giving them private advice on how they could distribute their literature without infringing the complicated press laws.

---

[1] Reports of the sub-prefects of Loudun, Châtellerault and Montmorillon, 15 January 1865: ADV M.4.71.
[2] Damay, 10 February 1865: BB.30.385.
[3] Damay, 10 February 1865, 11 January 1866: BB.30.385.

In 1864 Casimir de Sèze died, and the Presidency of the Court passed to a solid Bonapartist, M. Fortoul, a brother of the former minister of *cultes*. The prefect Levert was moved to Arras in the same year but his successor, M. Tourangin, proved to be almost as effective from Damay's point of view. Prefecture and *parquet* together managed the elections of the last years of the Empire without any great difficulty, and succeeded in replacing almost all of the *réfractaires* on local councils with supporters of the government. Surveying the results of the council-general elections of 1867, in which in some cantons all the candidates announced themselves as *Napoléoniens* and the winners were the ones who laid the most stress on their liberalism, Damay clearly felt that his own interpretation of 'Napoleonic ideas' had been vindicated in practice, and his final reports under the Empire were written in a tone of steadily rising optimism.[1]

At the proclamation of the Republic in 1870 Damay had to retire with the other senior officials of the Empire. Some of his colleagues at the *parquet* fled to avoid reprisals, but he stayed at Poitiers, confident that his reputation for fair dealing with the left would protect him. He died in January 1872, genial and irreverent to the last, and was given a funeral service at the church of St Hilaire which his friends who attended did their best to secularize.[2]

Pie saw the fall of Napoleon III as a stroke of divine retribution. When the news arrived of the capitulation at Sedan he announced to his clergy: 'At the public prayers after mass last Sunday the invocation for the emperor was said for the last time. *Justa sunt judicia tua, Domine.*'[3] In the last decade of his life, under the Third Republic, he was to play a very active part in national politics. As chief adviser on political theory to the comte de Chambord, as intermediary between Chambord and the Pope at the time of

[1] Material in the preceding paragraphs represents a digest of Damay's quarterly reports from 1866 to 1869, especially those of 14 July and 24 October 1867: BB.30.385.

[2] Report of the service, and the address given by the *avocat-général* Moreau: *Journal de la Vienne*, 20 January 1872. Damay's two adopted sons were at the Poitiers Bar during the first decade of the Republic.

[3] Baunard, *Pie*, ii. 405.

the attempted restoration in 1873, as leader of the movement for the *Voeu national* and the most formidable opponent of the Catholic liberals, he was to be constantly on the public stage until his death in 1880 at the comparatively early age of sixty-five, and for many years afterwards his teaching on Church-state relations had a profound influence with the traditionalist right in France. His obituarists, however, might have come closer to the true lesson of his career if they had looked beyond the national champion of ultramontanism, and paid more attention to the bishop of Poitiers. In the more significant conflicts of local politics Damay and the prefecture had won; twenty years of Bonapartism had left their mark, and Pie was never able to recover any serious degree of social or political influence in the Poitiers region. The cardinal's hat, for which he was nominated in the last year of his life, and which now hangs above his tomb in the darkest of the great Romanesque churches of Poitou, was an ironic prize for his resolute but ultimately fruitless struggle against the current of the nineteenth century.

CHAPTER IV

THE CONFLICT
IN THE VILLAGES

POPULAR ANTICLERICALISM IN THE ISÈRE (1852-70)

ROGER MAGRAW

1. *Introduction*

The nineteenth-century French clergy were never able to shed their dreams of a return to an idealized ancien régime in which, in the words of one bishop of the 1830s, 'all Frenchmen were brothers because all were Christians'.[1] The myth of a Christian rural France was the basis of much *ultra* royalist political thought during the Restoration, when some went to the point of advocating universal suffrage as a tactical device to drown Paris, the 'modern Babylon', in a damp wave of loyal Catholic peasant votes.[2] The illusion never died completely.[3] But it was an illusion —and one whose persistence gave a perpetual ring of unreality to legitimist politics throughout the nineteenth century. In brief,

---

[1] Pastoral letter of Mgr Beauregard, bishop of Orleans. Cited by Gabriel Le Bras in 'Preface', p. xiv, to C. Marcilhasy, *Le Diocèse d'Orléans au milieu du dix-neuvième siècle* (1964).

[2] Well illustrated of course in Stendhal's *Le Rouge et le noir*, notably part 2, Ch. 23: 'The clergy and the woodlands'. Cf. R. Rémond, *The Right Wing in France* (Philadelphia, 1966), 43.

[3] In the early days of the religious sociology of Le Bras and others in France in the 1930s the discipline, which aimed at presenting a detailed empirical survey of religious practice in France as an aid to pastoral work, was bitterly attacked by the Catholic right which denied the existence of a 'mission problem' and insisted that France was still the eldest daughter of the Church with her faithful masses intact and merely led astray by freemasons, Jews, socialists. G. Siefer, *Church and Industrial Society* (1964), 47.

the French peasantry was no longer—if it had ever been—the devout loyalist mass of *ultra* dreams.[1]

The process by which large sections of the rural population were alienated from the Church is still obscure and not yet fully understood—and obviously varied from region to region. A number of local studies provide at least a framework for the religious history of the department of Isère. The department seems to have resented—and in some cases resisted—the militant dechristianization campaigns attempted by popular societies during the 1790s.[2] Mute hostility and sporadic violence greeted attempts made from Grenoble to suppress Sunday observance or to enforce '*décadi*'.[3] Refractory priests were supported in several mountain cantons. On the other hand fears of a religious counter revolution—a '*Vendée dauphinoise*'—failed to materialize outside one or two of the mountain areas. By 1802 over one-quarter of the churches in the department were closed or unusable and clerical recruitment was in serious decline. Prefectoral reports spoke of the 'surly' attitude of many of the younger generation toward the clergy.

The reaction of the department toward the Restoration provided clear evidence that any sympathy shown to the clergy during the 'persecution' of the 1790s would not be forthcoming in a situation where the clergy themselves threatened to be the persecutors.[4] In Grenoble churches priests insisted that the Bourbons would restore all *biens nationaux*. The peasantry were alarmed by the return to the nobility of unsold émigré lands. An anonymous writer in late 1814 prophesied a new peasant revolu-

[1] For a brief survey of the available evidence for religious observance in the period before 1789 see F. Boulard, *An Introduction to Religious Sociology* (1960), 28-44.

[2] Pierrette Paravy, *La Faillite de l'église constitutionelle et de la déchristianisation dans le département de l'Isère*, Diplôme d'études supérieures, typescript, Archives départementales de l'Isère, 2 J 16 (henceforth ADI).

[3] Jean Georgelin, *Histoire religieuse du département de l'Isère 1797-1802*, ADI 2 J 34, pages 95-117; A. M. de Franclieu, *Histoire de la persécution religieuse dans le département de l'Isère* (1904), 3 vols.

[4] Mme Rolland, *Le Département de l'Isère sous la chambre introuvable*, Diplôme d'études supérieures, typescript, ADI 2 J 18.

tion against the nobility and the clergy. A society for the defence of holders of *biens nationaux* was set up.[1] In rural areas rumours of the restoration of the tithe were rife.[2] Many clergy were physically threatened. In Bourg d'Oisans peasants cut down the clergy's woodlands. A police report noted that 'through fear of seeing themselves stripped of their property [the peasantry] regret that they did not kill the nobles and the priests and dream of revenge at the earliest possible opportunity'.[3]

The experiences of the Restoration left an indelible stamp on the peasantry's relations with the clergy for the remainder of the nineteenth century.

As Marcilhasy's study of the diocese of Orléans shows, the anticlericalism of the 1830 Revolution, a revolution very largely provoked by the throne-altar alliance, could be as violent in a rural department as in Paris.[4] But in her estimation it was the events of the Second Republic which applied the *coup de grâce* to what remained of the religious practice of the ancien régime and which 'consummated the divorce between clergy and people everywhere that the notables did not throw their weight in favour of the former'.[5] As a number of recent studies have shown the Second Republic—in sharp contrast to the traditional picture of urban radicalism stifled by the apathy of a property-owning anti-socialist troglodyte peasantry—saw the last great rural jacquerie of French history in many areas of central, south-eastern and south-western France.[6] And as studies elsewhere have shown, the mass peasant vote for Louis Napoleon in 1849 was not for

[1] Rolland, *op. cit.*, p. 92. This was particularly strong in Vienne, which until 1790 had been a diocesan centre. Its fifteen religious houses had been confiscated, sold to the local bourgeoisie and used as workshops so that 'there were very few families who did not possess some portion of church property'.

[2] ADI 52 M 5, *Rapport sur la situation du département de l'Isère.*

[3] ADI 52 M 5, *Police politique*, 1 November 1815.

[4] C. Marcilhasy, *op. cit.*, 453.

[5] *Ibid.*, 479-80.

[6] P. Vigier, *La deuxième république dans la région alpine* (1963); A. Soboul, 'Les troubles agraires de 1848' in *Paysans, sans culottes et jacobins* (1966), 308-50.

a 'saviour of society' against urban 'reds' but for a guarantee of the 'revolution' against legitimism and the local notables.[1] Peasant Bonapartism was the guarantee of equality, the revolt of rural democracy against its traditional ties. As Vigier has stressed the February revolution in Isère and elsewhere in the Alps was decorous, merely substituting one group of notables for another. The true revolution came with universal suffrage which offered the chance of making the Republic *rurale et paysanne*.[2] This left-wing Bonapartism of the peasantry was to be a constant factor in the politics of the Second Empire.[3]

The aim of this study is to attempt to illustrate the type of conflict which arose between this nascent rural democracy and the society of notables which it confronted. The notables were the pillars of French Catholicism. They deformed religion by tying it to the narrow conception of the throne-altar alliance and to the conservation of a social order. Inevitably therefore for anyone opposed to legitimism or to the existing social order, anti-Catholicism became a foundation stone of class-consciousness. Since religion, in the eyes of its friends as well as those of its enemies, was secularized, 'it became a party and, at a time when parties had little substance, the most organized party. It was treated as such by those outside it.'[4] The process by which the French Church, by espousing political reaction and social conservatism after the June Days, uprooted the fragile plant of social Catholicism and created the final chasm between itself on the one hand and the urban artisan and working classes and republican intellectuals on the other, is fairly well known.[5] But

[1] E.g. L. Chevalier, *Les fondements économiques et sociaux de l'histoire politique de la région parisienne 1848-1851* (1951), typescript.

[2] Vigier, *op. cit.*, *passim*.

[3] See for example P. Barral, 'Forces politiques sous le second empire dans le département de l'Isère', in *77e Congrès des sociétés savantes* (Grenoble, 1952), 159-174.

[4] C. Marcilhasy, *op. cit.*, 492.

[5] J. B. Duroselle, *Les débuts du catholicisme social en France 1822-1870* (1951); Vicaire, 'Les ouvriers parisiens en face du catholicisme 1830-1870', in *Zeitschrift fur Schweizerische Geschichte* (1951); F. A. Isambert, *Christianisme et classe ouvrière* (1961).

France's retarded industrialization meant that she was and remained predominantly rural, not urban, and the plebiscites showed that she was Bonapartist not republican. The incessant anticlericalism of the governments of the Third Republic, installed by universal suffrage in a predominantly rural country, cannot be attributed solely to the tastes of urban workers or positivist politicians. This study is an attempt to show how and why anticlericalism found a rural audience.

The department of Isère falls naturally into two distinct sections. The north and west—the Bas Dauphiné—is a region of low hills and plains orientated towards the Rhône. Its population was relatively dense in the mid-nineteenth century. The proximity of the urban market at Lyon and the extensive road building of the July monarchy stimulated the growth of commercial agriculture. Although the department was still approximately seventy per cent rural, the Bas Dauphiné contained a large number of industrialized communes, some close to the Lyon agglomeration. The largest of these was Vienne with a population of some 17,000 and with silk weaving, textile and metal industries. Tullins, Voiron, Rives, Bourgoin and Jallieu were other communes with similar industries. This was the area of the department most susceptible to the influence of the radical ideas of Lyon.

The southern and eastern sections of Isère make up the alpine Haute Dauphiné—its population less dense, its communications much more primitive, its agriculture almost entirely of a subsistence nature in mid-nineteenth century. It was an area where national politics meant little. Its orientation was towards Grenoble, a city of as yet only 25,000, without the heavy industry of the Lyon plain.

We do not possess any full statistics on church attendance comparable to those given by Dupanloup's thorough survey of his Orléans diocese in 1852.[1] Impressionistic reports from prefects

---

[1] Marcilhasy, *op. cit.*, 488-91. These figures, which apply to the rural sections of the diocese, are very striking confirmation of the extreme inroads made into rural religious observance by the mid-nineteenth century. In all 11 per cent of the population attended church on Easter Sunday—67 per cent of the girls in the 13-20 age-group, 20 per cent of the women over

and bishops in 1877 have enabled Gadille in a recent study to compile a national map of religious practice in that decade.[1] In general, the Bas Dauphiné stands out as an area of barely average religious practice—though it was higher than in Orléans or any of the ten dioceses round Paris. The alpine regions show a much higher level of religious observance—yet even so reports from eighty-nine mountain parishes for 1855 indicate that the large majority of men were absent from Easter services. The seventeen parishes for which we possess reports both from 1855 and from the only other such enquiry in 1827-29 show a substantial drop in attendance in the interim. A prefectoral report of 1883 notes that the observance of much of the rural population of Isère was limited to rites of passage—baptism, first communion, marriage and funeral. The *procureur général* summarized the attitude toward the clergy as 'a mistrust which was not sceptical but completely reserved—so adopting a form of self-defence for fear of being less free arbiters of their consciences, their families and their municipal interests'.[2]

II. '*Anticlericalisme de clocher*'—*administrative conflicts in local politics*

This essay attempts to investigate the factors and issues at the local level which can explain the depth of hostility to the Church which underlay the Ferry legislation. At the national level the main causes were briefly the clergy's nostalgia for legitimism, its political and social conservatism, its highly unpopular ultra-montanism during the Italian question and its pretensions to dominate primary education. But at the communal level it is perhaps unrealistic to imagine that rural populations with a very limited range of political interests shared the opposition to the

20, 23 per cent of youths 13-20 but only 3·8 per cent of the men above twenty years of age. Two-thirds of the girls who practised ceased to do so after marriage. See also Barral, *Le Département de l'Isère*, 255-7 and Archives épiscopales de Grenoble B 15 and D 30.

[1] Jacques Gadille, *La Pensée et l'action politique des évêques français 1870-1883* (1967), 152-3.

[2] Archives nationales F.19 5812 30 May 1883. (henceforth AN.)

'intellectual obscurantism' of congregational education, or the sympathy with Italian unification or republican intellectuals. The roots of anticlericalism are to be found, not invariably but extremely often, in rural areas, in squabbles which in themselves are of a nature so parochial as to appear unimportant. Yet if one traces the courses of these innumerable petty disputes it becomes obvious that by a logical sequence they progress towards the sort of issues which comprised the national politics of the Third Republic.

A municipal council, at odds with the curé over the expenses for the re-roofing of a church, instinctively protests when the curé starts a campaign of propaganda for a congregational school. A mayor whose protests about the interference of a curé in local administration have produced no remedies from prefect or bishop sees in a rash sermon defending the Pope's temporal power an opportunity to discredit the priest in the eyes of the government. The opportunities for friction within the village were infinite. The state officials complained: 'the clergy involve themselves too much in temporal matters and create discord in the villages'; clergy of the department were seeking 'to control the mayors'. Such observations provide a constant threat in the reports of sub-prefects to the prefect. The sub-prefect of St Marcellin said that in his *arrondissement* the influence in politics was slight, but 'in administrative questions, on the other hand, it is sufficiently strong to contribute to divisions in many communes. All too often, where there is a party in conflict with the local administration, the curé can be counted among its main members.'[1]

In the villages no question aroused so much friction as the expenses involved in the rebuilding of churches, provision of new bells, the siting of new cemeteries. Year after year the sub-prefect of St Marcellin was forced to reiterate his protests in his terminal reports.[2] 'The clergy are generally too much inclined to consider religious buildings, churches and priest's houses as belonging to them personally—a tendency which leads them to undertake all sorts of work without the agreement and sometimes even against

[1] ADI 52 M 44
[2] ADI 52 M 38, 1859.

the wishes of municipal administrations. It is not possible to refrain from protesting against their tendency to consider the cemeteries as belonging to the church.' Citing disputes in Réamont and St Romans, he stressed this as a constant source of friction 'above all in small villages'. Frequently the root of such clashes lay in the curé's domination of the parish council. Legal forms would be ignored. The parish council would be controlled permanently by the curé's sympathizers, election deferred indefinitely. Very frequently one encounters protests that the parish council has not been re-elected for six years or more.[1] Having escaped from communal control, the parish council, then 'considering communal funds to be at their disposal', undertook rebuilding schemes which created financial deficits for the commune which they were often unwilling to meet. 'The irregularities of the running of parish councils, whose recruitment is often done not by way of election at all but simply by choice of the bishop, and which often buy, borrow and carry out all their financial transactions without either authorization or control, often rebounds on to the heads of the communes. These latter, who have not been consulted at all, refuse to bear the consequences of actions to which they have not agreed and such circumstances have been the cause of skirmishings in a great number of communes. All too often the ecclesiastical authorities claim the benefits of the rights allowed them by law but refuse to accept the obligations these entail. The parish councils regard the communal budget as being at their disposal—from this spring perpetual difficulties between mayors and curés.'[2]

In La Frette, the polarization of the commune into warring factions seems to have occurred early in the 1850s. However, it was the Italian war which provided the municipal council with the opportunity to denigrate the curé in the eyes of the government. In 1859 we find the bishop writing to the minister of *cultes* concerning the curé's alleged outrages against the government— refusal to sing the *Te Deum* and 'equivocal comments on the

---

[1] See, for example, ADI IV v 53, Parish Records of Fontaine, 1869.
[2] ADI 52 M 44, December 1862, monthly report.

Italian war'.[1] The bishop, while insisting with apparent certainty that 'no one is more distressed than myself to see the pulpit become a platform and the most important political questions broached and dealt with before a village audience', said that he thought the charges exaggerated and the request of the population for the curé to be moved unacceptable.

The *procureur général's* report, while emphasizing the *instituteur's* evidence that the curé had indeed called for prayers for the Austrians, 'since they are Catholics like ourselves', tended to place the cause of the incident 'on the divisions for which the commune of La Frette has been the stage for several years'. He said that soon after the arrival of Abbé Drevet, a friend of his, M. Romanuet, treasurer of the parish council, had gone bankrupt, owing ninety-six francs. In order to prevent the parish council from acting against M. Romanuet the curé adopted the simple device of refusing to call it together. 'From that incident one can date the struggles which, since then, have become progressively embittered' with Abbé Drevet refusing to keep parish council accounts and insulting the municipal administration periodically from the pulpit.

The canton of Grande-Lempes in the Bièvre has been seen as a traditionally conservative area with a high vocational ratio and an obstinate tendency under the Third Republic to vote for 'Order'.[2] The commune of Longchanel was one of the few in the Isère to put up any resistance to the making of inventories after the Separation. Yet it was this area of the *arrondissement* that the sub-prefect of La Tour du Pin noted for conflict with its curés, perhaps for the very reason of the local pretensions of the clergy.[3]

---

[1] AN F.19 5812, Letters of Bishop and *Procureur général*, July 1859.

[2] Barral, *Le Département de L'Isère*, 501-4.

[3] A. Siegfried, *Tableau politique de la France de L'Ouest* (1964 edition), 390-400, notes the existence of areas of high religious practice which nevertheless succeeded in remaining independent of the political and administrative control of their priests. This paradox rested on their ability to maintain a logical distinction between their Catholic religion and its local representative. All too often, in Isère at least, a single long-serving unpopular priest was sufficient to destroy local churchgoing habits which then never afterwards revived. For example, at St André' le Gaz where there was 'open war' for

In his report of 5 October 1857[1] he lamented that 'this part of the *arrondissement—"la terre froide"*—has always had the sad privilege of providing a public spectacle of its inveterate hatreds. I would add that unfortunately one does not find at all in this canton people of a sufficiently exalted social position or with a sufficiently firm and independent character to raise himself above these petty local rivalries and whom the administration can consult when necessary.'[2]

In Longchanel, for example, 'it would appear that reconciliation is impossible'. The contestants were the curé 'a man of spirit, too much perhaps', and the mayor, 'a violent man, very jealous of his authority'. The curé had used all his possible means to get money for a new church bell: his success 'exasperated the mayor'. The curé pressed for the reconstruction of the church and from the pulpit criticized the municipal council for their opposition. He then interfered in the local elections in an effort to overthrow the mayor. His failure left him open to further administrative pressure so that 'he would have done much better to have kept out of it.' The prefect's report to the minister blamed the curé for the coming 'all-out war'. 'His haughty and pretentious character . . . has created numerous enemies in the parish.'[3]

In October 1858 the sub-prefect of La Tour du Pin wrote to the *commissaire de police* at Grande-Lempes urging him to protect Abbé Chalons against a threat from twenty-five *pères de famille* who had 'made it known that they had made up their minds to go to the priest's house to evict Abbé Chalons, without doing him any harm, on the pretext that he was disliked by all his parishioners'.[4] A month later the sub-prefect protested at the violence

twenty years between a priest of violent character who charged excessive burial fees, etc., the sub-prefect reported: 'At St André they no longer believe in religion. Religion is very largely the example set by the priest.'

[1] AN F.19 5812.

[2] Cf. Barral, 92. Well under twenty per cent of the Bièvre was held in estates of more than twenty hectares. This contrasts with nearly fifty per cent in the neighbouring canton of Valloire, to the west.

[3] AN F.19 5812, 7 October 1857.

[4] ADI 52 M 35, October and November 1859.

which had been permitted to occur by the police and the *garde champêtre* and at the fact that the 'guilty have not been found'.

Just to the south of Grande-Lempes at Marnans, in the canton of Roybon, the curé was driven to pulpit polemics against the municipal council for their failure to undertake satisfactory church repairs.[1] In St Gervais the curé made use of the mayor's temporary lack of attention to build a fresh cemetery, demolishing the walls of the old one in the process. Challenged by the municipal council to explain this and similar actions, he told them not to interfere in parish council affairs. Though the sub-prefect assured the mayor that the curé's action was indeed highly irregular, the curé refused to give way. Despite strong protests from the local authorities the priest 'claiming that the cemeteries belonged to the parish council, would not agree to the commune having anything to do with them'.[2]

Grande-Lempes itself was the scene of protracted conflict in the early 1860's. Here Abbé Ballet was accused of misappropriating funds collected by the charity society for victims of a fire.[3] The curé became the target of a flood of caricatures, abusive verses, cartoons, distributed and sung year after year in the cafés and cabarets of the town, or sent through the post from Grenoble. Typical was the verse which appeared in March 1860 which began

> 'Tu avais donc, adroit, gredin,
> Sans tambours, ni trompettes,
> Porté ton impudente main
> Sur le don céleste.'

(So, cunning villain, without drums or trumpet accompaniment, you laid your shameless hands on the holy gift.)

The sub-prefect in 1860 lamented that the affair had already 'produced the very worst results in this district'. In an act of considerable tactlessness the local clergy openly supported a 'legitimist' in the local elections of 1861. In 1862 a ministerial enquiry on

[1] ADI 52 M 43, Sub-prefect of St Marcellin, 12 March 1861.
[2] ADI 52 M 44, Sub-prefect of St Marcellin, November 1862.
[3] ADI 52 M 35; 52 M 42; 52 M 44; IV v 57, Parish Records of Grande-Lempes.

the question of the funds cleared the curé from the charges, but his guilt had already entered too deeply into popular mythology for the court decision to have any effect. In October 1862 the sub-prefect noted that 'this priest, who is so disliked by the population, continues to be caricatured and lampooned in a truly scandalous fashion'. The latest caricature placarded round the commune showed him wearing devil's horns, trampling on books marked 'Law Book' and 'Scriptures' and waving a banner inscribed 'First prize for telling lies'. 'It is superfluous to add that religion and public morality suffer from this deplorable state of affairs.' The sub-prefect complained of the bishop's reluctance to change the curé when it was so obvious that 'Abbé Ballet can no longer carry out his evangelical mission'. Not, indeed, until 1866 did the bishop sanction a change.

The Bièvre had no monopoly of such conflicts. One finds the same pattern repeated in disputes in, for example, St Martin d'Hères,[1] now a suburb of Grenoble, or in La Ferrière, south of Allevard in the mountainous east of the department, where municipal politics were wrecked in the 1860s by the interference of Abbé Ballet, described by the local *justice de paix* as 'an un-educated man, full of prejudices, immensely full of himself, who assigns himself the right to dominate everything in the village, public and private business as well as consciences. The municipal authorities have wanted to retain their independence.'[2] On September 19th the mayor asked the prefect that the curé be moved. The parish council, he said, 'cannot remain with the members the curé wishes, for he makes his choices out of pure spite against the commune'. Though not treasurer of the parish council, the curé was constantly buying objects for the church without permission. He was trying to dominate public life, insulted the municipal council, and even slandered women who wore crinolines. Simultaneously the *inspecteur d'académie* pro-tested to the prefect that the curé was trying to get the *institutrice* removed although she was popular with the villagers, and was

[1] ADI IV v 94.

[2] ADI IV v 52, Parish Records of La Ferrière, J.P., to Prefect 12 November 1867.

trying to make her take time off from school to sing in the choir and numerous other '*tracasseries*'. By January 1868 the sub-prefect was reporting an accusation that the curé had refused to celebrate the *fête de l'Empereur* and that he was rigging parish council elections.

Such examples could be repeated in an endless list of local variations on a very similar theme. The point which emerges is that though anticlericalism in France has generally been thought of in terms of the working classes of the urban areas and the artisans, lawyers, doctors, café owners, etc., of small *bourgs*—the type of conflict described here was more intense in smaller rural communes.[1] Although it is undeniable that, in the Isère, the workers of Voiron or Vienne tended to have a greater ideological hostility to organized religion, their near-atheism in the context of a large commune meant that they could spend much of their lives without needing to come into any direct contact with the Church. In smaller communes, where the curé was one of the notables, the consequences of any divergence of opinion had greater impact on a larger proportion of the community. Hence the frequency of conflicts in rural Bièvre, despite its reputation as a 'Catholic' area. However, it would be misleading to suggest the paradox that 'anticlerical' areas produced fewer anticlerical demonstrations than 'Catholic' areas. One of the most virulent conflicts over church construction comes appropriately from Corbas, on the plain of Lyon, midway between Lyon and St Symphorien, a 'rural' area, but one highly influenced by the advanced left-wing tendencies of the city which found an audience among local shoemakers.[2] The area had been subject to a fit of violent anticlericalism in 1848, when many priests were driven from parishes—for example at Chaponnay and at Villeubanne—and St Symphorien elected a fervent republican, Etienne Buyat, as *conseiller général* in 1864.[3]

---

[1] See, for example, Marcilhasy, *Le Diocèse d'Orléans sous l'épiscopat de Mgr Dupanloup 1848-1878* (1962), 340-472.

[2] See Barral, *op. cit.*, pp. 524-6.

[3] F. Rude, 'L'Arrondissement de Vienne en 1848' in *La Révolution de 1848 dans le département de l'Isère*, edited by E. Esmonine (1949), 417.

The conflict at Villeubanne which culminated in the expulsion of the curé in 1848 is of interest as an example of the greater polemical sophistication of anticlericalism near Lyon. In 1845 the municipal council went to the trouble of having printed a long *Reply to Abbé Deléon's latest libel*. Its aim was 'to reject the lying accusations with which you are trying to brand our commune'. The issues are familiar—municipal council's refusal to build a church, curé's misuse of funds of the parish council and so on. The curé claimed that he was generous to the local poor. The municipal council retorted: 'As for your generosity, if we admitted it as genuine it would be only a farthing set aside from the gold which you amass from our village—because for many years it has passed into proverb that your living is profitable. The lease is good we say, in our vulgar language, all the farmers going into it poor come out rich. Thus you can easily give to the poor the thousandth part of what you levy from all the inhabitants.' They denied the curé's accusations that he had been physically threatened. 'The era of martyrs has gone. But Tartuffes still exist. Permit us to correct your pious mistakes.' After refuting all the curé's claims, the pamphlet contained in its final paragraph a withering criticism of the 'style' in which priests all too often waged these local conflicts. 'We have finished, M. le curé, but, poor sinners that we are, we are unable when concluding to drape ourselves in the oh-so-noble, oh-so-Christian sentiments which you express at the end of your writing. The beginning of it was a slander, an outrage against the entire commune. The end, on the contrary, is full of evangelical unction. With hands crossed on your breast, eyes piously lowered to the ground, you take God as your witness that you are committing an act of violence by writing at all, that you feel loath to use phrases that may wound. We were profoundly moved, M. le curé, our eyes are filled with tears; we wanted to re-read your communication. We compared the beginning with the end—then all of a sudden, enlightened by sudden inspiration, we cried out, full of enthusiastic admiration: Oh Molière, you are the greatest of writers and Tartuffe is immortal.'[1]

Many of the communes in the area were given to bouts of anti-

[1] AN F.19 5812.

clericalism in the Second Empire. In 1857 Genas demanded the immediate removal of its curé 'who has not been capable of confining himself within the limits of his office'.[1] In St Priest, where the church, 'is on the point of collapse' and the curé's house 'is cracking in a manner very disturbing for the safety of the priest', the municipal council looked on with bored detachment and showed no willingness to contemplate repairs.[2]

Before discussing one or two of the more violent explosions in this region, perhaps the attitude of the church hierarchy ought to be discussed. Frequently the departmental authorities regretted that the bishop of Grenoble was so reluctant to comply with requests from mayors, municipal councils, village petitions, sub-prefects or even from the minister of the interior himself to move curés who had become involved in local conflicts.[3] Given that the prolongation of such disputes tended to empty churches, discredit religion itself among populations incapable of making a logical distinction between religion and its local representative, and to create a village tradition of hostility towards the clergy in general, it seems at first sight astonishing that the ecclesiastical authorities remained so obstinate. It is possible that one source of difficulty was simply a communication problem. Once a dispute had started the bishop's immediate sources of information were the priest himself, local sympathizers and local clergy—most frequently the curé or dean of the canton. Too often these were men too intimately involved in the dispute to give a balanced judgement—and too often the bishop made his decisions on information refracted through such a vision. On occasions the local dean would send in valuable reports giving advice on how to nip such disputes in the bud. In 1869 the dean of Bourg d'Oisans, for example, pointed out that many priests failed to adapt themselves

[1] AN F.19 5812, Prefect to Ministère des cultes 1857.
[2] ADI 52 M 38, Sub-prefect of Vienne, 26 May 1859.
[3] On occasions there was a strange variant on this. From Venrey in 1870 the *vicaire* wrote to the bishop begging him to move the curé who was well meaning but old and deaf. But a group of 'free thinkers, scourges of the district, buried in materialistic slime, want him to stay because his presence makes a mockery of religion'. Archives épiscopales de Grenoble (henceforth AEG), Vicaire of Venrey to Bishop.

to life in mountain parishes. M. Berlious in Clunis was stiff, un-bending and had accumulated many enemies. M. Giraud at Livet had let relations get so strained that it 'prevented him from doing all the good he wanted to do among the population'. In all he advised the bishop that it would be expedient to move seven priests to prevent a deterioration in the situation.[1] This was the type of information on administrative questions which the dio-cesan authority needed more often—and which, if acted on, could have deprived militant anticlericals of a large section of their audience. Such advice was received on occasions from other deans. For example, the dean of Bourgoin wrote to the bishop to urge him to move the curé of Chateauvillain, saying that although the specific charges against him—raising pew rents, slandering families from the pulpit—were not true, nevertheless the curé had made it obvious that he wanted a change of mayor and in conse-quence the clash could only get more violent unless the bishop intervened. But examples of such advice are very rare.[2]

The habitual response of the episcopal authorities was the very reverse of this. In part this firmness stemmed from the bishop's suspicion that all too many of the charges made against his priests were false. At Ornacieux the sub-prefect was finally forced to agree with the bishop that 'contrary to information received' the curé had not been guilty of the various irregularities alleged.[3] Again it would appear that the bishop was well aware that the easiest administrative course open to the departmental authorities faced with such disputes was to sacrifice the priest for the sake of peace and quiet in the locality. In Masson the mayor and municipal council exceeded their powers in control of the parish council. The bishop urged a prompt redress of grievances and then demanded the mayor's resignation because of his 'threats and violation of all rights.'[4] The sub-prefect recognized fully where the legal rights of the case lay but insisted that the mayor's dis-missal would be 'very badly interpreted in the neighbouring

---

[1] Parish Records of Bourg d'Oisans in AEG, 9 July 1869.
[2] Parish Records of Chateauvillain in AEG, May 1865.
[3] ADI IV 4 77, December 1870; AEG Parish Records of Ornacieux.
[4] ADI IV v 69, 2 June and 10 July 1870.

countryside and would be sufficient to arouse further conflicts between the curé and his parishioners—which would do little to facilitate his ministry'.[1] The mayor acted illegally but 'under the pressure of popular opinion'. In these circumstances was it 'opportune to instigate legislative measures against the offenders'? In face of an attitude which suggested that the anticlerical faction in the village had only to be the larger, the more vocal or the more influential in order to persuade the departmental authorities to turn a blind eye, then perhaps episcopal stubbornness in such a dispute can be understood. A further example may illustrate how complex such a decision could be for the episcopal authorities. In Oyties, where the curé was forcibly expelled in July 1866, there seems sufficient evidence from a variety of sources to suggest that his own character was very largely at fault.[2] A similar but less decisive riot had occurred four years previously in protest against the priest's interference in local elections. By 1865 the curé was claiming that his house was uninhabitable and that the municipal council ought to supply funds for its repair. The sub-prefect visited the parish to investigate the long-standing dispute and reported that the house was the 'finest and best maintained in the *arrondissement*' and complained to the prefect that the curé had ranted at him that no one was going to tell him how to behave, 'neither the mayor, the sub-prefect, the prefect nor Mgr the bishop himself'. On 2 July 1866 the village gave the curé a two-week ultimatum. He was forcibly prevented from conducting several masses and drunks burst into the church to disrupt those services he did hold. The sub-prefect blamed the bishop.[3] During the period before the expiry of the ultimatum he remarked: 'Let's hope that Monseigneur will finish by waking up; once this respite is over we must expect the consequences of the inactivity in which the episcopal administration has seen fit to take refuge'. The moral responsibility therefore for any violence lay with the bishop. After the expulsion the local *gendarmerie* noted that the inhabitants

---

[1] *Ibid.*, 19 August 1870.
[2] IV v 77 1287 7:0 AEG, Parish records of Oyties.
[3] Letter of 17 May 1866.

had at last made sure that justice was done. All would be well provided the curé stayed away.[1]

The reasoning behind the bishop's refusal to change the curé thus appears at first sight to contain little more than stubbornness. However, if one traces the dispute further back the motives of the departmental administration itself become rather dubious. In 1864 the sub-prefect had agreed in a letter to the prefect that the curé's demands were not altogether ill-founded, that the whole dispute rested on a clash of temperament between curé and mayor.[2] But the main consideration of the sub-prefect was not really with the rights of the particular case at issue but with questions of administrative convenience. 'M. Emerard, the mayor of Oyties, is a *conseiller d'arrondissement*, an influential man throughout the canton of Heyrieux. I am afraid that if we act too strictly with him he will resign as mayor—which would be highly regrettable since it would be extremely difficult to find anyone to succeed him. I really do not know which side to take to conciliate all interested parties. . . .' In the period between this letter and the expulsion of the curé the sub-prefect obviously decided that it was easier to snub the episcopal authorities than to risk offending a local notable and denied his original admission that the curé had a legitimate case. In these circumstances the curé's letter to the bishop complaining of illegible letters from the prefect, and banalities from the sub-prefect is not surprising. 'I now understand that those people (*ces gens-là*) have a very strange view of justice and common politeness.' The bishop himself as early as 1857 had described the 'deplorable and degrading condition of the curé's house. I have seen it myself and can assure you that there are no exaggerations.'[3] The original request for repairs had been made in 1847.

In such a case the curé himself was obviously far from blameless. Although five men were fined at the trial in Grenoble for the riot, the fines were very light because of the extreme violence of

[1] Letter to Prefect, 24 July 1866.

[2] Letter of Sub-prefect to Prefect, 4 October 1864, and AEG, 11 July 1866.

[3] Bishop to Prefect, 30 August 1857.

Abbé Meunier's behaviour in court. The *procureur général* washed his hands publicly of any future disorder should the curé return to the village.[1] Nevertheless, it seems undeniable that the departmental authorities were willing in such cases to connive at behaviour that was, strictly, illegal on the part of municipal administrators and local populations. The resistance by the episcopal authorities becomes more comprehensible. The wisdom of it is much more doubtful. A month before the final expulsion the dean of Heyrieux had begged the bishop to remove Meunier from Oyties where 'his perhaps excessive zeal stirs up almost continuous opposition'.[2] The bishop's laconic footnote on the letter is revealing: 'We cannot give way to riot'. This insistence on the necessity of firmness lies at the heart of episcopal response to all local disputes. As the dean of Heyrieux himself had advised the bishop when consulted about the Oyties situation four years earlier, 'In all cases of this sort, when these types have boasted that they will get rid of their curé, I think it is best to leave him at his post. Failing that we would all be exposed day in and day out to denunciations each more stupid than the last.'[3]

This policy of 'no surrender in the face of violence' and of 'wise firmness' was the standard response of the episcopal authorities to local disputes. Applied without flexibility, it could lead to the sort of long-standing conflict which bedevilled the local politics of Corbas, a small commune near Lyon which assumed proportions sufficient to attract *L'Univers* and other national clerical journals. Here there was a smouldering feud between the village and its curé, who started repair work on the old church, ignoring the municipal council's decision that what was needed was a church situated rather nearer the centre of the commune.[4] The mayor was determined and well supported. 'Except for a feeble minority . . . the mayor has won the support of almost all the local inhabitants. He is a sensible man, loyal to the government, and one who is in

[1] Parquet to Prefect, 31 August 1866.
[2] Dean of Heyrieux to Bishop, AEG, 19 June 1866.
[3] Dean to Bishop, 1862 (undated), AEG.
[4] (*a*) AN F.19 5812, (*b*) ADI 7:0:442, (*c*) ADI IV v 44, (*d*) AEG Parish records of Corbas.

no way prepared to submit to the tyranny of the curé', reported the sub-prefect.[1] Already in 1864 a petition from some seventy *pères de familles* had been sent to the prefect expressing resentment at the possible cost to the village of the curé's schemes.[2] The mayor simultaneously sent a letter of protest to the emperor himself which began by insisting on specific issues—that he, as mayor, had the right to approve all building schemes—but which broadened into something which can stand as a virtual manifesto of the viewpoint of local administrations vis-à-vis the clergy in these decades. Why, he asked, was the departmental authority so slow in seeing that justice was done: 'Perhaps no one attributed any importance to a dispute which was boiling up unnoticed in a tiny commune? Or was it not rather that, since it was a curé who was at the root of all the trouble, no one wished to come into conflict with the bishop? I cannot positively affirm anything, but I attribute the hesitation which has been shown in this case to this second factor. I am not quite certain why it should be so—perhaps they are afraid of the influence of the clergy in the event of some political upheaval or other. Your Majesty, this is not the first time that I have noticed such hesitation in legal cases in which a priest is involved. Everyone seems scared to cross the diocesan authority even in the person of one of its lowliest members. I am not afraid of bringing this matter to your Majesty's attention: this way of going about things loses you many supporters. Much too much tolerance is shown to the *parti clérical* which would like to dominate and rule everything. The people fear this domination, which is the most humiliating of all, and one against which no resistance can ever be too strong. It is a domination to which I intend to submit neither as individual nor as mayor. From this latter viewpoint no administration would any longer be possible. I would prefer to resign rather than be incapable of making the authority which has been given me respected. Furthermore this antagonism exists in many communes in Isère. There is a perpetual war between mayor and curé and it is almost always the latter who is

---

[1] AN F.19 5812.
[2] ADI 7:0:442, Petition to Prefect, 26 July 1864.

"right" because the bishop does not care to admit that any of his priests can be in the wrong.'[1]

The case was taken to court in Vienne, where it was judged that the curé had exceeded his powers and that the work ought to be demolished. The court decision was the signal for the release of pent-up hostility. While the curé barricaded himself in the church with a handful of pious women and threw stones at the demolition workers; these, supported by a large crowd of villagers proceeded to smash the windows with ladders and to knock the roof off.

Predictably relations became even more strained. The curé refused to baptize children of the mayor's supporters. The attitude of the episcopal authorities was at once transformed. Two years before the 'riot', the sub-prefect had implored the bishop to tell the curé to be more restrained. The bishop had been prepared to be conciliatory to the extent of urging the curé to drop a just but inexpedient claim for a lodging allowance, warning him against regarding the church and the cemetery as his personal possessions and reprimanding him for writing direct to the minister of *Cultes*.[2] But the bishop stressed that, despite the curé's flouting of a valid court decision, the 'riot' was a crime, a revolutionary act which cancelled out any errors the curé might have made. He shrugged off the prefect's suggestion that the 'riot' was 'in some small way linked with the illegal rebuilding'. Although claiming that 'I have made myself a rule never to demand the dismissal of a mayor, whatever type of man he may be', he did try to secure the mayor's resignation.[3] He withdrew the curé but refused to send another

---

[1] ADI 7:0:442, Petition of mayor of Corbas to Napoleon III, August 1864.

[2] ADI 7:0:442, Bishop to Prefect, 22 February 1866, 19 March 1866, 17 May 1866.

[3] ADI IV v 44, Prefect to Minister, 20 February 1869, Bishop to Prefect, 17 February 1869, AEG Minister of Interior to Prefect, 5 March 1867. The reaction of the ministry to this idea is very interesting in view of the light it sheds on the government's awareness of the strength of anticlericalism in France in the 1860s. 'Though it may be desirable to do something conciliatory and impartial in the commune of Corbas in punishing all the guilty parties, it would be inexpedient from another point of view to strike down a mayor who replied with an irregular action to even more

until such time as the mayor and commune apologized collectively for the 'crime'. He hoped to make use of this device to turn the village against a mayor responsible for creating a *pays sans prêtre*, thus following the advice of a local clerical. He insisted that he was being lenient in not using his legal right of excommunication. When worship was finally restored in 1869 he insisted that the same curé should return there and that the commune should restore the old church to its pristine condition for occasional use for burials, despite the fact that the new church had been completed.[1] Not surprisingly the village protested at the expense involved in this, insisting that no other commune of that size had to keep up two churches.[2] The curé aggravated the situation further by starting to construct a belltower (despite further court injunctions) and by saying that the bishop was using the chapel to 'punish' them for 'having committed an outrage against public worship'.[3]

Consequently by July 1871 the sub-prefect was reporting that, despite a new mayor, feelings in the commune were again running high. He had consulted with a local mayor, 'a conservative . . .

irregular behaviour by the curé. Indeed the press is proving wide-awake these days in picking up the slightest event of this type. The *Siècle* and the *Opinion Nationale* make themselves the daily mouthpieces of complaints against the clergy and these two newspapers would have eagerly seized the opportunity to attempt to win over to their side all the mayors and all the municipal councils of all the communes in the Empire by pointing out that the central government was abandoning its officials in cases where they had right on their side. Our electoral position could suffer seriously from a discussion carried out on these terms.' Nevertheless, the minister's earlier spontaneous reaction to the dispute tends to confirm some of the fears expressed by the mayor of Corbas in his petition to the emperor. The riot, said the minister, 'will have caused displeasure among the clergy in the diocese of such a nature as to deprive you of its support in the next legislative election. Faced with numerous difficulties which you can foresee, and also by the increasing efforts made by the democratic party it is necessary to humour the susceptibilities of the section of the conservative party which obeys the lead given by the clergy.' Minister of Interior to Prefect, 22 March 1867.

[1] ADI IV v 44, Bishop to Prefect, 19 October 1871.
[2] ADI IV v 44, Sub-prefect to Prefect, 7 September 1871.
[3] ADI IV v 44, Sub-prefect to Prefect, 30 September 1871.

very little given to supporting the views of the mayor of Corbas, who admitted that the curé used the old chapel more than the new. This mayor had consulted with 'several very moderate local men' who were fully determined that if the old church were to be used it should be as a communal school. From personal visits the sub-prefect insisted that 'two-thirds of the inhabitants are supporters of the mayor, and most want to demolish the old chapel'. Reports from the *gendarmerie* insisted that the curé was widening the gulf by slandering the morals of some of the girls in the commune, insulting the lay *instituteur*, and claiming that 'blood ought to be spilt to wash away the curse which has been hurled at the parish'. In conclusion the sub-prefect stressed that there was an obvious need for a new curé 'less compromised, less violent'. Only then might the commune be willing to accept the bishop's decision to continue to make use of the old church. 'If you bring these facts to the attention of Monseigneur explain to him fully that I have no intention of harming a churchman. You know that I am not anti-Christian. My brother is a bishop and I cannot be accused of hostility to the clergy. I am merely doing my job. I am convinced that the present curé of Corbas cannot be useful to the cause of religion.'[1]

The episcopal authorities remained adamant. In 1873 the dispute was still smouldering. Why did successive bishops—Ginoulhiac was replaced by Paulinier in 1870—risk provoking further anticlerical outbursts by this type of uncompromising stand? One might suggest that they were convinced that an innocent priest was being victimized were it not for several clear indications to the contrary. The curé of St Jean de Bornay described the curé of Corbas as a 'quarrelsome muddler', and another curé said in 1868 that the bishop was making a mistake by not being conciliatory—the new church was sufficient reparation for the damage to the old.[2] It was unreasonable to expect an apology: 'Such an act of humility is inconceivable on their part. In all that happened at Corbas none of the protagonists ever had the intention of insulting religion or the religious authorities. They were merely

[1] ADI IV v 44, 25 December 1871.
[2] ADI IV v 44, Prefect to Minister 20 February 1869.

annoyed at the behaviour of one priest.'[1] On the bottom of a letter received by the bishop in 1871 he scrawled that the curé was 'very cunning but neither "prudent, frank or honest".'[2] Yet this was never admitted in public correspondence—indeed here he was allowed to have 'an impressionable and sensitive mind'.[3] The starting-point of the episcopal attitude to the case lay very close to that of the proclerical minority on the Corbas parish council and to that of the dean of St Symphorien—that the mayor's rule was a 'horrible tyranny', aiming at 'blatant hostility' to the Catholic religion, that the commune was divided into 'agitators' and 'honest Christian families'.[4] The commune was 'a miniature 1793 and getting worse'. Thus the riot of 1866 was an 'illegal and revolutionary act', a 'crime' which nullified all irregularities of the curé, past, present or future. Though one must admit that the mayor, by his own admission, was 'professionally anticlerical' and that there was a degree of both administrative and political expediency in the attitude of the departmental authorities and of the ministry, it appears undeniable that in such cases episcopal overreaction in defence of 'religion and public morality' was self-defeating.

One other aspect of the reaction of the clergy and of the episcopal administration to criticism needs to be stressed. In a report on the dispute at Corbas, in July 1871, the sub-prefect of Vienne reported that similar conflicts existed in neighbouring communes such as St Sorlin, St Alban les Roches, Les Roches.[5] Much of the trouble came from curés who poured oil on the flames by violent language. 'They treat peaceable republicans as though they were *communards*.' During the Second Empire the episcopal administration used 'men of 1848' as their bogey. At Brezins, where the curé wanted to build a new church and raised pew rents to help

---

[1] AEG Curé of Marennes 1868 (undated).

[2] AEG October 1871.

[3] AEG Bishop to *Procureur-général*, 25 November 1866.

[4] AEG Bishop to *Procureur-général*, 25 November 1866; Dean of St Symphorien to Bishop, November 1867. ADI 7:0:442 Parish council to Bishop, 18 August 1866 and 31 July 1868.

[5] AEG Sub-prefect of Vienne to Prefect, 8 July 1871.

pay for it, the bishop was prepared to conciliate the anti-curé faction by limiting the new building to being an auxiliary chapel until it was reported to him that the villagers had marched on the new building hurling insults and singing the *Marseillaise* and other revolutionary songs and that the centre of opposition was a café which served as a republican nucleus in 1848.[1] At Veyrins the minister and the prefect agreed that the bishop ought to move the curé who constantly attacked the new municipal council against whose election he had campaigned from the pulpit.[2] The bishop refused to comply with this request for the curé had informed him that the municipal council was made up of 'revolutionary rabble, affiliated to secret societies' and had warned him that if the commune succeeded in having him disciplined 'What a triumph for the enemies of the clergy, since all that needs to be done is to accuse them and brand them as guilty'.[3] 'It would be easier for me to deal with Russians or Turks than with my beloved parishioners. . . . I have against me only those who are hostile to religion. Persecution by types such as these is glorious rather than humiliating.' Eventually in 1867 the bishop was prevailed upon to end the conflict by moving the priest. The municipal council had insisted that they were the representatives of universal suffrage and that the curé was a legitimist who had maintained that he would 'never bow down his head to the tricolour'. In this case the bishop finally admitted that 'now more than ever priests ought to be reserved in their comments on universal suffrage'.[4] This was a rule which the episcopal authority would have done well to have urged much more forcibly on its clergy.

A final source of irritation between local populations and their clergy was the puritanical condemnation of dances, wine shops, festivals, amusements of all kinds—perhaps an expression of the last vestiges of Jansenism? For many clergy the local *cabaret* was

---

[1] ADI IV v 33, Prefect to Minister of *Cultes*, 3 May 1860.

[2] ADI IV v 19, Minister to Prefect, 26 April 1867. Municipal Council to Minister of Justice, reported by Sub-prefect to Prefect, 8 February 1866. Minister of Justice to Bishop, 28 October 1865.

[3] AEG Curé to Bishop, 26 November 1865.

[4] AEG Bishop to Prefect, December 1866.

at one and the same time a 'talking shop' and a platform for agitators, and a rival centre of attraction on Sundays when the population should have been at mass. From Moidieu the curé triumphantly sent to the vicar-general the 'confessions' of a 'wretched old reprobate of ninety-two' who stated that the curé was right to preach against dancing and against wine shops, for these latter were centres of 'conspiracy against public order and against religion' where many in the village, including the mayor, spent their Sundays.[1] From Cordian, near Lyon, the priest protested to the prefect against a population that spent 'the larger part of its days and nights in wine shops and cafés. You were asking, *M. le Prèfet*, what do the representatives of the civil authority do? Alas, *M. le Préfet*, I must complain that they behave like the others.'[2] At Goncelin in July 1857 the curé tried to get the local *'fête baladoire'* prohibited.[3] At Oyties (see above, p. 185) one of the reasons for the curé's unpopularity was his attitude to such matters. The local curé of Heyrieux backed him up.[4] There would always be excessive dancing: 'We cannot abolish totally the inveterate scandals of our countryside but we ought to be allowed to fight against them, and *above all not to approve of them*'. At La Ferrière the curé slandered the character of women who wore crinolines.[5] At Villemoirieu the curé wrote urging the bishop to give financial support to the school run by the nuns, the only civilizing force among a 'wild, coarse' population. Should the school disappear, 'this hamlet will become worse than ever: the great majority no longer go to mass. They work all day Sunday. They spend their evenings in *cabarets* feeding themselves on the devilish doctrines of evil newspapers and listening to scurrilous attacks on religion and its priests.'

Such trivial, yet passionate and commonplace conflicts were the daily background from which militant anticlericalism on issues such as the schools question was to emerge.

[1] AEG 29 September 1854.
[2] ADI 52 M 35, 2 January 1857.
[3] ADI 52 M 35, July 1857.
[4] AEG Curé of Heyrieux to Bishop, 1862.
[5] ADI IV v 52, J.P., to Prefect, 12 November 1867.

III. *Anticlericalism and the School Question in Isère 1852-70.*
On 30 March 1848, forty-five *instituteurs* from Isère met in some
school premises in Vienne. They declared the 'phalange' of
schoolteachers to be the avant-garde of civilization and called for
one of their number to stand in the next legislative elections, not
merely to advocate the cause of education but:

1. to bear witness to the contempt and indignation they felt for
   the scandalous and tyrannical obstacles which the '*coterie
   jésuitique*' had raised against them;
2. to demand prompt and genuine suppression of all the religious
   teaching orders, both of men and of women;
3. to call for the complete independence of the teaching body
   from all religious authority and to insist that education administration and inspection be placed entirely in the hands of
   teachers.[1]

Here was a lay programme thirty years before Ferry: a striking
testimony to the resentment felt by the teachers of the Isère at the
spread of congregational education and at the supervisory powers
allowed to the clergy by the law of 1833. But for 'laicity' it proved
a false dawn. Carnot's projects for the suppression of the 'letter
of obedience', which allowed those in religious orders to teach
merely by virtue of presentation of a letter from their superiors,
for free compulsory education, for public libraries, higher teaching salaries—all fiercely denounced by the clerical press in the
Isère[2]—were the victims of the Second Republic's rightward
swing after the June Days.

Instituteurs had been not infrequent participants in the outbursts
of anticlericalism in the Isère in the early months of the republic.
With political reaction came systematic reprisals by local notables
and clergy against *instituteurs* who had shown too overt a taste for
suspect newspapers, expressed too vocal a disdain for the Church.
In Morette, for example, the *instituteur* had taken his chance in

---

[1] ADI 2 J 59.
[2] *L'Union Dauphinoise*, 4 July 1848 and 6 July 1848. For Carnot's educational reforms see P. Carnot, *Hippolyte Carnot et le ministère de l'instruction
publique de la deuxième république* (1948).

February to settle old grievances by inciting the commune against the curé.[1] By late 1848, labelled a 'red' he had been ousted by curé and municipal council. The March 30th meeting, a gesture of collective professional solidarity by the lay teachers of the department was nullified by the events which followed. Isolated in his village, subject to the pressure of local notables, cut off by salary from the middle class and by education from the peasantry, the *instituteur* was a prey to retaliatory persecution, encouraged by successive government measures—the *petite loi* of January 1850, the loi Falloux, the imperial decree of 1852 giving prefects wider powers. (The republican *Patriote des Alpes*, soon to be suppressed, tried to oppose the *petite loi* by setting up an '*Association pour la conservation des écoles laïques*' and by drawing attention to the plight of the *instituteurs* subject to clerical pressure.)

The example of Morette was typical of many communes in the Isère. The price paid for the momentary gestures of radicalism or anticlericalism was the systematic administrative 'purification' of 1850-53 carried out with such efficiency that, for the remainder of the Empire, reports on the political conduct of the purged teaching corps were to indicate an almost unanimous loyalty to the government. In 1848 only three *instituteurs* were dismissed or suspended, in 1849, six—only two described as 'political'.[2] In 1850 the figure rose to forty-five, of which thirty-five were specifically 'political' or for reasons of 'irreligion' or conflict with the curé. In 1851, thirteen were disciplined, one explicitly for hostility to the curé at Roche Tuir but several for '*inconduite*', '*mauvais principes*', irreligion, and similar vague charges. In 1852 nineteen were disciplined, in 1853 eleven.[3] By 1852 they had been cowed. None was reported as voting against the plebiscite. Thereafter only the occasional *instituteur* had to be weeded out for social, political, or religious subversion. This forcible weaning from militant republican anticlericalism did not imply any improvement of relations with the clergy in the Isère. Rather,

[1] ADI T.364.
[2] See, for example, ADI T.14, 17, 27, 29, 38, 361, 364.
[3] AN F.19 5812, ADI T.364.

hostility to clerical influences in education had to be muted for fear of government reprisal. It was deprived of outlet other than in factional struggles at communal level. Only when the Italian question forced the imperial government to give its attention to the clerical viper which the loi Falloux had nurtured in its breast did the laic sympathies of Rouland and Duruy allow an explicit anticlerical attitude.

The persecutions of radical *instituteurs* did not pass without indications of popular unrest. The Inspector Mathieu noted on 19 January 1850, 'To strike them down might perhaps be an unwise action which would sow unrest in the communes where they work and there the majority of them are protected by the sympathy of the population'.

The advantages given to the Church at the departmental level by the loi Falloux are too familiar to require more than a brief outline here. They included most notably, the place given to the bishop on the departmental council, the retention of curé-mayor supervision in the commune, the recognition of the '*lettre d'obéd-ience*', the choice between academic and congregational lists allowed to communes, the exemption of congregational schools from pedagogic inspection by laymen. The insistence that all communes of 800 people (Art. 51) should have a communal school for girls was to be a further provision which accelerated the expansion of congregational education in the Isère. This said, however, one must beware of emphasizing too strongly the subservience of imperial education policy to the Church, however strongly Thiers may have insisted that the purpose of the 1850 act was the subordination to the clergy of the '36,000 anti-curés, frightful little village orators'.

In the first place, the decree of 9 March 1852 and the law of June 1854 readjusted the balance of 1850. In the *conseil supérieur* the elective aspects of the 1850 law were suppressed and two *inspecteurs généraux* created to make the minister's weight felt in primary education. Surveillance of primary education was transferred to the prefects who, through *inspecteurs d'académie*, could nominate and change *instituteurs* and so on—hence the complaints by militant ecclesiastics such as the bishop of Montreuil that the prefects not the Church were confiscating powers once held by the *université*.

The avowed aim of Falloux was to moralise 'education too cut off from religion'. Hence the supervision by the curé, the emphasis on scripture and catechism at the expense of history, the insistence that the *instituteur* should be and be seen to be a Christian and should take his pupils to church. The ideal teacher in Fortoul's 1852 circular did not wear a beard, 'symbol of anarchy', avoided 'political clubs and cafés' and was full of respect for authority. The ideal *école normale* produced not intellectually advanced, but '*sages instituteurs*' who could teach the catechism as well as arithmetic. Such an ideal seems to have been scarce in the Isère. In 1855 Inspector Richard lamented that 'the great art of moulding the heart at the same time as the mind is understood and practised to its full extent only by a very small number of lay schoolmasters and mistresses'. In a report of the same year the *inspector d'académie* wrote, 'good social relations existing between priests and schoolteachers can do nothing but consolidate the calming down of men's minds and the moral future of the country.[1] Alas among the majority of them there is insufficient feeling of Christian resignation towards the difficulties of their position.' Inspector Chateauneuf lamented that 'the religious devotions of the majority of schoolteachers are limited to an occasional prudent appearance at church'.[2] As will be seen below it was the contrasting emphasis stressed by lay and congregational education that caused many of the local disputes in the department.

If the majority of the *instituteurs* were to prove unwilling to play the role of passive moralizers to the rural masses, the higher echelons of the educational establishment in the Isère were themselves never as devoted as a Montalembert might have wished to the cause of clerical control of education. From 1859 onwards the Isère had in Massy a prefect little disposed to aid the congregations' 'invasion' of primary education, who had lost his previous post in Lourdes for determined opposition to the Lourdes

[1] ADI T.17.
[2] ADI T.14.

'miracles'.[1] The departmental council played its part in the dis-
ciplining of radical *instituteurs* in 1850-53, but during the Empire
came under the control of the *inspecteur d'académie* and of his
inspecteurs primaires—often extremely critical of the intellectual
level of congregational education. Both Cresp, the *inspecteur
primaire* of St Marcellin for thirteen years, and Habans of la Tour
du Pin won a reputation with the local sub-prefect for indulgence
to lay *instituteurs* and bitter hostility to congregational education.
'I have had the chance to see yet again on my recent tour of the
communes that the primary school inspector's attitude scarcely
improves. He shows himself much too openly hostile to the
clergy, preaches to the *instituteurs* that they ought to be independent and gets them to mistrust the administration,' reported the
sub-prefect of la Tour du Pin about Habans in October 1862.[2]

Although the *inspecteur primaire* of the Isère had complained
in 1847 of the 'invasion of public education by the religious
teaching orders', neither the régime nor the department was too
favourable to their expansion in the 1840s.[3] The freedom allowed
by Article 31 of the loi Falloux to communes to choose congregational education, and the recognition of sixteen teaching orders
as '*établissments d'utilité publique*' cleared the way for their rapid
growth in the Isère. In 1848 there were thirty boys' public schools
in congregational hands. By 1860 the figure was seventy-one.[4] In
1861 the sub-prefect of St Marcellin insisted with some plausibility
that 'the clergy is moving towards the complete absorption of all
primary education on behalf of the teaching orders. In the communes where the schools are still in the hands of lay schoolteachers
the clergy busy themselves obtaining favourable circumstances
for the setting up of church schools. If we are not very careful
this movement will continue imperceptibly everywhere and lay
education will, in practice, be annihilated.'[5]

The expansion was most striking in girls' education. In 1852

---

[1] J. Maurain, *La Politique ecclésiastique du Second Empire* (1930), 233.
[2] ADI 11 N 32.
[3] ADI 52 M 44.
[4] ADI T.167, 168.
[5] ADI 52 M 43, 14 November 1861.

there were 160 lay *écoles publiques de filles* and 116 congregational. By 1860 there were 226 lay *écoles publiques* and 179 congregational. In addition there were 110 lay private schools and sixty-four congregational. 336 lay schools taught 14,000 girls; 243 congregational schools taught 17,000.[1]

It must not be assumed that every establishment of a congregational school provoked the resentment of local populations, lay *instituteurs* or departmental authorities. The more militant anticlericals among the *instituteurs* had been purged. The imperial authorities in the early 1850s were anxious to keep on friendly terms with the Church. The congregations themselves may well have lacked the personnel to make a frontal attack on all communes and tended to withdraw in cases where their projected arrival was arousing hostility. Financially harassed municipal authorities welcomed the arrival of congregations supporting themselves from pious legacies of legitimist or bourgeois notables anxious to see mass education in safe hands. On occasions, as in Pont de Beauvoisin, the curé was also able and willing to pay the *frères'* modest salaries from his own pocket.[2]

The substitution of nuns for lay *institutrices* rarely produced local resentment. Intelligent, unmarried, independent lay *institutrices* scarcely harmonized with rural conceptions of woman's role in society. The nuns, coming in groups of three, made themselves part of village life, looking after the curé's washing (as at Montfalcon)[3] or tending the sick (as at La Combe des Eparres),[4] or keeping kindergartens for younger children. The Isère lacked an efficient *école normale* for *institutrices* whilst a leading family of the department, Murinais, had founded an *école stagière* for nuns of Notre Dame de la Croix. However by the late 1850s the communes were beginning to resent the hold of the congregations on girls' education. Habans' reports frequently expressed dissatisfaction that the 1850 law allowed no powers of pedagogic inspection, resentment at the fact that barely one-fifth of the *directrices*

[1] ADI T.8, 14, 358.
[2] ADI IV v 84.
[3] ADI T.447.
[4] ADI T.447.

had diplomas, distaste for excessive concentration on the cate-chism and religious studies.[1] The Italian question brought Rouland round to a similar way of thinking. His circular of 11 May 1860, founded on the suspicion that the congregational schools might be teaching legitimist or ultramontane ideas, gave the *inspecteur primaire* a measure of control over congregational schools and examinations. The staunch Bonapartism of the majority of the lay teachers in the 1860s, contrasting strongly with the ultramontane leanings of the clergy, helped redress the balance of 1850.

The lay *instituteur* merged more easily into village life than his female counterpart. Frequently he supplemented his income by acting as secretary to the mayor, helping peasants with their accounts, or measuring fields. On the many occasions when the curé's conduct had divided the commune into rival factions the *instituteurs* sided almost without exception against the curé. The *inspecteur d'académie* commented in 1856: 'The relations of *instituteurs* with mayors are better than their relations with curés. They know by bitter experience that in conflicts that arise between communal and religious authorities it is the former which usually come out on top. The *instituteur* thus chooses the stronger side.' He added, 'The *instituteurs* do not always have the necessary deference and respect for the curés. In some rural communes they align themselves alongside the large number which shows neither veneration for the priest's office nor sympathy for his person. It is not rare in this department to see the curés the target of slanders as soon as someone gets it in mind to attack them. Petitions con-taining odious accusations are hawked around covered in signa-tures—and the *instituteurs* do not remain aloof from these goings on.'[2]

But it was not simply in order to side with the dominant factions in local politics that so many *instituteurs* in the Isère became involved in bitter struggles with the curés towards the end of the 1850s. Perhaps for many mayors the roots of opposition to the

[1] ADI T.14.
[2] AN F.17. 10. 779.

congregational school may have been an *anticlericalisme de clocher*, a still bitter memory of recent conflicts over church repairs or the site of a graveyard. But for many lay *instituteurs* the struggle appeared to be one for the very survival of lay education. The congregations in many cases appeared to have raised their target to complete annihilation of lay education even in communes where the lay school was popular, efficient, and sufficient for local needs. From the resistance of local populations to calculated clerical attempts to undermine lay *instituteurs'* positions sprang a wave of local anticlericalism in the Isère in the 1860s. As will be seen later, the hostility to congregational education was to find its most lucid ideological expression in the larger industrial *bourgs* such as Tullins, Voirin and Vienne, among militant republicans influenced by the wave of laicisation in Lyon in 1870-73, in the foundation in the Isère of branches of Macé's *Ligue de l'enseignement* or in the pages of the radical *Réveil du Dauphiné* in 1870.[1] What is perhaps more important is the way rural populations in the Isère, not basically hostile to clerical education, were antagonized by the congregations' attempts to destroy existing lay schools. Later in the decade, they also came to resent clerical resistance to widely approved reforms suggested by Duruy. This reaction was not limited to traditionally republican areas—resentment at clerical pretensions in the educational field was marked also in rural 'Catholic' areas.

The degree to which the struggle between lay school and congregational 'invasion' could dominate local politics is well illustrated by the case of La Buisse. In December 1863, the mayor wrote to the *inspecteur primaire* complaining of the curé's refusal to participate in drawing up a list of 'free pupils' for the communal school and of the 'continuous agitation of the curé who has never stopped attacking my administration'.

By 1865 the curé had made a more determined assault on the lay school by soliciting the donation of property and 1600 francs per year from a local legitimist lady, the comtesse de Michalon, in order to set up a congregational school to 'save the area from the

[1] See, for example, Gontard, *'Une bataille scolaire au XIXe siècle'*, in *Cahiers d'histoire* (1958), Vol. 3.

devil', and then by denouncing in the pulpit the municipal council's refusal of the offer. The municipal council wrote to the prefect that this had been 'announced very pompously to over-throw the municipal council'. The prefect was also informed that 'Disorder continues . . . could it be otherwise when it is widely known that the curé only induced Madame de Michalon to make this donation to get rid of the *instituteur*. But he is so well liked by his pupils and so sympathetic to their families that despite the fact that the congregational school is free he has kept many more pupils than his competitors. Providence, *M. Le Prefect*, never blesses works born amid passion and lies.'

In the following year the municipal council renewed their correspondence with the prefect to defend the lay *instituteur* from slanders which the curé sent to the school inspectors. Already, they insisted, enquiries by the justice of the peace and by the prefect himself 'have clearly shown the innocence of the *instituteur* despite the defamation of his character by the curé from the pulpit and elsewhere. In short, the Brothers were invented to get rid of the *instituteur* and of the mayor with him.' In La Buisse, as in so many communes, the *instituteur* acted as the mayor's secretary. The municipal council went on to describe the curé's attitude as one of trying 'to rule us like a new court of the Inquisition. Already the majority of people in villages no longer go to church on account of the sermons they hear there.'

According to the municipal council the Brothers were not themselves disliked by the populations of the communes, 'but they have become unpopular because they were imposed on us after denunciations and defamations, all the proof of which you have in your hands'.

However, a petition signed by over two hundred *pères de famille* in 1866 struck a more positively anticlerical note.[1] After saying that in their opinion the 'free school' had been founded specifically 'to endanger the communal school from which our children draw a firmly based education' and describing the zeal, devotion and popularity of the lay *instituteur*, M. Baudet, and the

---

[1] ADI 7:0:244, 1866 (undated).

success of his adult evening classes which attracted audiences of upward of sixty in a population of 1200, the signatories concluded that all this 'bears loud witness to the fact that our district will only live with lay education, and that all pressure which might end in turning it away from this would only produce bad effects'. They feared that the fact that the new school was free would cause the authorities to withdraw the lay *instituteur* but insisted that nothing could induce them to send their children to a religious school: 'in the event of lay education being withdrawn from our commune . . . we will see ourselves forced to send our children to be taught outside the commune, which would involve us in heavy cost'. They ended by pleading to the minister 'to maintain lay education in our commune, as the only type which is suited to the needs of our younger generation'.

The struggle, however, had scarcely started. The *procureur général* reported that the curé was refusing first communion to pupils from the lay school. The 'incessant conflict' between the two groups of partisans, each seeking to 'destroy the other's establishment', made local administration difficult. The mayor protested that the pupils of the lay school were being discriminated against by being placed in the side aisles of the church. The curé protested that the *instituteur* allowed his pupils to shout offensive remarks outside the congregational school—and a retaliatory petition of 125 signatures informed the authorities that the curé was hostile to the Republic. Madame de Michalon stepped up her campaign by a further sizeable donation to the congregational school.

The question arises as to the extent to which this type of campaign received the backing of the episcopal authorities. Mlle Marcilhasy has shown that the 'liberal' Dupanloup undertook a positive campaign to oust lay education in his Orléans diocese.[1] There is no evidence at hand for Isère to suggest that Ginoulhiac went to these lengths. However, in La Buisse he gave tacit support to the assault on the lay school by a blunt refusal of the *justice de paix's* request to change the curé and replace him by a

[1] C. Marcilhasy, *Le Diocèse d'Orléans sous l'épiscopat de Mgr Dupanloup* (1964), Ch. VII.

man of 'less violent character[1]'. Any accusations such as the twenty-four page dossier which the municipal council sent to the prefect against the curé were 'manifestly false', and the mayor put himself beyond the pale, said the bishop, when he said there was a 'powerful influence' stopping the course of justice and that before 'this type of criminal (that is, a priest) justice was disarmed'.

Of greater interest is a letter addressed to the bishop's vicar-general from a M. Morel in Vizille, which described a meeting of more than one hundred legitimists in his brother's house and continued: 'If we can keep together in the next local election we hope to get the municipal council kicked out by a handful of votes. . . . It is said that the lay *instituteur* works very hard and that his pupils make much better progress than those of the Brothers. . . . I have spoken to Brother Philomène, their superior in Grenoble, about this but he tends to treat all criticism as slander. At the same time the headmaster of the congregational school is in Madame de Michalon's pocket so the evil is difficult to remedy. Nevertheless the *great aim* of the *parti noir*, its principal basis for hope of a future triumph, lies in demonstrating to the country the undeniable advantage of having a free con-gregational school founded in the communes. Therefore the tactics in La Buisse should be to demonstrate to the population that the behaviour of the mayor and the laic faction might deprive them of Madame de Michalon's donation in the hope that this financial blackmail might lose the mayor votes in the election. At present it is the intellectual weakness of the Brothers which gives the mayor an excuse for resisting the establishment of the congregational school as the communal school.'[2] The suspicions of the supporters of lay education about a 'clerical plot' were obviously not totally unfounded.

The lay *instituteur* of La Buisse was fortunate to find a large enough body of militant lay support to offset the financial advan-tages of the clericals and the pulpit violence of the curé. In Péage-de-Roussillon the young *instituteur* was less fortunate in

[1] ADI 7:0:244 (1) 18 November 1868, Prefect to Minister of Interior; (2) Bishop to Prefect, 24 October 1868.
[2] AEG 28 November 1867.

his struggle against curé, congregation, and local notables. After some four years of conflict he was forced to leave in 1863. The tactics employed by the clerical party were even more ruthless. In July 1860 in a letter to the *Inspecteur Primaire* he complained bitterly of the curé's methods which included household visits to mothers of pupils at the lay school, threats that such pupils would not be given first communion, insistence that pupils should go to the Brothers for confession, pulpit defamations of the *instituteur*. The curé and the Brothers were free to 'go into the houses and exercise their "divine" influence on the mothers'. By contrast, the influence of the *instituteur* was 'very limited. . . . Nowhere is one as isolated as I am here. These poor inhabitants of Péage, who nevertheless flatter themselves that they are in tune with modern ideas, are so much dominated by the threat "if your child goes to the communal school he won't get his first communion" that it is truly preaching in the desert to assure them the contrary.' The *inspecteur primaire* confirmed in his April 1862 report that, 'the communal authorities and above all the curé are using all possible means to destroy the school'. The *instituteur* stressed that the opposition was backed by the substantial landowners of the area. 'The ten or twelve large landowners or merchants keep the bakers, wheelwrights, etc., under with a rod of iron and if these latter do not comply with the slightest whims of these gentlemen then it is goodbye to their business. We would have the larger proportion of the people on our side but they are tied to these gentry by links which are too delicate for them to attempt to break them so soon.'

The *instituteur*—described by the *inspecteur primaire* of Vienne as 'both able and full of enthusiasm'—insisted throughout that he had no personal animosity towards the curé 'but merely the enthusiasm I feel to make lay education triumph'.[1] By 1863 the pressure of landowners and clergy, despite the wishes of most of the local population, forced the lay school to shut.

In St Jean de Bournay similar pressures were exerted but came up against more determined resistance.[2] The mayor backed the

[1] Report of 15 April 1860.
[2] ADI T.451. AEG Parish records of St Jean de Bournay.

opponents of the local congregations and the conflict, spread over more than a decade, polarized communal politics into two factions over these issues. In May 1856 the curé wrote to complain to the *inspecteur d'académie* about the relegation of the hitherto communal school run by *Frères de la Doctrine Chrétienne* to the status of mere *école libre* while the new communal school was lay. 'Since the partisan mentality which splits this commune has filtered down into the two schools, and since it is that which has inspired this change, I have become a mere spectator of the state of conflict which has just been set up around the boys' school. The essentially religious nature of our population will disappear under the influence of these various lay schools.'

The atmosphere in the commune was not improved in 1858 when, as the prefect protested to the bishop, 'the curés of Charantonnay, Calin, St Agnin, Châtonnay, together with the curé of St Jean . . . contested not only in public but from the pulpit the official candidate' in the elections for the *conseil général*.[1] The bishop replied that these priests had merely voted for a man who was devoted to the government but also 'a friend of religion and of the clergy, whereas they considered the official candidate to be hostile to themselves'. The priests had been booed and cat-called as they made their way to vote and greeted by cries of '*à bas la calotte*' and '*à bas la soutane*' from cafés as they left. The bishop quoted a letter from a handful of local Catholics who blame the disturbance and the protest to the prefect on 'a number of men who for many years have taken on themselves the task of disrupting the peace of the district'—even threatening to bring in a Protestant preacher! In July 1856 the *instituteur* asked for permission to start the next scholastic year earlier to try to prevent the attempt of the congregational school to attract away all his remaining pupils. In 1859 the curé was protesting to the bishop about numerous street fights in the commune between pupils of the two schools which, he claimed, the *instituteur* encouraged.

In 1860 the chaplain of the local Ursuline convent addressed a letter to the empress claiming that in 1854 the mayor had asked

[1] AN F.19 5605, July 1858. Also AEG Correspondence of Prefects and Bishop in St Jean de Bournay parish records.

them to build a sort of kindergarten for the very young children and that now he refused to pay the agreed sum for this. Simultaneously the pro-clerical *délégué cantonal* wrote to the departmental authorities, 'the *Frères de la Doctrine Chrétienne*, after all sorts of local disputes, have seen themselves forced to purchase at their own expense an establishment where they give a religious education to almost 200'—whereas the lay school had barely thirty.

When on February 10 the *inspecteur primaire* of Vienne wrote to the *inspecteur d'académie*, his version of the affair stressed the other side of the question. He saw the lay school and the lay nursery school as living under a state of siege, targets of the same sort of clerical pressure which we have observed in La Buisse and in Péage-de-Roussillon. 'The communal boys' school is besieged and under attack by all imaginable ways and means. St Jean de Bournay is at this moment divided into two distinct parties, the party of the Church and that of the communal authority. But the division concerns more than the schools; it is like a political party, evidence of which was noted in the last elections for the *conseil général* and which will be seen even more keenly in the elections for the municipal council which are about to take place. The ecclesiastical authorities in St Jean and all their supporters are ruthlessly opposed to the communal school. They even go into homes to recruit pupils for the Brothers' school: all methods are employed to remove children from the communal school— promises, threats, secret influences, anonymous letters and defamation of the character of the *instituteur* and his assistant, the mayor and his deputy—no efforts are spared.' With regard to the nursery school, the primary inspector denied the story of the Ursulines and insisted that they were trying to undermine the position of the young lay *directrice* of the communal nursery school. 'These women, one might say, spend a lot of their time on the things of this world. They are furious at the setting up of a kindergarten outside their control.' By 1862 the nuns had succeeded in making life so difficult for the lay *directrice* that she was considering leaving, but the *inspecteur primaire* notes that the mayor remained as reluctant as ever to hand the kindergarten over to the nuns: 'If control is handed over to them it will become a nursery where the Brothers' school will come to recruit its pupils to the detriment of the communal school, all the more easily since the children will hardly be trained to fit into the latter'.

The factor determining the failure or success of the clerical campaign in such a dispute was whether or not it could attract the active support of influential local notables who could not merely supply funds but continue to pressure their dependants— tenants, customers and so forth—into supporting the Catholic school. At both St Jean and La Buisse the combination of a strong municipal authority, an influential mayor and popular resentment at clerical tactics saved the lay school. The Isère was, broadly speaking, a department of small property and as such was obviously less susceptible to pressure from legitimist notables than were areas with greater concentration of landed property.[1] The map of congregational education in France was very nearly the map of legitimism.[2]

It was not that there were no legitimist notables to supply funds. La Buisse was one example. Another was the village of Moidieu, where a certain Madame de Montauban donated in 1859 money and buildings for a congregational school at the instigation of the curé.[3] But the response of the commune to the attempt was violent. Already in 1854 the commune had tried to get the curé dismissed, accusing him of being more of a businessman than a priest. The Vienne police chief after fresh complaints in 1860 commented in amazement: 'I thought that since 1789 the tithe, like all other feudal rights, had been abolished. It seems that it still exists in the rural communes of my district under the name of *cueillette*. The curé of Moidieu 'either after the cereal crop or the wine harvest goes from house to house where the inhabitants each

---

[1] Barral (*Le Département de l'Isère*, 90) estimates that it would come sixteenth among the departments in a nineteenth-century league table of small landowners. The area held in estates of over 20 hectares was 35 per cent of the total in 1840, 26·5 per cent in 1869.

[2] A. Prost, *L'Enseignement en France 1800-1967* (1968), 181-2.

[3] ADI 53 M 15, Police report from Vienne 17 March 1860; IV v 69. ADI parish archives of Moidieu.

give him a proportion of the crop. Curé Bonneton also gathers quite a few insults.'[1] The curé was unpopular already on further grounds in that he met with some twenty-two other priests at a local village and 'it is believed that this meeting had its purpose more in politics than in religion'. Six years earlier the mayor had already sent in a petition for a change of curé with 120 signatures, demanding a priest who taught Christianity, not one who got mixed up with local legitimist high society and 'wetted his lips amid the cups of sumptuous hospitality with the fortunate ones of the century'. Once there was a choir; now only two people in the village cared to sing in the church. He charged exorbitant burial fees and pew rents.

When such a priest tried to use his influence to get the existing lay schools removed the commune's resistance was predictable. They objected furthermore to the tactics he used to try to get the *institutrice* dismissed, which consisted of writing letters to the bishop claiming that she was having an affair with a young man with whom she had been seen in a café and to whom she wrote letters whilst she was away in Lyon. The municipal council denied these slanders and retorted that she 'enjoyed much more public esteem than he did'. In March 1860 the curé was denounced for visiting parents to tell them not to send their children to school and for attacking the mayor in his sermons. The dispute dragged on for a further five years, by which time the local police appealed to the prefect to intervene with the bishop to take the necessary measures to prevent violence. The episcopal authorities for once

[1] The continued efforts of the rural clergy to collect tithe in some communes ties in with the fears expressed by the peasantry in 1815, and with rumours of its possible return in the 1869 election campaign. It is interesting that in his appeal to the French nation in 1874 the legitimist pretender Chambord included a specific denial that a Bourbon restoration would involve such a return—which seems to indicate a very widespread peasant suspicion of it in late nineteenth-century France (quoted in Falloux *Mémoires d'un royaliste* (1925-26), 3, 237). See also C. Marcilhasy, *Le Diocèse d'Orléans au milieu du dix-neuvième siècle* (1964), 127-8, for this type of feudal survival. This seems to throw doubt on Maurain's assertion (*op. cit.*, 57, n.3,) that only in strongly clerical regions was such tithe collection attempted.

took the easy way out, feigning surprise at the state of unrest, claiming that it was a case of personal enmity towards the curé by the mayor, but securing his dismissal nonetheless.

Similarly at St Pierre de Chardieu, the efforts of the curé to set up a congregational school with the aid of a large donation from a Madame Gavinet were resisted by the local population.[1] As the bishop was informed, 'The municipal council . . . has refused this gift and is trying to persuade the academy to give them a lay *instituteur*. Since the communal school is their own work they are proud of it and prop it up.' As at Moidieu the curé slandered the character of the *institutrice*—the third consecutive teacher he has tried to 'annihilate', insisted the mayor in a long complaint to the bishop about refusal of first communion to pupils from the lay schools. Six years earlier the curé had tried to get the *instituteur* dismissed on similar grounds—that he was a pillar of the wine shop, taught his pupils dubious songs whilst ignoring their catechism and that he had actually been seen dancing and had never expressed any shame at the fact! Throughout the 1850s the curé had failed to get the municipal authorities to make adequate provision for the upkeep of the church. They showed 'a hostility to anything to do with religion. There is a type in the village for whom the altar is always too rich, religious services too well attended, who would like to banish from our solemnities all luxury, all comfort, in short anything that might make an impression on the popular imagination.' The *instituteur* and the mayor had great influence on the rest of the village, 'uneducated people, always mistrustful of the well-off . . . but on the other hand of a more than sheeplike docility towards those who flatter them in their evil prejudices'. Only two of the twelve municipal councillors had ever been to mass in eighteen years.

The ideas of the curé on how this hostile population was to be

---

[1] ADI IV v 96. AEG Parish archives of St Pierre de Chardieu. AEG Letter of Curé of Heyrieux to Bishop, March 1865. AEG Mayor, etc., to Bishop, 23 March 1865. AEG Curé to Bishop, 30 March 1859. AEG Curé of Heyrieux to Bishop, 15 January 1856 and 30 January 1857. AEG Curé of St Pierre to Bishop, 13 July 1853.

won back to the Church shed an interesting light on the mentality of the nineteenth-century French clergy. No attempt was made to understand the roots of the 'revolutionary' mentality which he attacked. The remedies were firstly to set up a congregational school, secondly to raise money to 'reconstruct a beautiful church in the interests of worship, religion and beauty of ceremony which makes such a big impression on the mentality of our rural populations'. Not surprisingly this attitude, reminiscent perhaps of England's slum ritualists, was worse than useless in winning back an alienated population who merely resented church rebuilding as an additional expense.

At Villemoirieu one finds yet again a pious legitimist benefactress, Mademoiselle Comte, donating 6,000 francs to set up a congregational school in 1869.[1] By the early 1870s the curé protested to Grenoble that the municipal authorities were doing all they could to replace the nuns with a lay *institutrice*—a virtual persecution, he called it. For decades this had been a 'wild, coarse' population. The only hope in the 'fight against evil' was to maintain the religious school. Otherwise 'this hamlet will become worse than before: the great majority will no longer go to mass'. Already 'they work all day Sunday, spend evenings in wine shops feeding themselves on devilish doctrines of the evil newspapers and listening to dreadful accusations against religion and priests'. Here was a commune unmoved by many of the tactics which the clergy used in such conflicts. When he refused communion to pupils of the lay school, one replied, 'Very well, keep your precious God'. The situation worsened when the curé made an unsuccessful attempt to oust the mayor. In consequence the mayor demanded a change of curé. The reaction of the local dean whom the bishop consulted for advice is again an interesting example of the higher clergy's attitude towards such disputes. He said the curé had tried to overthrow the mayor, that he was driven on by 'an often excessive zeal' and that a change would have been for the best were it not for the fact that the mayor might regard this as

[1] AEG Parish records of Villemoirieu, Mayor to Bishop, 1868, Curé of Crémieu to Bishop, 1868 and 20 October 1872, and Curé to Vicar General 27 October 1875.

a victory. Consequently any change at that time was 'inopportune'.

These examples should not be seen as isolated phenomena, but rather as among the more striking illustrations of a process which repeated itself regularly in many communes of the department when the congregations attempted to establish themselves under the Second Empire. The conflicts arose not because of the arrival of the congregations themselves, but because so frequently the congregations gave the impression not of fighting to set up *écoles libres* but rather of attempting to annihilate well-established lay *écoles communales*. In 1860, fifty-seven of the seventy-one congregational boys' schools and 168 of the 229 girls' schools were communal. By 1875, 290 of the 400 congregational schools were communal.[1] The reports of *inspecteurs primaires* in 1867 mentioned conflicts similar to those described above, in Savas Mépin, Villeneuve de Marc, Seyssuel, Chonas, Beauvoir de Marc, and St Prim—where the lay *instituteur*, 'well thought of both in the district and by the authorities, sees his school almost empty'.[2] In December 1864 the sub-prefect of St Marcellin in the course of a long complaint to the prefect about the growing pretensions of the clergy in all aspects of departmental life, insisted that 'the clergy direct their efforts in particular against primary schoolteachers. Under the clergy's inspiration, often with the decisive benefit of donations made specifically for that purpose, the majority of the important communes have called in religious Brothers to control their schools.'[3] Where there were popular objections to this direct process, the *école libre* was set up as a basis for destruction of the lay school. 'This process has already been followed many times. It is what is happening this moment at Renage, a populous industrial commune where the priest, assisted by aid from several factory owners, has just called in the Brothers and set up a school without fees—and already that of the communal schoolteacher is deserted.'[4] In January 1866 he insisted that

[1] ADI 2 J 74.
[2] ADI T.167.
[3] ADI 52 M 44.
[4] ADI 52 M 45.

there were conflicts over congregational infiltration 'in all the large communes'. The archives contain numerous examples.[1]

Even in areas traditionally conservative and deferential to notables and clergy, the tactics employed by the clergy and the Frères produced bitter local resentment. This was most apparent in the canton of Crémieu. Here the clerical-legitimist party had always been dominant.[2] The chef-lieu contained many religious houses and had the largest percentage of religious vocations of any urban centre in the Isère. Nearly fifty per cent of the canton was held in estates of over twenty hectares—nearly twice the departmental average. It was in this unpromising milieu that lay anticlericalism made one of its more surprising appearances in the 1860s—a profound reaction which culminated in the victory of the freemason, Marion, in the 1869 elections over the clerical, de Vaulserre. Here, as in many other areas of the department, the rise of vocal resentment of clerical pretensions seems to have been incited by the clergy's attitude to the Italian question. In 1859 the Abbé Bouchard of Crémieu made a series of violent pulpit attacks on Piedmont which caused sufficient local hostility for the sub-prefect to remark that as a consequence, 'the clergy has no political influence in this district, which is nevertheless religious'.[3] In 1866 the opposition succeeded in electing four members of the municipal council of Cremieux. The commissaire de police attributed this change to the influence of M. Fabre, head of the local lay college, founder of an eighty-member musical society and société de bienfaisance in the town.[4] One of the issues in the elections was the stagnation in the town's economy 'which arises from the fact that the aristocracy puts obstacles in the way of all industrial enterprises'. But the question which aroused the bitterest conflict was that of M. Fabre's lay college. The mayor protested to the sub-prefect of the attitude of the curé who 'has gone so far as to say from the pulpit: "How do you expect me to support an institution whose pupils emerge rotten to the marrow of their bones?"

[1] For example, ADI T.361, 447.
[2] ADI 52 M 45. See Barral, Le Département de l'Isère, 521-2.
[3] ADI 52 M 38.
[4] ADI 52 M 45.

This last incident has ended by exasperating the population which is very proud of its college.'

The curé refused to say mass in the chapel of the college. The mayor's continued efforts to get the curé changed still met with no response from the bishop. Consequently the school question became the central subject of conversation in local cafés and cabarets. The mayor in a letter to the sub-prefect insisted that the situation was worsening: 'almost the entire population, which sticks by the college, is very exasperated'.

An interesting indication of the mood of the more vocal of the supporters of the college is furnished in a letter written by one of them to the sub-prefect in September, attributing the struggle not to the personal malevolence of the curé but to a determined, co-ordinated clerical plan to destroy lay education in the department. As a pointer to the attitude of the growing number of militant anticlericals in the Isère in the late 1860s it deserves quotation. 'The curé has done what every priest in France would have attempted to do. Since they all obey the same instruction, all are forced to act in similar ways and to show the same hostility to the institutions and personnel of lay education. One might put a bit more fire into it, on the other hand another adds not a bit more tolerance—for he has not the right to do so, and he would keep himself from doing so—but a bit more mildness. It is not a difference of principle or of rules, but only a matter of temperament. . . . Since it is a question of a ceaseless conflict against the college and against all lay schools we must not blame our curé any more than all the others. It is the clerical spirit which wants it to be that way and it will be like that, as in all political matters, for as long as our clergy, while finding solid support and inexhaustible protection in the French government, continues always to receive its orders and inspiration from abroad.' The writer claimed that the clergy were trying to undermine the school by overthrowing the present municipal administration.

The surprise defeat of the marquis de Vaulserre by Marion in the 1869 general election can be largely attributed to a widespread popular reaction in the rural areas of the canton, as well as in the *chef-lieu*, against clerical pretensions. Crémieu presents in microcosm the entire range of abuses which provoked the rise of anticlericalism in the Isère—an ultramontane, legitimist clergy, interfering openly in local and national elections, and trying to destroy lay education.

The educational conflicts worsened in the late 1860s as Duruy's education policy won much lay support and provoked much clerical antagonism. The reports of the *Inspecteurs primaires* for the last four years of the Empire illustrate how widespread in the Isère the friction over such issues as the extension of free education, the establishment of girls' secondary education, and the founding of *bibliothèques scolaires*.[1] In a terminal report of 1866, the *inspecteur primaire* of Vienne insisted that 'the wishes of the population with regard to primary education are the same as those that I have already made known—free schooling and teaching given by lay *instituteurs* and *institutrices*'. Unfortunately, 'the clergy in the *arrondissement* of Vienne views lay teaching with very little favour'. In November, he noted the warm welcome for measures such as 'adult evening classes among the working class and among men with generous ideas. But the setting up of adult education courses, which are such a powerful means of spreading civilization and morality, has displeased the clergy immensely—they seem to fear the extension of education.[2]

By December 1869 the *inspecteur primaire* of Grenoble was reporting as 'the only fact worthy of note . . . the reaction in people's minds in favour of lay schools', and he ascribed this to the

[1] ADI T.489.

[2] Cf. G. Duveau, *La Vie ouvrière en France sous le Second Empire* (1946 445: 'The bitterness of the social struggle makes the worker want to be educated'. Cf. also C. Emérique, *Essai sur la vie ouvrière dans le département de l'Isère 1871-1914* (Grenoble D.E.S. typescript), 84-6, notes a great deal of working-class concern with education in the latter years of the Second Empire. Foundry workers in Pontcharra gave support to free, compulsory, lay education—so did a number of militants in Vienne. It was a worker, Alphonse Ailloud, who organized the visit of Macé to that town in 1871 and who supported the *Ligue de l'Enseignement*. In 1869 a *Cercle d'étude progressif des travailleurs* was set up in the department (p. 109). In the 1870s another group *Le sou des écoles*, which was specifically anticlerical, contained a number of Grenoble workers.

fact that 'congregational education is too exclusively religious', and the popular questioning of the value of teaching theological 'abstractions which are incomprehensible to children' at the expense of all else. In his third terminal report of 1870 he again emphasized that 'without a doubt religious instruction ought to be the basis of popular education: but not everything ought to be sacrificed to it. That is, however, what happens in almost all congregational schools and in those where the curé lays down the law to the *instituteur*. They do not go beyond scripture, catechism and religious history.'

In September 1869 the *inspecteur primaire* of Vienne, while commenting on the existing uneasy calm, added: 'as soon as a change comes, then immediately the hostility which exists underneath will be brought out'. The 'liberalization' of the Empire provided the first favourable opportunity for criticism of the Church's role in education in the department. The fall of the Empire was to release the accumulated resentment of two decades in which the two streams of anticlericalism—the 'ideological' hostility of committed republicans to the Church's obscurantism, and the strictly parochial resentments of local populations to the tactics used by the clergy to dominate communal education—reinforced each other to produce many attempts at laicization in 1870-1. The campaign conducted by the *Ligue de l'Enseignement*, or by the radical *Réveil du Dauphiné* gained its strength at the communal level. In the Isère, at least, laicity was not the brainchild of liberal intellectuals thrust upon sturdy Catholic peasant masses, whatever Catholic historians might claim to the contrary.

IV. *Working-class anticlericalism*

It is a commonplace of criticism of the French Church that, after its brief flirtation with democracy and social reform in 1848 it linked itself unequivocally with social and political reaction. Archbishop Affre of Paris had given his support to the democratic wing of Social Catholicism in the 1840s[1] but, with rare exceptions like Mgr Giraud of Cambrai, the vast majority of the hierarchy closed its eyes to the implications of industrialization

[1] J. B. Duroselle, *Les Débuts du catholicisme social* (1954).

and urbanization.[1] The 'liberal Catholicism' of Dupanloup stopped short of an understanding of social problems, and Montalembert apostasized briefly from his liberalism to support Louis Napoleon's dictatorship as a safeguard against the gales of socialism which threatened to overturn the frail raft of civilization and culture.[2] This espousal of the cause of social conservatism by the hierarchy after the June Days wrecked the nascent Catholic democratic movement centred round the journal *L'Ere Nouvelle* and including, for example, Ozanam who had stood for election at Lyon on a platform which included 'the right to work', and progressive income tax.

As Duroselle has shown, in provincial France democratic priests were severely disciplined. Social Catholicism fell back into paternalistic charity. The links which in the 1840s had developed in Paris between the Church and such working-class journals as *L'Atelier* were snapped.[3] The ideological gulf between urban workers and the Church created a mission problem in the cities which the inflexibility of the parish system, incapable of coping with the influx of rural migrants, merely accentuated.[4] Proudhon epitomized this working-class bitterness with his rhetorical question: 'Is there a single honest man in France today who does not say to himself: "Shall I die without killing a priest"?'

The revolution of 1848 in Lyon contrasted with Paris in having

---

[1] P. Droulers, 'L'Attitude de l'épiscopat' in *Le Mouvement social* (November–December 1966). Cf. his *Action pastorale et problèmes sociaux sous la monarchie de juillet chez Mgr d'Astros, archevêque de Toulouse* (1954).

[2] C. Marcilhasy, *Le Diocèse d'Orléans sous l'épiscopat de Mgr Dupanloup 1858-78.* Dupanloup's colleague Montalembert, who spent his life trying to marry Catholicism with constitutional government, confessed to sharing 'not the indifference but the ignorance of the majority of the politicians concerning the working class'.

[3] For the bitter rejection of Catholicism on account of its acceptance of dictatorship and social exploration see the eloquent testimony of a member of the *Atelier* group, Corbon in *Le Secret du peuple de Paris* (1863) and *Pourquoi nous vous délaissons* (1877).

[4] See, for example F. Charpin, *Pratique religieuse et formation d'une grande ville* (1964), a study of Marseilles.

strong anticlerical overtones,[1] and the influence of the city extended to the industrial communes of Bas Dauphiné where more than twenty communes evicted their curés.[2] Claude Emérique has stressed that the working classes in the industrial communes around Lyon had already drifted away from the Church and that in those aspects of life in which contact was maintained they saw it as a tool of capitalism. In the textile industry, for example, employers used nuns to supervise institutions for orphans who worked in the silk factories of Vizille and Voiron. These children were lodged and fed but not paid. The Church was exposed to the double accusation of exploiting the young and of helping to undercut wage rates.[3] The religious and administrative authorities made frequent despairing reference to the popularity of wine shops (*cabarets*) among the workers and the serious effects this had on religious practice, in Vienne and other towns.[4]

A number of priests in the department in the 1840s had followed a certain Abbé Clavel who had favoured more democratic structures both within the Church and in society and had been severely critical of the conservatism of Mgr de Bruillard.[5] In 1848 Abbé Koenig of Tullins stood as a radical candidate in the national elections. But a prefectoral report of 1850 stressed that he had few

[1] Roger Voog 'Les Problèmes religieuses à Lyon pendant la monarchie de juillet et la seconde république' in *Cahiers d'histoire* (1963), Vol. 8, 405-21.

[2] F. Rudé in E. Esmonine, *La Révolution de 1848 dans le département de l'Isère.*

[3] C. Emérique *Essai sur la vie ouvrière dans le département de l'Isère 1871-1914* (1953), 78. A report in the ministry of *cultes* (in September 1858 complained of 'feeble religious spirit among the workers' in Isère and of workers 'in the workshops who have escaped from moral control'. ADI 52 M 42. Attempts by employers to remedy this by introducing religious orders to teach child workers in the factory proved unsuccessful. ADI 52 M 42, Sub-prefect of St Marcellin, 4 December 1864.

[4] ADI 162 M 8, ADI 16 M 3. For example, Sub-prefect of La Tour du Pin, 26 October 1882, lamented that the enormous numbers of *cabarets* in his *arrondissement* (1,025) kept workers away from church, wasted their money, etc. Cf. Duveau *La Vie ouvrière en France sous le second empire,* 499, 510-11, 521.

[5] Vigier, *op. cit.,* vol. I, 142-6; vol. 2, 94-118.

supporters among the clergy in the department.[1] The handful of left-wing priests who survived into the Empire soon found themselves harassed and dismissed by the bishop, Ginoulhiac.[2] This latter supplies a fine example of the virtues and inadequacies of liberal Catholicism in mid-nineteenth-century France. An Orleanist, a one-time youthful admirer of Lamennais, a tactful and moderate opponent of legitimist extremists during the Italian crisis of the 1860s, a scholarly opponent of infallibility at the Vatican Council, he nevertheless stopped short of an understanding of social problems.[3]

The career of Abbé Koenig in Tullins raises the interesting possibility that the French working class might have been attracted back to the Church had its ministers shown themselves more sympathetic to their genuine grievances. Tullins was a steel and textile commune with a population of some 4,500. It had a past history of radicalism—food rioting in 1847, a radical mayor Masson during the Second Republic, a majority vote for Ledru Rollin in the presidential election and against Bonaparte in the 1852 plebiscite.[4] What makes its history of interest is the presence there of an *abbé démocrate*, Koenig, who had taken up his post in 1835 and who made himself an extremely popular figure in the town. The sub-prefect in a detailed report on Koenig's career written for the prefect on 14 December 1860 outlined the features of Koenig's twenty-two years in Tullins, culminating in his removal in 1857. The sub-prefect had no illusions as to Koenig's unusual qualities—'gifted with a remarkable degree of intelligence and with a rare cunning, he had not hesitated to recruit an army of evil acquaintances in order to enhance his personal influence'. These contacts he used in order to arouse in the masses of Tullins

[1] AN F.19 5813, Prefect to Minister of Interior.

[2] ADI 52 M 36, Report of *Juge de Paix* of Mens, 16 February 1858, on dismissal of Abbé Laval of La Mure for radical sympathies.

[3] Droulers L'Attitude de l'épiscopat' in *Le Mouvement social* (1966), comments that his pastoral letters in his industrial archdiocese of Lyon, to which he was elevated in 1870, lack the social awareness of his legitimist predecessor, Bonald.

[4] ADI IV v 115, Parish records of Tullins, Sub-prefect of La Tour du Pin, 1860.

hatred 'against their social superiors and against the rich'. He accused the upper classes of Tullins 'of greed and of indifference to the sufferings of the needy classes. It is in this way that he had succeeded in creating for himself a large party from among the uneducated section of the population and among the lower middle class.' Among the latter he had not scrupled to arouse 'jealousy and the desire to substitute their own authority for that of the important families. Even among the clergy M. Koenig has left behind a reputation as a propagator of socialist doctrines.'

He had made himself the intermediary between the charity society and the poor, had contracted considerable debts, borrowing money to distribute to workers, 'jealous to preserve his popularity among the poor'. The sub-prefect noted that Koenig had shown himself more reserved in the 1850s though this was more from a spirit of self-preservation than from actual adherence to the Empire. He blamed Koenig for the votes in Tullins for Ledru-Rollin and the opposition to the *coup d'état* shown in the plebiscite—commenting laconically that since Koenig obviously enjoyed vast influence there, either he was hostile to Napoleon or his influence did not stretch to elections.

In the early years of the Empire, Koenig had restrained his criticism against the emperor but had manifested his radicalism in other ways, notably by holding meetings in 1853 against the La Salette miracle which he saw as superstitious obscurantism being exploited by legitimists.[1] The depth of hostility to the Church among the Tullins workers is perhaps nowhere better illustrated than in the fact that even so radical a priest as Koenig was not wholly exempt from the sort of administrative conflicts which we have seen to have been so prevalent in the department. In 1853 Koenig had carried out various repairs to the church without asking for administrative approval. 'The curé who thinks that he is exempt from obeying common law has acted without consulting the authorities, thus overstepping all legal methods: afterwards he asked that the local authority should pay his costs.' In a superbly disingenuous stroke Koenig tried to lay the blame for the attacks on him on to local legitimist notables, 'enemies of a

[1] ADI 52 M 45, *Bureau de Police* of Tullins to *Commissaire de Police*.

government which has saved them, these men still dream of fresh disasters with fresh dynasties'. The *Commisaire de Police* refused to accept such stratagems and insisted that Koenig was still associated with many ex-republicans while in his frequent provocative sermons 'it seems to me that there is incitement of hatred against one class of society'.[1]

By 1854 Koenig's relations with the municipal administration were improved by the presence of mayor Masson who shared his political predilections. The years 1854–57 were thus marked by incessant republican propaganda in Tullins and adminstrative hostility to all clergy other than Koenig. In January 1858 the head of the *gendarmerie impériale* of St Marcellin wrote to his commander in Grenoble his impressions of the political situation in Tullins.[2] He said that when he had arrived in the *arrondissement* in 1854 'I was not long in noticing the hatred which exists between rich and poor in that commune, and above all between the police and the municipal leader, the mayor M. Masson, who since the revolution of February 1848 unfortunately exerts a fatal and disruptive influence on the least honourable section of the community, belonging to the demogogic party, which was previously led by the curé, Koenig. He has never been willing on several very difficult occasions to lend his assistance to the police when they requested it.' Masson delighted in freeing prisoners arrested by the police. With his assistance the police would have caught 'those who for several years past amuse themselves by spreading seditious writings about the Emperor and other insulting and outrageous pamphlets concerning the new priest'. He remarked on the degree of class conciliation which other areas of the *arrondissement* managed to achieve: 'At Tullins, on the other hand, the antagonism between the poor and the rich became more evident every day'. Koenig was cited as 'the prime cause of all these events'.

The anticlericalism of the local administration was well illustrated in its relations with the curé of Fures, a heavily industrialized suburb of Tullins two kilometres away, with a

[1] ADI 52 M 35, Police Commissioner of Tullins, August 1853.
[2] ADI 15 M 82, 1 June 1858.

population of some 1,500 and rapidly growing textile factory.[1] The prefect and the bishop agreed that the moral welfare of the workers required the building of a new church there. Masson was violently hostile. In 1854 he indulged in protracted polemics with the new priest who had acquired a plot of ground for a cemetery without administrative permission. In the summer of 1856 he refused the Fures parish council's request for financial assistance for the curé's lodging, font, and bell.[2] Masson insisted that the Tullins municipality was already in debt, had heavy commitments on roads and schools, and had no intention of making 'useless expenditure'.[3] The sub-prefect had to warn Masson that under no pretext could the municipal council escape paying for the curé's lodgings and then had to contradict the mayor's assertion that he had the right to be present at the financial meetings of the Fures parish council.[4] Masson tried to get the permission to build a church revoked by the minister of *cultes*, protesting that one church and one priest's house were quite sufficient for any municipal council to have to keep up.

Until 1857 the full extent of Tullins' anticlericalism was veiled by the fact that in Koenig it possessed one of the few radical priests in the department. In 1857 the departmental authorities in a despairing effort to remove such a subversive influence moved him to the parish of Domène. This news was met by violent popular protests, threats to sound the tocsin, petitions to the ministry of *cultes* (signed by Masson) which circulated in all the cafés.[5] Months after Koenig's departure the *commissaire de police* was protesting of 'violent unrest which time has not yet calmed'. The man who bore the full force of this hostility was the new curé, Abbé Mège. In December 1857 the sub-prefect reported 'a poster containing outrageous comments against M. Mège, the curé of Tullins, was found on 14 October in Rue St Laurent.

[1] ADI IV v 115, Sub-prefect of St Marcellin to Bishop, January 1854.
[2] ADI IV v 115, Sub-prefect of St Marcellin to Prefect, July–August 1856.
[3] ADI IV v 115, Parish Council of Fures to Prefect, 7 May 1856.
[4] ADI IV v 115, Prefect to Sub-prefect, 30 June 1856.
[5] ADI 52 M 35, 36, Sub-prefect to Prefect, October 1857 and February 1858.

This poster is the work of supporters of M. Koenig.' On October 20-1 further insults to Abbé Mège appeared together with 'seditious writings of such a nature as to insult the person of His Majesty the Emperor'. It contained the words 'Long live the Republic. Why always Napoleon? etc. Bring back our priest.'

Early in 1858 the departmental authorities forced the resignation of Masson, suspected of favouring this agitation or at least of showing total unconcern about apprehension of culprits. Leading republican families kept up a correspondence with Koenig who periodically appeared in neighbouring communes to be visited by his followers.[1] Mège's position got worse and worse. Caricatures were pinned on the church door and distributed in the commune representing him as a fish in a frying-pan who would assuredly poison those who ate him. 'Oh, the old beast. Oh, how tough he is to cook. He'll be poison for Tullins.'

In a letter of 9 April to the prefect, Mège commented that 'this area is the classic region of this petty meanness, because I am often informed that no priest, curate or middle-class person has been sheltered from this war of pin pricks'. However, in 1857 he still had pitiful illusions. With patience and charity 'the sheep will little by little return to the fold'. He still professed a belief in the ever-growing influence of the Church. The history of Tullins in the next few years did nothing to substantiate such optimism. Though in a letter of 10 March 1858 the *Commissaire de Police* of Tullins hoped that the removal of Masson would make Mège's enemies less 'bold', he had to confess that Koenig's influence continued.[2] Latest threats from the commune were to turn Protestant! By May he was reporting meetings in the house of M. Charanne, a republican, threatening letters to Mège, which 'have one sole aim, to prevent people from going to church and to induce them to hate the clergy and the upper middle class'. In order further to discredit Mège, rumours were circulated that Koenig had gone to Paris to apply for reinstatement at Tullins.

The Italian war brought another element to the conflict in Tullins. The republicans were enthusiastic about the first cam-

---

[1] ADI IV v 115, *Commissaire de Police*, 6 April 1858.
[2] ADI IV v 115, *Commissaire de Police*, 10 March 1858.

paigns. After Villafranca there were many complaints that the emperor had left his task half finished.[1] The local clergy, however, including those in rural areas of the canton, expressed strong ultramontane leanings.[2] In July 1859, Mège was bitterly attacked by the mayor for a supposed refusal to sing *Te Deum* to celebrate Austrian defeats.

But by comparison with what had gone before, Tullins enjoyed relative calm in the 1860s. It is true that in the elections in 1861 for a new mayor the clergy 'carried out an active propaganda campaign' and gave rise to a violent argument between ex-mayor Richard and Abbé Clel, when the former warned 'His Excellency the curate to indulge in less electoral agitation'. Thereafter, however, for several years, the only documented clashes were over the municipal council's continued reluctance to spend money on the church.[3]

However, the growth of militant anticlericalism in the 1869 legislative elections in Isère did not by-pass Tullins. Indeed, with Voiron, Tullins provided the nucleus of the radical campaigns of Nugues and Réal. Predictably the republican election committee was headed by Masson.[4] After 4 September 1870, a *conseil cantonal* was set up, dominated by the radicals of Tullins itself, suspicious of the 'apathy' of the local rural areas. A society for 'Republican Education' was established including Masson among its members. A secular secondary school was planned. In a report to the prefect in November 1872, the *commissaire spécial de police* described the popularity in Tullins of *Le Siècle* and *Le Réveil du Dauphiné*, papers which he criticized for 'that tendency to relate nothing but the shameful behaviour of clergy and of certain religious congregations. The canton of Tullins, and above all the town itself, contains a large party of radical republicans who approved of, and to all appearances still approve of, the Paris commune and all its works.'[5]

[1] ADI 52 M 38, Sub-prefect, August 1859.
[2] ADI 52 M 38, 18 May 1859.
[3] ADI 15 M 82, Sub-prefect to Prefect, 18 June 1861.
[4] ADI 55 M 1, *Justice de Paix* to Prefect, 9 May 1869.
[5] ADI 15 M 82.

H

Conclusion

There is much evidence to suggest that the years 1869-71 saw a strong wave of anticlericalism in Isère. This was most militant in industrial bourgs such as Voiron where, under the influence of a highly articulate artisan, Alexis Favre, St. Bruno's church was used as a Republican headquarters in early 1871 and local clergy 'insulted, struck, and dragged in the mud'. The administration lamented that Favre's anticlerical brochures were widely distributed in surrounding rural areas just as in northern Isère they were alarmed at the profusion with which the most 'advanced papers have spread to the most remote hamlets.' Rural suspicion of clergy had been accentuated by the clergy's hostility to the 1859 war and to Italian unification—for the Habsburgs were not popular in a border department which remembered the 1815 Austrian occupation. Rumours of secret gatherings of clergy and legitimists to support the Pope outraged 'men who know nothing except their work' in rural St. Laurent de Pont to such an extent that 'fathers stopped going to church and stopped their children attending,' calling for the dismissal of clergy 'whose political principles are diametrically opposed to our own . . .' Dozens of churches emptied in protest at sermons attacking Louis Napoleon's Italian policy.[1] The national elections provided an outlet for widespread anticlericalism. In 1869 the most striking result was the success of the 'advanced' Marion, a Freemason, in rural Cremieu, an area traditionally dominated by the power of nobles and clergy. The local rural population was not hostile to the Empire but could not stomach voting for an official candidate who was a Catholic noble. 'The only persistent rumour that has gone around is that M. de Vaulserre was a clerical, a friend of the clergy. With the best will in the world it is impossible to persuade a peasant in our countryside that a clerical can be a true friend of the government'. Marion's election campaign stressed that 'the clergy had too much power . . ., wished to restore the feudal regime and bring back the tithe.'[2] The local population, in

---

[1] ADI J. 516 Fonds Chaper, Dossier on Alexis Favre; ADI 8M. 16 May 1869 and February 1870; ADI 52. M 38: 52 M 42: 52 M 44: IV V 96.
[2] ADI 8M. 16 Justice of Peace of Beaurepaire July 1860.

some cases already involved in clashes over education agreed with this analysis. Already, a decade before Ferry, the Church was beginning to pay for its misconceived administrative and educational policies and for its political involvement.

CONCLUSION

THEODORE ZELDIN

This book has illustrated how violent and apparently complete the clash between the Church and its opponents could be, but its main conclusion is that the differences between the two were not as great as they believed. On closer examination, looking at what they did rather then at what they said they were doing, the distinctions between the two sides are not always clear. The Church in France was not as coherent, united or formidable an army as the republicans imagined. It did not dispense a radically different form of education in its schools; its syllabuses were not all that much more cut off from reality than those of the state schools and it had as much difficulty in presenting a clear view of the world as they did. The state schools for their part were on the whole not anti-religious, even if they might be anticlerical. This was true of primary schools as well as of the secondary ones Robert Anderson has studied. A state inspector wrote in 1898 of their moral education: 'The lessons are generally pale imitations of the homilies of country priests. . . . Morals are taught in the same way as the catechism once was, by question and answer.'[1] The state's secondary schoolmasters were generally very conservative men, as Paul Gerbod has shown in his important thesis.[2] In moral teaching, the two sides were both divided amongst themselves, and at the same time had quite similar views in their attitude to major problems of daily behaviour. In politics, it is true, bishop Pie talked of theocracy, as many others did too; and in local affairs the curés

[1] F. Lichtenberger, *L'Education morale dans les écoles primaires*, Mémoires et documents scolaires publiés par le musée pédagogique, second series, No. 28 (1898), 26.

[2] Paul Gerbod, *La Condition universitaire en France au dixneuvième siècle* (1965).

often longed to be able to run their villages without interference from the state officials. It was such ambitions that roused the anti-clericals to what they conceived to be the defence of their liberties. This was a real division in French life. But it is the concentration on politics that has given the impression of a struggle about irreconcilable principles, when often it was a struggle for power.

In order to get a true picture of the issues, it is important to stop thinking of the anticlerical quarrel as having just two sides to it. The religious party should not be counted simply from those who attended church. The sociologists of religion inevitably began their studies by doing just this, but they are becoming increasingly aware that the next stage is to assess the quality as well as the quantity of religion. The peasant who went to his village church in Brittany was not necessarily doing exactly the same thing as the businessman attending mass in Lyon. The Church itself expressed doubts about the piety of both categories. It complained of Breton peasants who fooled their curés into saying masses for magical purposes; it sometimes even destroyed ancient statues of saints which were shrines for pagan superstitions.[1] Though the Church profited from the return of the bourgeoisie to the fold in the second half of the nineteenth century, there were those who denounced the insincerity and superficiality of this movement.[2] It might be fairer to compare not just church attendance and abstention, but belief in miracles with the survival of superstitious folklore. Certainly, if one looks at attitudes to science—a large subject, on which I plan to write elsewhere—one does not find the clergy uniformly opposed to or sceptical of new discoveries, nor—which is more significant—the liberals universally readier to accept them. The intellectuals were exceptionally endowed with brilliance, curiosity and originality but at the time the weight of the past was strongly present amongst them. One of the most fascinating aspects of French society is the way the innovators were torn by conflicting forces at work within

[1] Emile Jobbé-Duval, *Les Idées primitives dans la Bretagne contemporaine* (1920), 52, 109.

[2] For example, J. B. Cloet, *L'Arsenal catholique, ou démonstration des dogmes et de la morale de l'église* (1857), 1. 317-26.

them. Renan, whose *Life of Jesus* and *The Future of Science* made him appear a leader of secularism and of the critical rejection of religion, was of course a former seminarist: he was always obsessed by religion, he devoted most of his life to its study and he never quite knew where he stood with regard to it.

The writings of men like him suggest that there were several different levels of anticlericalism. Roger Magraw has shown that the intellectuals of Paris had very little to do with the village anticlericalism he has studied. Certainly Vacherot, who had vigorous battles with the Church during the Second Empire, expressed dissatisfaction with the more simple of his followers. To philosophers like himself, wrestling seriously with metaphysical problems, that epitome of the anticlerical—Monsieur Homais—was a figure of fun, naïve, absurd. But in the village M. Homais was a philosopher. Vacherot thought him terribly out of date, perpetuating the crude sarcasms of the eighteenth century, but M. Homais considered himself an advanced thinker.[1] There were numerous gradations between these two, and there were of course extremists on either side of them. To understand anticlericalism therefore it is not enough to read the anticlerical newspapers—or indeed to consult any single source. Nor is it enough to deduce from the fact that there were Church schools that their pupils necessarily took up and retained Catholic values. If that were so, there would have been no revolution in 1789, nor a separation of Church and state in 1905. Combes and Caillaux, leaders of anticlerical radicalism, were products of Church schools.

What then caused anticlericalism? There can be no simple answer. Recent research has shown how the establishment of state lay schools in religious areas in the region of Montpelier has made no difference to the extent of church-going[2]: it is necessary therefore to reconsider the effectiveness of anticlerical propaganda, to discover not simply what the anticlericals said, but also what real results they achieved. Detailed investigations have shown likewise that urbanization and migration have not always destroyed

[1] E. Vacherot, *La Religion* (1869).
[2] G. Cholvy, *Géographie religieuse de l'Hérault contemporain* (1968), a model study.

230

religious practice.[1] The collapse of traditional society had much to do with decline in religious faith, but this decline had often already occurred in the ancien régime. The spread of anticlericalism cannot be seen simply as the triumph of modernity, science and education over obscurantism. René Rémond, in his illuminating analysis of *The Right Wing in France*, has a suggestive introduction on the problem of the varieties of political conservatism which can be broadly classified under that general head: it would be worth while attempting a similar dissection of the varieties of anticlericalism. However, much research will first have to be done. The influence of the clergy and attitudes to them are difficult to assess. Austin Gough's essay makes the point that though there are strong regional traditions in this matter, the Church might at one point appear to be highly influential over the masses until some crisis suddenly reveals the weakness of its hold. Roger Magraw stresses how important the personality of individual priests was. The wide generalizations which some historians and sociologists have sought do not always stand up to close scrutiny. The progress of knowledge in this field must be in detailed studies of the whole variety of cultural and social phenomena.

---

[1] F. Boulard, *Pratique religieuse urbaine et regions culturelles* (1968).

NOTES ON CONTRIBUTORS

ROBERT ANDERSON, formerly a Scholar of The Queen's College, Oxford and a Student of St Antony's College, Oxford, is Lecturer in History at the University of Edinburgh.

AUSTIN GOUGH graduated from Melbourne University and was subsequently a Student of St Antony's College, Oxford. He is now Reader in History at Monash University, Australia. He is completing a book on *French Catholics and the Papacy during the Second Empire.*

ROGER MAGRAW, a graduate of Worcester College, Oxford, is Lecturer in History at the University of Warwick.

THEODORE ZELDIN is Dean of St Antony's College, Oxford. He is a former Scholar of Christ Church, Oxford and Research Fellow of the Centre National de la Recherche Scientifique, Paris; in 1969-70 he was Visiting Professor of History at Harvard University. His publications include *The Political System of Napoleon III* (1958, to be reissued shortly in paperback), *Emile Ollivier and the Liberal Empire of Napoleon III* (1963), *Journal d'Emile Ollivier 1846-69* (2 volumes, ed., 1961), *Napoleon III* (ed., in the press) and numerous articles. He is now writing a volume on *France 1848-1945* for the Oxford History of Modern Europe.

INDEX